AN ORAL HISTORY OF UNIVERSITY COLLEGE GALWAY, 1930–1980

An Oral History of University College Galway, 1930–1980

A University in Living Memory

JACKIE UÍ CHIONNA

OPEN AIR

Set in 10.5 pt on 12.5 pt Ehrhardt MT for OPEN AIR
an imprint of FOUR COURTS PRESS LTD
7 Malpas Street, Dublin 8, Ireland
www.fourcourtspress.ie
and in North America for
FOUR COURTS PRESS
c/o IPG, 814 N Franklin St, Chicago, IL 60622

A catalogue record for this title is available
from the British Library.

ISBN 978-1-84682-812-6

Printed in England by
CPI Antony Rowe, Chippenham, Wilts.

Table of contents

Acknowledgments

This project was initiated by the University Management Team of NUI Galway, who deserve great credit for their vision in tapping into the rich oral history of the university.

I wish to acknowledge the generosity of a donor who kindly supported this project through the Galway University Foundation.

Professor Daniel Carey and Martha Shaughnessy of the Moore Institute for Research in the Humanities and Social Studies at NUI Galway not only provided me with a wonderful space in which to work, but also provided invaluable guidance and support whenever it was needed, for which I will be forever in their debt, and thank them most sincerely.

Dr Caitriona Clear of the History Department, NUI Galway, showed unwavering support of the project from the outset, and her guidance in relation to the methodology of oral history contributed significantly to the success of the project. Go raibh míle maith agat a Chaitríona.

The staff of Special Collections in the Hardiman Library were, as always, unstinting in their help in providing access to a variety of sources, including college calendars, college publications, written memoirs of students and photographic archives. I thank them all most sincerely for their assistance.

Four Courts Press, and in particular the book's editor, Sam Tranum, did an exceptional job of steering the manuscript to publication stage, for which I am immensely grateful.

Finally, this book would not have been possible without the input of all of those who agreed to be interviewed, and who gave so generously of their time, not only during the interview process itself, but also in reading transcripts of the interviews, and providing clarifications where necessary. It was both a pleasure and a privilege to have been allowed access to the memories of such a wonderful cohort of students and staff. Sadly, a number of those interviewed have passed away since the interviews were conducted. Their legacy remains, however, and this book is dedicated to them. Ar dheis Dé go raibh a n-anamacha dílse.

Introduction

This book is an oral history of a university in the words of those who taught, studied and worked there over a fifty-year period, 1930–80. It is based on the results of 'The University in Living Memory', an oral-history project begun in 2007. Over two years, more than sixty interviews were conducted, with everyone from college presidents to grounds staff, from students who began their college lives in the 1930s, to the post-free-education student-union activists of the 1970s. The project began with an invitation being extended to anyone who had ever taught, worked or studied at UCG to participate and be interviewed. It says a great deal about the affection which people have for the college that there were no shortage of volunteers coming forward and offering their memories of their time here – indeed far more people came forward than could be accommodated given the time and resources available to us.

The interviews were conducted in both English and Irish, and for the purposes of this publication, edited highlights were selected from the interviews, and were grouped thematically and chronologically so as to form a logical, and hopefully compelling, narrative. The narrative reflects the experiences of several generations of staff, students and employees, and in reflecting their own personal experiences, also serves to chart the story of how the university evolved over a critical fifty-year period in its history. Thousands of students, and staff, passed through the gates of UCG in the years 1930–80. This study reflects a representative cross section of students, academic staff and general employees of the college who were here at various times. Every effort was made to identify interviewees from across the academic disciplines and across the decades. We were particularly fortunate in finding so many alumni from the 1930s, whose recall of the events in those formative days between Irish independence and the Second World War has added so much to this study.

Most of the interviews ran to approximately one hour thirty minutes, and in some cases second interviews were required. The interview with the late Prof. Pádraig Ó Céidigh was a case in point. The former professor of zoology sadly passed away in the course of the project, but not before leaving a wonderful record of his time at UCG. After a three-hour recording session, which began with Prof. Ó Céidigh talking about his arrival at UCG in 1956, the interview had to be terminated when the voice recorder's capacity had been reached. But Prof. Ó Céidigh was adamant that there was a lot more ground to cover: 'Ah you'll have to come back,' he said. 'Sure, we're only up to 1959.'

In almost every case, the interview process was relaxed and relatively easy for the interviewer because the interviewees themselves were so relaxed. They each had a story they wished to tell, and in every case any initial shyness or reticence which existed was quickly dispensed with once they began talking about their college days. For students, the sense of fun was palpable – quite simply, they had a great time at UCG, regardless of which decade their own experiences occurred in. They worked hard certainly, but they also loved the freedom and challenge of their college days, and they loved it largely because they felt they were all in the same boat – sharing experiences, sharing what little money they had, and sharing the joy of learning new subjects with their fellow students.

For academic staff, the strongest sense to emerge from the interviews was the feeling that in UCG anything was possible if you were determined enough to make it happen. For obvious reasons there were no staff interviewed who would have taught here in the 1930s or 1940s (although many later staff were students here at that time), and it is only from the 1950s to the early 1980s that we get a sense of what the college was like for academics. It was a quite remarkable time, with unprecedented development of faculties, departments and the college infrastructure, and all in the context of a changing society. Some extraordinary men and women came to work at UCG, and for many it was not the easiest of the career paths they could have chosen. They could have earned more, gained greater prestige, even had an easier time of it, had they chosen to take up opportunities elsewhere. But they didn't – they chose to come to UCG for a variety of reasons, and most importantly they stayed. And they made sometimes remarkable things happen.

The interviews with non-academic staff revealed much of the family atmosphere that existed in the college. Whether it was Ma Creaven, keeping a strict motherly eye on her 'charges' in the coffee shop, George Deacy being schooled in the Irish language by his boss prior to the interview that would confirm his appointment, or Peadar Ó Fátharta, who literally grew up in the college – all of those interviewed have wonderful, happy memories of working at UCG. They admired and respected the academics they worked for, they enjoyed the friendly banter with their co-workers, and they felt very much part of a well-oiled machine, which collaborated with ease and became a formidable team in serving the needs of generations of staff and students. And of course they liked the students – they derived great pleasure from seeing students do well and progress. They consoled them when they were distressed, they enjoyed their youthful exuberance, and they ensured that students' time in college was as supported and stress-free as possible. They had a real sense that they were indeed fortunate to work in UCG, and even when, inevitably, issues arose with college management or individual academics, they stood their ground, brought about the necessary changes, and got back to work

This book is not, nor did it ever intend to be, an academic history of the university. That role has already been ably filled by a previous college publication, *From Queen's College to National University: essays on the academic history of QCG/UCG/ NUI Galway*, published in 1999.[1] Rather, it is an oral history, recording people's experiences of their time spent here – in essence 'living memories' of their college days, whether they were spent studying, teaching or working at the university.

1 Tadhg Foley (ed.), *From Queen's College to National University: essays on the academic history of QCG/UCG/NUI, Galway* (Dublin, 1999).

The historical record is always incomplete, and historians constantly strive to fill in the gaps. The recording of oral history is but one way in which these gaps may be filled, although there are obvious difficulties attached to the process in terms of both the subjectivity of the interviewee, and the nature of human memory itself. Memory is a strange thing – it can be random, alternately searingly clear or blurred, it can be selectively edited either by choice or the vagaries of time, but it is, at its core, essentially personal. And it is the personal stories of people that we sought to record in the course of this project, and thankfully our interviewees did not disappoint. In sharing their memories of UCG they have added considerably to our knowledge of the history of this educational institution.

A REMARKABLE STORY

Founded in the part of the country most badly affected by the Great Famine of the 1840s, under-funded, and considered very much the 'poor relation' of the so-called 'Godless Colleges', Queen's College Galway – which would later become University College Galway and then National University of Ireland, Galway – struggled to survive from the very outset. In welcoming the new college, the *Galway Vindicator* reflected something of what the first president, and his staff, were up against. The *Vindicator* hoped that the college would 'advance the Irish people from the 'Gothic barbarism' and the 'presumptive ignorance of the *hedge*, to the bright polish and intellectual refinement of the university'.[2] Clearly expectations were high.

The college, however, experienced real difficulty in attracting students to the significantly less affluent west of Ireland, which had been decimated by the Famine. Successive college presidents struggled to save the college in the face of government pressure to close it. The stresses of maintaining the university as a viable educational institution were such that its first two presidents – the Revd Joseph W. Kirwan (1845–1849) and Edward Berwick (1849–77) – both died in office, their deaths being attributed to the strain associated with keeping the college from closure. But QCG survived, and, in the face of all the odds stacked against it, produced some very fine students, many of whom went on to success in the competitive British civil service exams, thereby enhancing the college's reputation.

By the 1930s the college had faced yet more crises, but was optimistic that under the new Free State administration the college would finally come into its own. As president from 1899 to 1934, Alexander Anderson oversaw the transition from QCG to UCG, and from a university of the United Kingdom to the designated Gaelic university of Saorstát Éireann. Anderson's hopes for the college appear to have been well founded, for at the time he became president, QCG had fewer than one hundred students, whereas on his retirement, there were over six hundred – still a relatively small number, but nonetheless a significant increase.

2 Ibid., p. xi.

A staunch advocate of multi-denominational education, Anderson successfully defended his college against the threat of closure on two occasions.

The next college president, and one about whom we will hear a great deal in the course of this book, was Monsignor John Hynes. Prior to becoming president in 1934 Monsignor Hynes had already proved his worth, when, in 1910, at a time of acute financial crisis for the college, the government offered to double any funding for UCG that might be raised locally. Monsignor Hynes lobbied the county councils of Connacht until they agreed to strike a rate to support the college. His efforts resulted in an annual increase of funding of £3,000, thus guaranteeing the survival of UCG. By the time Monsignor Hynes retired in 1945 student numbers had risen to close to eight hundred.

While it fell to Monsignor Hynes' successor as president, Monsignor Pádraig de Brún, to save one college faculty – the Faculty of Medicine – from closure in the 1950s, the efforts of most presidents from the 1930s onwards were largely directed towards the development of the college in both an academic and a physical sense. Throughout the decades, and the problems in attracting sufficient numbers of students in the early days, the college survived, and indeed thrived. And it did so largely by playing to its strengths. Over time these strengths alternated between the college's unique position with regard to its commitment to the Irish language, its location adjacent to one of country's finest maritime environments, and its inherent willingness to innovate and take on new challenges. And above all, from the perspective of students, it was a wonderful place in which to study, and experience the many and varied facets of student life.

As a university, UCG has always been different. UCG must surely have been the only university in Ireland where a rowboat on the river was deemed by students to be a perfectly logical extension of the college library as a place to study. It was a university where, as we shall see, an entire new department, and groundbreaking research, could begin with makeshift sheds and hastily improvised electrical extensions – and a determination on the part of the academics to make it work. It was a college where the live-in college president could, if needs be, borrow the proverbial cup of sugar from the live-in porter – or vice versa. A college where the significance of the Irish language both defined – and ultimately saved – the college on more than one occasion.

In many respects this book is a record of experience, recalling a journey in education and in life. But it is also the story of the college itself. The college grew, both physically in terms of the construction of new buildings and new facilities, and in terms of its academic reputation, and yet it was an institution that was extraordinarily maternalistic/paternalistic in its relationship with its students. It was surely no accident that so many of the college's staff were known to students as 'Ma' or 'Pa'.

But the stories recounted in this book reveal so much more about what made UCG 'tick'. There are tales of lady superintendents, who supervised the moral well-being of female students; of dodgy digs and quirky landladies, eccentric professors, and all-seeing, all-knowing tea ladies. There are stories of bright scholarship students coming to Galway with a single change of clothes and very little else, except a keen desire for knowledge; of American GIs coming to study medicine in the 1950s and creating quite an impression on the female population of Galway; of army cadets, nuns and brothers who made up quite distinct strands of the student population. And there are the stories of the generations of ordinary students, from every part of the country and every socio-economic background, who came to Galway for a good education – and to have some fun in the process. These stories are at times revelatory, funny, poignant and inspiring. And each one reflects the interviewee's experience of what it was like to study, work or teach at UCG. All in all it is a remarkable story.

The beginning of the big adventure: early days

SCHOLARSHIPS AND FEES

In the first half of the twentieth century the single biggest factor in whether a student was in a position to study for a university degree was money. The cost of sending a student to university – in terms of course fees, books, accommodation and subsistence, not to mention the loss of a worker and potential wage earner at home – was a major consideration for a great many Irish families. Although university fees were relatively modest by the standards of the time, they were still prohibitive for the vast majority of families in the 1930s, '40s and '50s. Obtaining a scholarship was very often the only way a bright student could avail of a third-level education. There were various types of scholarships available to students, most of which were based on the results of the Leaving Certificate. Eibhlín Uí Chionna (née O'Malley), who came to UCG in 1942, recalls that the grants system was somewhat skewed in favour of those who excelled at mathematics:

> If you wanted to get [a grant] off the Leaving really you were at a big dis-advantage unless you were doing honours maths, because honours maths counted for 600 marks, and other subjects like Latin were 400, Irish was 400, English was 300 and so on. So anyone going for a scholarship had to do honours maths. Now a person who wasn't up to the maths, they'd no chance of getting the scholarships, which was unfair.

Over a decade later, the situation regarding scholarships had not changed a great deal, and Bobby Curran, who came to UCG in 1955, was typical of many students who went to university in the 1950s:

> In Dungarvan CBS there was very little history of people going to univer-sity, virtually none. People did the Leaving Cert and hoped to get a job with the county council, or the civil service. An odd person would win a schol-arship to university and might go, but certainly the couple of years before I did my Leaving Cert, there was nobody from Dungarvan CBS went to university.

It was a combination of factors – the wider availability of scholarships, the tenacity of some teachers in ensuring that particularly bright students applied for them, and the quality of teaching which ensured that the students got the results needed in the Leaving Cert in order to secure the scholarships – which finally began to turn the tide, as Bobby explains:

> The principal of CBS at the time, Brother Tommy Keane, had a great record of producing people who were good at mathematics. He would have put us in for everything. He had a view that you should be in for everything, if you weren't in you couldn't win. So you were in for the civil service, I did the Junior Ex, and I got fifth in that, there was three other fellas from CBS Dungarvan who were in the top twenty.

Having come in the top five in the Leaving Cert in Ireland, Bobby had a number of other choices:

> I had county council scholarships which were tenable to any of the universities. Anyone who got the county council scholarship generally went to Cork. An odd one would go to UCD, and nobody, but nobody, went to UCG. But Sylvester Murray and myself, being from Ring, and of course Dungarvan CBS at that time was an 'A' school, everything was done through Irish, we had also won Gaeltacht scholarships, and I had won an Aiken [Scholarship] as well, which would have been on the Leaving Cert results. But it was all about money. The county council was worth about £120 a year, and the conditions on it weren't too stringent. The Aiken was worth £150 and the conditions were very stringent. And the Gaeltacht one was worth £175 and not as stringent. There was still a requirement that you do your courses through Irish, but that one was definitely ... no contest. The First Science fee was £18 and the First Engineering I think was £25, and medicine would have been the same. So I came to Galway. I also, by the way, accepted the Junior Ex as a kind of a *ceann sa phóca* [one in the pocket].

The role of the Christian Brothers schools in producing excellent students was significant. As Bobby Curran notes, his school, CBS Dungarvan, had a reputation for producing students who were particularly strong in mathematics and the sciences. CBS Dundalk was another such school, which produced a significant number of excellent mathematicians and scientists – and at least one linguist, in the person of Seán Mac Iomhair, who came to UCG to do a combined BA/B. Comm. in 1961.

In 1951 Tony Bromell was another student who was fortunate in securing two scholarships to attend university – a Limerick corporation scholarship and a state (Department of Education) scholarship. A student of CBS Sexton Street in Limerick, Tony recalls that both he and the other Limerick corporation scholarship recipient – a woman – opted to accept the state scholarship, and as a result the Limerick corporation scholarships were offered to the next highest students on the list, with interesting results:

Do thug mé fhéin agus [an macléinn eile] na scoláireachtaí Bhardas Luimnigh ar ais, agus beirt as mo rang fhéin a fuair an dá cheann. Agus smaoinigh nach raibh ach dhá scoláireacht ar fáil don chathair iomlán i 1951. Bhí Sexton Street ar fheabhas.

Myself and [the other student] handed back our Limerick corporation scholarships, and it was two lads from my own class who got both of them. And remember, there were only two scholarships available for the whole of the city in 1951. Sexton Street was excellent.

In the majority of cases of CBS past pupils who were awarded scholarships to UCG the fact that they attended schools which had both A and B streams, i.e. where classes were taught, in the A classes, entirely through the medium of Irish, gave these students a distinct advantage in doing well in their Leaving Cert exams, and hence in the competition for the much-coveted scholarship places. It also meant that many extremely bright students were attracted to UCG, where it was possible to study a number of subjects entirely through the medium of Irish.

Medicine, given the length of the course and the number of practical subjects involved, was a particularly costly course. Here again a proficiency in Irish, and the fact that so many courses were available through the medium of Irish at UCG, was to prove a significant factor in making the course more affordable for students. Prof. Seán Lavelle recalls that his fees for doing medicine in 1946 were mitigated by the fact that he had been awarded a scholarship – and was taking the course (at least in the first year) through Irish: 'I got an entrance scholarship, and my fees the first year were £8, because I got reductions for doing it through Irish. And about half the incoming class did it through Irish.'

While a proficiency in Irish was clearly a major boon to some students, Jo Burke (neé McGowan), who won an entrance scholarship in 1933, recalls that when she first arrived one of her friends advised her that not all scholarship holders were the same – and to be careful whom she befriended:

Some of them thought they were superior to the people who came in from Connemara. A pal met me when I arrived, 'Ah it's only like when we were in school,' she said. 'But be very careful – don't get in with the people from Connemara, they're a different breed.' I remember that distinctly now. There were Gaeltacht scholarships, which was rightly so, they deserved it more than any of us, to get a scholarship.

The replacement of scholarships with grants in the late 1960s brought about a significant change in the numbers entering third-level education, as Pat Rabbitte explains:[1]

1 Pat Rabbitte graduated with an honours degree in arts and law in 1970.

I was the last intake of the pre-grants generation; '67 was the last year. We had huge protests on democratic access to education throughout '67 and the beginning of '68, and if memory serves the first grants scheme came in the autumn of '68. I don't think you could notice it immediately in my time, you know, but the explosion started to happen fairly quickly after that. I mean the population, I think, from memory, was about 2,200 when I was there, and to be honest I think I personally knew most of them. And it was after that that the explosion happened. So you wouldn't see the impact of the grants thing immediately, but of course looking back on it, say ten years later, you would indeed.

Not all students who came to college were fortunate enough to have scholarships. For those who did not, it was generally down to a great deal of hard work and sacrifice on the part of the families of those students to find the fees and the money to keep the student in Galway for the duration of the course they were studying. Christy Hannon recalls that in his case it was his mother's determination – and foresight – that led to his being able to attend UCG in 1961:

My mother felt that I should go to third level, and I was happy to go there myself. But she was far-seeing, she had an insurance policy matured that year, so that covered it ... I didn't have a scholarship so I was largely supported from home. I was the eldest of a family of ten, and I had another brother who went, but he was in Maynooth. I was the only one who went to UCG.

FIRST IMPRESSIONS

For some students their first impression of UCG had happened well in advance of them actually coming to study at UCG. Prof. Seán Lavelle was one such student, as he explains:

I went to the Bish,[2] and [for PE] we went up to the pitch in front of the college, and we did our exercises there. There were over 100 boys in it. So one of the lads in the class, his father was a professor there, and he said, 'There's stuffed animals inside in the Archway,' so we went in to have a look. And we saw the Canadian bush canoe, and we saw the whale's jawbone, and the big anchor, and that sort of thing, they were under the stairs on the left-hand side as you go in. And when we were there a man came in, he had a priest's soutane on him, and a biretta, and he was well able to talk to children, and he says, 'Hello boys, what are you doing?' and we told him. And he showed us what was there, but he didn't let us up to the stuffed animals, which at that time used to be above where the staff room is now.

2 St Joseph's Patrician College, know to generations of Galwegians as 'the Bish', is an all-male secondary school, run by the Patrician Brothers and located in Nun's Island, Galway.

The priest in the soutane was Monsignor John Hynes, who was, at that stage, president of the college,[3] and his easy manner with the schoolboys was indicative of his warm, friendly manner with the college students – he proved to be an extremely popular president.

For those arriving in to UCG for the first time the impression given was one of a laid-back college, intimate, open and welcoming, as Joe McGrath, who came to the college in 1945 to study engineering, recalls:

> It was very free … You could be at lectures for a week before you'd sign on to do anything. It was very casual. And there was only about seven or eight hundred students in the whole college. Sure we all knew one another, and 'twas easy to get around.

Sr Mairéad Murray, who came to do arts in 1959, was similarly impressed, not just by the friendly atmosphere of the place, but by the imposing architecture: 'I arrived, as a greenhorn I suppose, in Galway. And I loved the old look of the place, the Gothic architecture. And I never cease to marvel at the friendliness that there was everywhere, it was wonderful.'

For Seán Mac Iomhair, coming to UCG was something of an event. He arrived, as he explains, at the tail end of a hurricane in 1961:[4]

> Thaining mé ar d-eireaball Debbie. Thaining mé an lá in dhiaidh Debbie agus bhí m'athair ag tiomáint tríd na tuillte, agus crainnte laghta ar fud na h-áite, agus do réir mar a thuigim leagadh leath do crainn na choláiste leis an ngaoth mór sin.

> I came at the tail end of Debbie. I came the day after Debbie and my father was driving through the floods, with fallen trees all over the place, and as far as I understand it about half the trees in the college were blown down by that hurricane.

Christy Hannon,[5] from Roscommon, also came to UCG in 1961 and his first impressions remain with him vividly:

> I remember the registration day very, very clearly. There was a huge crowd there, huge to my eyes anyhow. And we were all in the Aula Maxima,[6] and

---

3 Monsignor John Hynes served as president 1934–5. 4 Hurricane Debbie hit Ireland on 17 Sept. 1961, causing the deaths of eleven people in Ireland, and widespread destruction of property. 5 Christy Hannon graduated with a BA in Irish and English in 1964. The following year, he graduated with a H.Dip. in education from UCD, and in 1992 he began an M.Ed. course via the Open University, graduating in 1996. 6 The Aula Maxima ('Great Hall') is located in the oldest part of the university, known as the Quadrangle. It was traditionally the venue for many formal events, such as registration, exams and conferrings.

Professor [Jeremiah] Murphy, who was the professor of English, was advising students as to what subjects they might take. And so I opted for Irish, English, Latin and economics, or *géilleagar* as it was known then. Everything in the Commerce Faculty that time was through Irish. The dean, the professor of commerce, was Liam Ó Buachalla, and there were no English lectures for commerce, so economics was through Irish.

Pat Rabbitte remembers his first day on campus in 1967 clearly:

It was a great thrill to get to university. I was quite overawed by the university ambience, and quite excited and thrilled about it to be honest. I probably was with the guys with whom I was in digs. One of them was a guy who played rugby for Ireland subsequently … He was staying with me and a couple of guys from science, and you know it was an amazing period. It was a very friendly place, there was a tremendous relationship between town and gown in Galway at that time.

Brendan Smith, from Carrickmacross, who came to do a BA in 1975, recalls a memorable introduction to the college, courtesy of a local taxi driver:

When I first came to college I had never been west of the Shannon in my life, and I remember getting a taxi from the train station to my digs, dropped my luggage off there then, and was brought up to sign on, because I was late arriving. And I remember the taxi driver saying to me as he was bringing me up, 'They're all at it there,' and I said, 'What do you mean?' 'Sexually, they're all at it there,' you know? So I'd these visions of the free-love thing happening on the campus, and it was not like that at all.

REGISTERING AND CHOOSING SUBJECTS

Having arrived at the college, the next step for new students was registration for the courses and subjects they had chosen. Choosing subjects was a relatively simple matter for some students, who had specifically chosen a particular career path to follow, or whose scholarships required them to study specific subjects. For others, it was an infinitely more relaxed, even arbitrary, affair. Certainly in the 1930s, when student numbers were small, there appears to have been a casual approach to the choosing of subjects at UCG, as Budge Clissmann,[7] who came to the college in 1931, explains:

7 Elizabeth Mulcahy (1913–2012), always known by her nickname 'Budge', was from Co. Sligo. She married Helmut Clissmann in 1938.

> I studied Irish and French for degree, and English as a pass subject. And
> there were other trimmings. I did chemistry because I had got first place
> in Ireland in science in my Intermediate Certificate, and so they said you
> had to study science anyway, because science teachers were so rare, and
> they were much better paid, you have to do science, but I didn't really
> want to. I was willing to try a bit so I did chemistry for First Arts, and
> you could always have one science subject for arts, and vice versa in sci-
> ence you could have one arts subject. So that would give me two subjects
> that I was doing for First Arts and I did First Science when I was doing
> Second Arts.

Dr Sheila Mulloy (née O'Malley) came to college in 1939, and was one of six of
the seven children of Prof. Michael O'Malley who took degrees from UCG, their
father being the professor of surgery at the university for many years. The manner
in which Dr Mulloy chose her course of study is interesting, as she explains:

> I arranged to go up with a girl I used to know at school in Galway. We hadn't
> a clue what we were going to do, nobody had in those days. You went into
> the Aula Maxima and a few professors were around, and you talked to them
> about different subjects, and all I knew was that I wouldn't do anything that
> one of the others had done, because I never doubled. We all did different
> things, deliberately. So my father had thought I should be going in to busi-
> ness but I'd no notion of it. But to please him anyway I put my name down
> for a B.Comm. And at the same time you could do an BA, and that gave you
> greater choice.

For others the choice of subjects proved to be somewhat more arbitrary, and as the
following anecdote recalls, it was not even necessary to have any prior knowledge
of the subject in order to register to study it at third level. Dr Sheila Mulloy's sister, Eibhlín Uí Chionna, came to UCG in 1942, as the second youngest of the six
siblings who studied at the college,[8] and her choice of subjects indicates an almost
pioneering willingness to take on a new challenge:

> I did science, and I chose science largely because I'd never done science
> before, it wasn't available. Boys' schools had science but lots of girls' schools
> didn't have it. And if they had it, it was at a very low level.

The fact that she had no background in the subject was not a major deterrent, as
Eibhlín explains: 'If you decide that you want to learn something, you could do
in one month what you spent five years at in school. I wanted to do something I

8 The eldest of Prof. O'Malley's seven children had opted to study architecture in Dublin, largely,
Eibhlín maintains, because it was a subject not available in Galway, 'and she picked architecture so she
could go to Dublin'.

hadn't done before.' A keen interest in a subject aside, for some students the choice of subject was something that required careful thought, as there were cost implications if it required practicals, as Eibhlín explains:

> It was £2 per subject, I think the practical might have been more. I know it was £2 per subject through English, and £1 per subject through Irish. And that meant a subject with practicals was more costly, and that would be one reason why people who were not really well-off went and did Arts to become a teacher. Because they could do all the subjects through Irish, five or six subjects, £5 or £6 for the year. So I would say that people doing medicine on the whole had to be better-off. And that was the impression that they gave you too, you got the feeling that they were the ones with the bit of money in their pockets. And also medicine was long, and how would the parents not only pay the fees, but also have to do without somebody maybe who was going to help them back home? Medicine was costlier from all points of view, and therefore the people doing medicine did tend to come from a better-off level, I'm sure of that.

Adrian Ryder,[9] who came to college in 1963, recalls some students choosing their subjects quite arbitrarily:

> You walked into the Aula Max and there were various people sitting around at tables. Now I knew where I wanted to go, but I'm told that people had gone in, and looked around, 'Where's the shortest queue?', and gone there, and paid their fees. Imagine, the shortest queue.

The idea of choosing a course of study based simply on whatever was the shortest queue for registration might sound like an incredibly casual approach to a course of study which would take up at least three years of a student's life, but there is plenty of evidence to suggest that students adopted this, and other similarly arbitrary approaches, in opting for a particular course of study. Peadar O'Dowd, for example, who came to UCG in 1959, recalls the manner in which he and two of his former classmates at St Mary's secondary school decided what they were going to study at college:

> I didn't know what to do in the college. There was no career guidance, nothing at all. The only career guidance I got in St Mary's, I was told by the president that I'd make a very good priest, and I said, 'You probably think so Father, but I don't.' Now I'd two friends, and we decided that we were fed up looking at each other. So we had three subjects we could do. We could do

9 Adrian Ryder graduated with a H.Dip. in education in 1964, having previously graduated with a B.Sc. from Maynooth. He subsequently returned to UCG to complete an M.Ed. in 1983.

science, commerce or arts. So we put the three things into a hat, and I drew commerce. That's basically how we did it.

Choosing a faculty was one thing – understanding what studying that subject would involve was an entirely different matter, as Peadar soon found when he met his prospective professor at registration:

> I remember coming in to do Commerce. Liam Ó Buachalla was the dean at the time, he was very strict as regards Irish. And I remember coming up to him and it was all in Irish, I was asked what was I going to do? Now, I knew the subjects you could do were *cuntasaíocht* [accountancy], no problem, *tráchtál* [commerce], no problem, and there was a name he had picked out for *eacnamaíocht* [economics], it had a special name, *geilleagar*. And I said I didn't understand that name, so it wasn't a very good start.

Pat Rabbitte was fortunate in that, having had no clear idea of what subjects he wanted to study, he was given advice, and was subsequently mentored to a degree, by a senior college academic, and fellow Mayo man:

> I ended up doing arts and choosing arts subjects, not for any great planning on my part. Michael Duignan was registrar at the time, and he was there advising us on what we might do and a predecessor of his was probably more influential in my decision, that was James Mitchell. He was the registrar before that. He was a very influential figure in the politics of the governance of UCG at the time, he was still on the Governing Body, and he was the senior statesman at that time. He used to walk with an old-style walking stick, and he was from Mayo, and I think for some reason or other he adopted me, insofar as I got any sensible advice at that time, it came from him. I ended up of course on the Governing Body with him.

The financial realities of pursuing a course in medicine were clearly prohibitive for many students, even with the availability of scholarships. Bobby Curran, who came to UCG to do one subject, ended up doing a different one. The story of how this came about says a great deal about Irish society at the time:

> I had intended to do medicine, I don't know why now. I would have had only the murkiest idea of what medicine involved, or any of the others for that matter. So I came to Galway and the day of induction the whole class of '55 stretched from the Aula Maxima out to the Archway, the total intake, about 200 people. And inside in the Aula sitting at different tables were different deans. And I was sent to the table where Professor [James] Mitchell, he was the registrar and secretary of the college, sat. And I had a form, I

remember ... I can see the form with my handwriting on it, and down I had *leigheas* [medicine] first and *innealtóireacht* [engineering] second, and so he said to me, 'You want to do medicine?' And I said, 'Yes.' And he said, 'And what's your background?' And I said, 'Well, my mother is a widow, a farmer, my brother's at home working and my other brother is in England.' And he said, 'You know if you qualify you'll have to buy a practice, and would your mother have the kind of money for that?' And I said, 'God no, she wouldn't.' That's what he said to me.

So with engineering now looking like his only option, Bobby Curran found himself with another major obstacle to overcome:

I said, 'Okay, I'll do engineering.' 'Well', he said, 'to get into civil engineering in Galway you have to sit an entrance exam'. And I said, 'I'd be glad to sit it.' 'Well', he said, 'it's a bit late now, it was held in August'. So, he said, 'What you'll do is do the subjects of First Engineering,' which were the academic subjects maths, maths physics, physics and chemistry, and then there was kind of practical subjects like surveying.

Having done very well in first-year exams, however, fate had one more roll of the dice for Bobby, which decided his future career, as he explains:

I was now going to do engineering, but in 1955/6 the Academic Council in UCG decided that the three-year civil-engineering course wasn't sufficient. It must have been the case that UCC and UCD, or maybe the National University of Ireland, as a policy, decided that it was going to be a four-year course. So the first inception to the four-year civil-engineering course came in '56 ... so now I was looking at five years in university.

Understandably, Bobby opted to stick with maths and maths physics, and completed his degree in 1958. He subsequently went on to have a long and successful career at NUIG, becoming director of computer services in the college in 1978.

Tuition fees at UCG, although beyond the means of most Irish families in the 1930s, '40s and '50s, unless scholarships were involved, were nonetheless remarkably low. Dr Ben Corballis recalls that he was thrilled to find that the fees for his medical degree in Ireland were significantly lower than those for a comparable course in the United States:

Tuition was $78. In the States it would have been $25,000. Anybody in my age group that went to a medical school would get student loans, and most of them came out $100,000, $125,000 in debt. And of course we didn't have anything, it was wonderful.

The registration process, which required that all students queue up in the Aula and sign on for their preferred course, was probably the first time students got some idea of what student numbers for that year were going to be like, and who their fellow classmates were likely to be. For female students coming to college for the first time, most of whom would have attended convent schools or all-female boarding schools, there was something of a rite of passage to be undergone as they entered a world where young men were now a major feature of the landscape. Eibhlín Uí Chionna recalls the earliest experiences of 'the GIBs',[10] as they were called when she first arrived in 1942:

> You were coming in to register, and all the fellas would be hanging around the Archway, eyeing them all up. So you'd run the gauntlet, you know? But you see there weren't that many girls. I would say it was even less than a third, because the total student body was in the order of 500 or 600. About a third of them were religious, now they were a class apart, they were neither male or female as far as the general public were concerned, they kept their heads down and worked.

Prof. Seán Lavelle, who came to UCG at a significant time in the college's history, was more methodical in his assessment of student numbers, as he explains.

> I came to college in 1946, and the new president, Monsignor de Brún, had just been appointed there. There were 808 students there that year. I counted them. I counted them to see how many I knew. I knew all but 30 I think, either by sight or reputation.

First years coming into the college had to find their own feet, but they in turn were 'found' by the more experienced – and opportunistic – second years, as Prof. Lavelle explains:

> You joined the queue when you came into the place, and then you were raided by the second years who wanted to sell textbooks, there were no textbooks available at that time. Kennys Bookshop would get the occasional one, but for the regular ones, the ones the first years had, they just weren't available. You just had to buy them second-hand. I still have my pathology book, which I got second hand, and as it turned out, it was held by my chief while I was in the hospital … and he got it from a stalwart of the Boxing Club, so it was third-generation.

INTERVIEW WITH THE PRESIDENT

Another formal aspect of the registration process is recalled by Christy Hannon, who remembers having to present himself to the president of the college:

10 GIB stands for 'green, ignorant and bashful'.

We had to queue up for President Newell's office. We went in and we had a letter attesting to character and academic aptitude from the principal of our secondary school, that was compulsory, that such a one would benefit from third-level education, or wording to that effect. There was a letter of recommendation from the school, and your matriculation certificate. That was a very brief meeting.

Christy went on to note of the president that, 'The next time I saw him was the day of graduation.'

Christy Hannon also recalled that as well as presenting themselves to the president, all first years had to make the acquaintance of another important figure on campus:

> All first-year students were expected to report to Fr Kyne. He was the college chaplain. He lived in a house directly across from the college main gate. He was a tall, very pleasant, kindly man, who remarked to myself and a classmate that the year would be quite pleasant for us provided we didn't fail the exams. Fortunately we passed.

Although most of those interviewed referred to Fr Kyne as the college 'chaplain', technically such a role did not exist at that time, and his actual title was 'dean of residence', as Dr Séamus Mac Mathúna explains:

> Bhí An tAthair Tomás Ó Cadhain anseo mar Dheánach Cónaithe. Ní raibh aon chead 'Séiplínigh' a bheith ag an gColáiste. Bhí bac ar na Coláistí faoin Irish Universities Act 1908 aon airgead poiblí a chaitheamh ar chúrsaí creidimh: sin an cur chuige ginearálta a bhí ann. Mar sin, is faoi scáth an teidil 'deans of residence' a ligeadh isteach iad siúd le haghaidh na gcreideamh éagsúla. Bhí siad ar fáil le comhairle ghineárálta a thabhairt do mhic léinn. Agus daoine mar iad siúd, bhí siad an-tuiscionach. Bhí Mary ('Ma') O'Driscoll ann mar 'lady superintendent' dos na 'cailíní' (seachas na 'mná' – bhuel, sin an blas a bhí ann).

> Fr Tom Kyne was here as dean of residence. The college was not allowed to have 'chaplains'. The colleges were prohibited under the Irish Universities Act 1908 from spending any public money on religious matters: that was the general approach. So, it was under the title 'deans of residence' that they were allowed in for the various denominations. They were available to give general advice to students. And people like them were very understanding. Mary (or 'Ma') O'Driscoll was there as 'lady superintendent' for the 'girls' (rather than the 'women' – well, that was the flavour of the times).

DIGS AND LANDLADIES

Finding digs in Galway was one of the first tasks facing students. Unless they lived within cycling distance of the college, and could continue to live at home, most students had to find accommodation in either digs, which were available in private houses, on a bed-and-board basis, or hostels, which tended to be run by the religious orders. The renting of houses or flats by students certainly did not feature until at least the late '60s or early '70s when the housing stock in Galway increased significantly.

Budge Clissmann recalled her experience of staying with the Sisters of Jesus and Mary in their hostel in Shantalla in the early 1930s, and the productive environment for study which it provided:

> I went to the hostel initially. And then the second year I didn't go to the hostel, I decided to go into digs. And they were very distracting. For my third year, my last year, I decided that I would go back to the hostel, because I could concentrate more on my work. The nuns were wonderful. Teresa was the cook, who went in lay clothes into town to buy the meat. We were always asked what would we like to eat. There were only about twenty-three of us. It wasn't a big hostel. It had been set up in order to facilitate the order, to send their young nuns to college. You didn't have your own room. You had about maybe three or four in a room. And the real snag was there were several toilets but there was only one bathroom – for twenty-three girls. And there'd be hell to pay when there was a hop. Everyone banging on the door, 'Come out, come out!'

According to Budge Clissmann, however, there was an alternative to the rather crowded bathing facilities afforded by the hostel:

> I'll tell you what there was in Galway, there were civic baths. They were a wonderful institution. They were down on the quays, and they had been installed for the emigrants going to America. There were baths there and you paid tuppence, and for tuppence you got a hot bath, a clean towel and a lump of soap. And you could be always sure of having a bath when you went, you didn't have to book. That was a wonderful facility for us. We came when the emigrants stopped. I came to college in '31, and the emigration to America stopped, practically, after the crash in '29, but they still maintained the baths.

What is most striking about this account of the hostel in Shantalla is that thirty years after Budge Clissmann stayed there, Maureen Langan-Egan also stayed at the hostel for the duration of her BA/B.Comm. degree, which she began in 1960 – and her experiences were similarly positive, with the Sisters of Jesus and Mary emerging as an order that provided a wonderful environment for the students in their care:

> I was singularly privileged. I stayed up in the hostel in Shantalla, I was there for three years, and you had absolutely fantastic people in that place. You had Sr Anthony, Sr Mel, may God be good to her, the other people who were running the place, and I've heard people say since that 'anybody could keep students'. They can't. I mean the standard of food and everything was superb. They had wonderful big, clean kitchens. You wouldn't get any salmonella out of those places I can tell you.

By the 1940s most students were in digs in Galway, with Salthill, College Road, Canal Road, Fr Griffin Road and Newcastle having a large concentration of digs accommodation for students. Prof. Sean Lavelle recalls what he paid for his digs.

> We all were in digs, except the fellas who lived in the town. And we would get our bed and breakfast, three meals a day, usually three to a room, for 35s., it had just gone up from 32s. and 6d., to 35s., that's about €1.75, thereabouts, a week.

Students and their parents usually tried to arrange accommodation before coming to Galway, but this was not always possible. Prof. Seán Tobin, who first came to the college in 1947, had something of a trying time in this respect:

> I turned up here in October of 1947, and I was 17 years old at the time, going on 18. And I had been away from home a couple of years before that at boarding school, so it wasn't my first time away from home. But I had hoped to have my father come up with me, you know we were somewhat insecure teenagers in those days. As things turned out he couldn't manage it but he said, 'I have an old friend there. I've written to him and he'll look after you, and he has a guest house in Lower Salthill in Galway.' Except that when I turned up he knew nothing about it. And there was nothing he could do for me, and he was loftily uninterested. I had a big suitcase, and there I was. But I went around looking for someplace to stay, and of course the student numbers were much smaller in those days, and I eventually wound up on Fr Griffin Road … and there were about three or four other students with me. Two of them from Cork became very great friends of mine, so I spent the first year there.

Unlike Prof. Tobin, Tony Bromell's father was able to accompany him to Galway from Limerick in 1951, and ensure that his son was settled into suitable accommodation in Galway, as Tony explains:

> Chuaigh m'athair liom an lá sin an an mbus, agus chuamar amach go dtí an lóistín, agus bhí an lóistín ceart go leor, agus ansin d'imigh sé sin abhaile. Dhá phunt agus deich scilling, agus ba mhór an méid airgid é sin. An scoláireacht a bhí agam, bhí céad caoga phunt sa bhliain. Na táillí, bhíodar an iseal, £35, nó rud éigin mar sin.

> My father came with me that day on the bus, and we went out to the digs, and the digs were fine, and then he went home. £2 10s., and that was a lot of money that time. The scholarship I had gave me £150 a year. The fees were very low, £35 or something like that.

Naturally, the cost of digs changed over time, and Christy Hannon, who came to UCG in 1961, recalls his digs being reasonably priced for what he and his fellow housemates were getting:

> I had digs got out in Salthill. A friend of mine who would be doing Second Ag. that year was in that digs and he recommended it, so I went there. Now the digs were £3 10s. a week. That was seven days, 10s. a day we'll say.

Landladies, in the main, took their duty of care to students very seriously, and there were very few instances of bad landladies, or landladies who shirked their duties. Most students appear to have rather liked and respected their landladies, who had to work extremely hard to meet all of the needs of the students. Prof. Tobin recalls one of his landladies fondly:

> We went home at Christmas, and I think at Easter, but you weren't going home every weekend the way they do now. But of course in those days it was quite different. We were looked after by landladies and I remember particularly the landlady I had in my second, third and fourth years, in St Mary's Road, a really lovely woman, very maternal lady entirely, and sure she had a hard time with us. Not that we gave her a hard time as such, but it seemed to rain incessantly in those days, and you'd come in dripping wet. And she had in her kitchen a great big range, with an enormous copper cylinder over it, and our overcoats, and if we were fortunate enough to have a second pair of trousers, the wet ones would be thrown up over that.

During the war years, and for some time afterwards, with money in short supply, the clothes worn by students were often very basic. Prof. Tobin has referred to the fact that having a second pair of trousers was something of a luxury. But girls were similarly curtailed in their dress in the hungry days of the '40s. He recalls that: 'We were all so young, and kind of impecunious too in those days, that sometimes girls would turn up in their first year in their convent uniforms. You couldn't afford anything else you know, times were tough.' Similarly, Dr Sheila Mulloy recalls that during her college years (1939–43) even the most basic item – a good winter coat – was often in short supply for some students:

> Of the boys, some of them hadn't overcoats. And the girls would have the same coat for the whole four years. They'd be there with you and you'd know them, you'd say, 'The girl with the green coat,' and so on.

While most students could ill afford to dress in the latest fashions, one affectation students could just about afford was the smoking of cigarettes. Dr Mulloy recalls one group of female students who were viewed with some awe by herself and some of her friends:

> There were three 'sophisticates' together that I knew well, and they all smoked. Most of the girls didn't smoke. They used to have their smokes held by a hairgrip so that they'd get it right down to the end you see.

Digs were generally divided into houses for boys and houses for girls, and although it was permissible for boys to visit girls' digs, a strict curfew was imposed for visitors, and a watching eye was kept by the landladies at all times. Jo Burke came to college in 1933 and recalls one of her male friends paying her and her friends visits in their digs:

> He christened our digs 'The Vestal Virgins'. They'd say, 'Where are you going tonight?' 'I'm going to visit the Vestal Virgins,' he used to say. We had a lovely landlady, and every night at half past 10 she'd knock at the door, 'Ladies, your supper is ready.' What she was really saying was, 'Boys get out, time to go.' Oh we had boys coming in, every night we had visitors.

Maureen Langan-Egan, who had been a student herself in the early 1960s, later kept students on occasion, and she recalls that even at that stage Mrs O'Driscoll, the lady superintendent, kept a very close eye on student digs, and was particularly keen that students of opposite sexes did not occupy the same house:

> She'd be very strict on the rule of boys and girls in the same digs. And I remember I had a student, a lady student, staying with me at one stage, and somebody asked me would I take this lad for a while, he was the son of a friend. And Mrs O'Driscoll checked the accommodation. She said, 'Maureen Egan – you should know better than that!'

The rewards for landladies were relatively meagre, given the work involved, but in post-war Ireland even that income was very welcome. Joe McGrath, who came to study engineering in 1945, recalls that there was no shortage of people willing to take in students:

There was no problem getting digs. I don't know how … word of mouth [I suppose]. When I went to Galway first I was in digs in Canal Road. And then afterwards we were out in Taylor's Hill. We were paying about 20s. a week, all found. And they were glad to get it. A lot of people involved were depending on the students year in, year out. And we knew nearly every digs in Galway because there was someone we knew in them. They were spread all over the place, from Salthill right into the college. I never heard of anyone being in a flat or an apartment, it was all digs.

With many students relying on scholarships and grants to support them through their college years, money was always in short supply, and Maureen Langan-Egan recalls that landladies sometimes had a long wait to be paid:

I stayed up in the Hostel in Shantalla for three years, and they would wait until the end of the year when the grants came in and get it in a lump sum. And an awful lot of the landladies around the town did the same thing. Indeed I remember very clearly one medical student who was fond of the horses, and he owed his landlady up in Shantalla an awful lot of money, and finally when a horse won he cleared the whole lot.

Students were generally very well behaved in their digs, because the consequences, if they were not, were grave: they would be asked to leave and have to secure other digs at short notice, and they would be reported to the college authorities. But there were occasions when students, unbeknownst to their landladies, somewhat misbehaved but escaped the consequences. The following story, recounted by Jo Burke, relates to one of her contemporaries in the early 1930s:

He was staying in digs in Salthill, and some of the neighbours had turkeys in for Christmas. They used to buy turkeys, and fatten them up themselves. One of the turkeys was cackling all night, and he went out and chopped its head off, he did, and presented it to his landlady. They had a turkey dinner. They had no idea where the turkey had come from. They thought it was a present he gave.

Most students were lucky with their digs, but occasionally students had to move when the accommodation was not up to standard. Dr Diarmuid Ó Cearbhaill, who came to UCG as an Aiken Scholar in 1947,[11] recalls that his first digs in Galway did not quite work out as planned:

11 In 1947 the minister for education, Frank Aiken, introduced new scholarships to encourage students to take university degrees through the medium of Irish at UCG. At £150 per annum they were 50 per cent more valuable than any existing scholarship and were eagerly contested. The first cohort of 'Aiken scholars' arrived in UCG in 1947, in the faculties of arts, commerce and science.

> An rud sa chéad lóistín, is cuimhneach liom nach raibh an bia rómhaith agus mí Feabhra amháin bhí anraith againn agus bhí dhá bluebottle ann. Agus bhí mé cúthalach go leor, ach is é an rud a rinne mé, chuir mé ar imeall an phláta iad agus tharraing mé ciorcal timpeall orthu.

> The thing about the first digs was that as far as I remember the food wasn't great. And one February we had soup, and there were two bluebottles in it. And I was shy enough, but what I did was I left them on the rim of the plate and I drew a circle around them.

Sadly his landlady did not appear to get the message. The food did not improve, and Diarmuid changed digs, and went on to stay with his next landlady, in Salthill, for the next three years.

The food served to students was basic, but generally good, with landladies experiencing particular difficulties during the war years when rationing was in force and food was scarce. Having come to college at the outbreak of the war in 1939, and commuted from her home in Barna each day, in her final year Dr Sheila Mulloy opted to take digs in Galway. She soon discovered that while being based in the town was a great boon to her social life, the quality of catering in her digs left a lot to be desired:

> This lady didn't know how to cook a potato. She was able to cook nothing. And every single day we got potatoes that were left in the water too long, and the skin falling off. And then a pork chop every single day, and baked beans every single day. And then in the morning you got a fry, and in the evening you got a fry. And the big thing was a big plate of biscuits was put out after the dinner, and we'd all eat into that.

Dr Mulloy's sister, Eibhlín Uí Chionna, who came to UCG in 1942, agrees that the menu was pretty much the same each day:

> In those days your first lecture would be at nine, and off you'd go. For breakfast you'd be given a rasher and egg, and then you'd come back, you'd be finished at one, and then between one and two that was dinner time, none of this fancy lunch stuff. And you cycled back to your digs and you were given dinner. You'd get soup and you'd get a piece of overcooked meat and you'd get potatoes and vegetable, which would often be tinned beans. There would be some kind of a pudding too, some kind of a milk thing, or stewed apple or something, and you'd eat that and then you'd go back to college for two. And then you'd come home and you were given tea, which was rasher and egg. Maybe there'd be sausages thrown in as well. And then on Friday you got a boiled egg, fish for dinner, and then you got another boiled egg for tea.

In later years, when wartime restrictions were at an end, limited menus were less of a problem. But the somewhat cosseted existence enjoyed by those living in digs did have its disadvantages, especially for the male students, when they eventually left college, as Prof. Tobin explains:

> We were fed very well by our landladies, well at least I was. I'd never complain about the treatment that I got. The same thing happened when I went subsequently to do postgraduate work in Manchester, and I was in digs there where we had landladies who looked after us splendidly. And I remember my mother saying to me, 'You've been spoilt rotten, you can't do a thing around the house.' Well you know, two years in boarding school, four years in UCG, and the next three years in Manchester, and all the time being looked after. I mean you get very lazy. I think it's much better now. My boys, they learned to cook for themselves because they had to. I never had to. So we had a privileged life in many ways.

Coming home, wet through in many cases, to a cold digs, was something students just had to accept. But in the early '50s Tony Bromell and his roommate found a way to keep warm, courtesy of the college:

> Bhí teallach againne sa seomra codlata, agus nuair a bhímís ag teacht abhaile istoíche ón ollscoil, bhí an mhóin a bhí á usáid ins an ollscoil ag an am, le haghaidh a' teasa, agus bhíodh crúacha móra móna ansin ins an Quad. So do thugfaimís cúpla fód móna linn, agus bheadh tine againn ansin ins an seomra codlata. Ach an deacracht ná fáil réidh leis na luaithrigh ar maidin, agus iad fós te, i ngan fhios don bhean a tí.

> There was a fireplace in our bedroom, and when we used to be coming home in the evening from college, the turf they used in the college for the heating would be piled in a big mound in the Quad. So we would take a couple of sods of turf with us and we'd have a fire in our bedroom. The problem was how to get rid of the ashes in the morning, as they would be still hot, without the landlady finding out.

GETTING TO KNOWN EVERYONE – AND GETTING KNOWN

Prof. Seán Tobin recalled that the student numbers in those post-war years were very small, amounting to approximately seven or eight hundred: 'In those days you'd know everybody, every student, if you didn't know them to speak to then you'd see them, so it was a small, neat little college in those days.'

Neat and friendly it may well have been, but there were disadvantages in everyone knowing everyone else, as Tony Bromell, who came to college in 1951, explains: 'Ar bhealach amháin bhí sé ar fheabhas an aithne a bheith chomh mór sin ar a chéile, ar bhealach eile bhí fhios ag chuile dhuine céard a bhí ar siúl agat.' ('On the one hand it was great that everyone knew each other so well. On the other hand it meant that everyone knew what you were up to.') As an honours student, and a pioneer, there wasn't much that Tony might have been doing to draw unwanted attention on himself, but the point is a valid one nonetheless. For any student, being anonymous on campus, at least until the 1980s, simply wasn't an option.

WAITING FOR GRANTS

Having registered for their courses, and found suitable accommodation, the students could settle in, attend lectures and begin their studies. But there was still one major source of stress for those students who were dependent on scholarships – the wait for the next tranche of funding could be agonizing. For many years, the administration in the college was handled exclusively by Máiréad Ní Dhonnchadha and her sister, Mrs Máire Brazil. Prof. Seán Tobin reflects the experiences of many when he recalls the anxious wait for much-needed scholarship funds to arrive:

> I remember two or three of us, as the time approached, going into the Bursar's Office. Máiréad was really lovely to us. But she'd say, '*Níor tháinig sé go fóill, ach b'fheidir amárach* [It didn't come yet, but maybe tomorrow].' And you'd be there waiting for your £30 or whatever it was. Oh I tell you that was wonderful, to get that into your hands.

Bobby Curran also recalls the anxious days waiting for payment of the scholarship money, and how students survived in the interim:

> The first moiety didn't come on the first of the month. We didn't get it until maybe the first week in December. How did we survive? We'd to fund ourselves, well … a lot of borrowing. I used to owe Johnny Ward a couple of quid for the odd fag or whatever. But Johnny was great. You'd come in and Johnny would have the chat with you, and, 'Ten fags,' and he'd give you them. And then years later Johnny would get a cheque in the post for ten fags for five years or whatever. Sure that's why Johnny Ward got an honorary degree, because people wrote back … well one of the reasons.[12]

The name of Johnny Ward, of Ward's Shop on University Road, is one that was invoked by very many of those interviewed, and in each case reference was made to the many kindnesses extended by this genial shopkeeper to generations of UCG students. Maureen Langan-Egan was one of those who remembered Johnny Ward with great affection:

12 Mr Johnny Ward was conferred with an honorary master's degree in November 2002 in recognition of his valuable contribution to the lives of students in NUI Galway.

Money was very, very short, and Johnny Ward bolstered an awful lot of
people over the years. I was so delighted to see him getting that honorary
degree, all the kindness that man did. You know he could pick up on where
there was distress very, very quickly. He just looked after people. And people didn't forget him for that, I'm sure.

THE AIKEN SCHOLARSHIPS

The introduction of one scholarship scheme, the Aiken Scholarships, in 1947
was to prove a turning point in the fortunes of the college. The scholarships,
which were initiated by the then minister for finance, a keen Irish language
enthusiast, Frank Aiken,[13] were provided to allow students to study for their
degrees entirely through the medium of Irish – and UCG was the only NUI
college that could facilitate this. Selection was based on Leaving Certificate
results, and only the highest achievers were awarded the scholarships, a fact
that led to the attraction of the very best students to Galway in certain
disciplines (although even in Galway some courses, such as engineering and
medicine, were not available through Irish). The amount – £150 – was the highest of any scholarship available at that time, and the Aiken Scholarships were
therefore much prized. One of the first recipients of an Aiken Scholarship, Prof.
Seán Tobin, recalls they were initially the brainchild of Monsignor Pádraig de
Brún:

> Frank Aiken … had introduced these scholarships, as far as I know at the
> behest of Monsignor Pádraig de Brún, who had not long before that become
> president of the college. He managed to persuade Aiken to provide these
> scholarships to try to gizz up UCG, which was more or less rumbling along,
> but more or less in the doldrums.

UCG was not the only Irish university in the doldrums. In the aftermath of the
Second World War, increases in university attendance were a worldwide phenomenon, and as O'Connor has observed 'the universities of the world, many of which
had spent centuries in semi-slumber, had been thrust into the forefront of national
and, indeed, international endeavour'.[14] In the case of Ireland, however, increases in
attendance were generally not matched with increases in state investment in third-
level education. Dr Arthur Conway, on assuming the presidency of UCD in 1940,
was confronted with what he described as 'a state of grim and unrelieved penury'
at a time when student numbers were rising and limited space and resources had to

---

13 Frank Aiken was first elected to Dáil Éireann in 1923 and at each subsequent election until 1973.
Aiken served as minister for defence (1932–9), minister for the coordination of defensive measures
(1939–45), minister for finance (1945–8) and minister for external affairs (1951–4 and 1957–69). He
also served as minister for lands and fisheries for a brief period in 1936.   14 S. O'Connor, *A troubled
sky: reflections on the Irish educational scene, 1957–1968* (Dublin, 1986), p. 47.

be spread thinner and thinner.[15] His colleagues in the other NUI colleges, including UCG, found themselves similarly stretched. Even up to the late 1950s it was
the case that the state's educational policy 'was informed by a conservative con-
census, shared by politicians, senior officials and educational authorities, which
dictated only a limited, subsidiary role for public authorities in providing education'.[16] As a result, all four university colleges were severely under-resourced, with
net state expenditure on higher education in 1958–9 amounting to 0.62 per cent
of overall appropriations.[17] In the context of such underfunding, it is hardly surprising, therefore, that the introduction of the Aiken Scholarships at UCG had a
particularly profound impact on the fortunes of the college.

Lucrative they may have been, but the Aiken Scholarships were also hard-won,
and hard to maintain, as Prof. Tobin recalls:

> We were this group of pretty … well, if we weren't very bright we were
> certainly hardworking after we got these scholarships. But you had to take
> your course tré Ghaeilge, so as I couldn't take engineering through Irish, I
> couldn't take engineering. So I decided that the next best thing, a subject
> which I liked and was reasonably good at, was mathematics, so I took sci-
> ence, and concentrated on mathematics. Furthermore, the conditions were
> extremely tough in that first year, you had to get a certain quota of honours
> in your first-year exam to hold on to your scholarship. Oh it was very tough.

The pressure on students to retain these valuable scholarships was sometimes so
great that drastic measures were called for. Prof. Tobin recalls one instance where
he was in danger of losing his scholarship because of a difficulty with lab work in
one of his science subjects:

> One of the subjects I took was chemistry, and for some reason chemistry
> and I didn't get on too well together. There was a particular procedure
> that you had to follow called titration, trying to filter out certain things,
> and this means you pour something through filter paper in a glass funnel.
> Now whenever I did that the wretched filter paper always dissolved and
> went down through the funnel too. I did well enough on the theoretical
> side of the chemistry, which involved a certain knowledge of mathemat-
> ics and so on. In those days the professors were approachable, and the
> students were very few. You could go to them and ask them how did you
> get on in the exam, while waiting for the official results to come out. So a
> friend and I called up to Tommy Dillon, a famous professor of chemistry,
> and Tommy looked at our results and he said to my friend, 'Oh yes, you

15 UCD had 2,400 at the time of Conway's appointment. By the time he retired, seven years later, that
number had risen to 3,200. E.T. Whittaker, 'Arthur William Conway. 1875–1950', *Obituary Notices of
Fellows of the Royal Society*, 7:20 (Nov. 1951), p. 339.   16 O'Connor *A troubled sky*, p. 237.   17 Ibid.,
p. 255, quoting Committee of Public Accounts, *Appropriation accounts, 1958–9* (Dublin, 1959), p. 88.

got your first-class honours of course, no question.' And then he looked at me, and he said, 'Well, you did well enough, you got second honours … but I understand you need a first honours?' I said, 'If possible, if possible.' 'Well', he said, 'you're not so far off', he said, 'are you going to take chemistry next year?' And I said, 'No Professor.' 'In that case you can have a first honours.' As long as he could get rid of me, he was willing to help me keep the scholarship.

The pressure to achieve honours in all subjects was particularly high in first year, when students on Aiken Scholarships had to achieve honours (including two firsts) in all their first-year subjects. The attractions – and more particularly distractions – of college life often took their toll at exam time, as Prof. Tobin explains:

> In the second year of the Aiken Scholarships quite a number of them lost their scholarships … because they just didn't make the grade. I remember one girl, who was a very bright girl, ah but to tell the truth I think she spent more time on the dance floor than in the study hall, so it wasn't surprising that she lost her scholarship.

For other more diligent students however the demands of the Aiken Scholarships were simply too exacting, despite their best efforts, and steps were taken by the college authorities to alleviate some of the pressure:

> After that there was a deputation up from the college, and it was led by the *léachtóir sa stair tré Ghaeilge* [lecturer in history through Irish], Síle Ní Chinnéide. She went up with some others to argue that the conditions on the scholarship were far too hard, and so they lowered the requirements, because people were coming in, good people, but they were being put to the pin of their collar, we all were, and we had to work like crazy in first year I remember.

The significance of the Aiken Scholarships in the development of UCG cannot be overestimated. The scholarships attracted exceptional students to UCG from all over the country, including areas that traditionally would not have been a catchment for the college, and it could be claimed, with some justification, that the subsequent improvement in the academic reputation of the college was due in no small part to the influence of this scholarship scheme and the academic achievements of its holders.

THE COMING OF THE AMERICANS

Another group of students who were attracted to the college in the 1940s, but for very different reasons, had an equally dramatic influence on the college's fortunes.

From the mid-1940s UCG began to admit a group of students who were to leave a very strong mark on the university – American medical students, most of them ex-servicemen. Having served in the US military during the Second World War, these men returned to the United States at the end of the war with the intention of either taking up training in one of the US medical schools, or of completing training begun before they were called up or enlisted. However, with intense pressure for places in the American medical schools, there were insufficient places available for the ex-servicemen. The 'GI Bill' guaranteed these young men (many of whom were by this time married with families) an education on their return from active service,[18] and in order to make good on this guarantee the US government had to look outside of the US for suitable medical schools to which to send their ex-servicemen. Following an assessment of all the medical schools in the British Isles, the decision was made to recognize only two as suitable schools for American medical students: the University of Edinburgh – and University College Galway.

The choice of these two universities is striking, given that they were up against very stiff competition from all of the major universities in the UK and Ireland. However, the assessors based their decision on a number of factors, not the least of which was the locations of the medical schools, both of which were in close proximity to the teaching hospitals where the medical students would receive their clinical training. This, the assessors felt, ensured that medical students would be more clinically experienced at the end of their training. And so the Americans arrived, and created quite an impression from the outset.

Dr Ben Corballis was one of those Americans who came to Ireland to study for a degree in medicine in 1950. Although not an ex-serviceman, the story of how he came to be a medical student at UCG is a fascinating one:

> I was planning to go into medicine, and was not a good student. My days in college were wonderful, but minimal. And I applied to medical school, and they had the very good sense to say no. A parish priest, Fr Hugh Morley, who'd come over from Mullingar, said to me, 'Would you go in Ireland?' and I said, 'Of course I would.' So my friend and I, we got applications, and we filled them out, and sent them in. That was in February. And they never responded of course, never heard from them. So in October I said to Fr Morley, 'What are we going to do now?' He said, 'I have my friend Fr Senan in Dublin, we'll send him a cablegram.' So he did. Later that day we got a cablegram back that said, and I quote, 'Should you arrive baggage in hand you would be assured of an old-fashioned Irish welcome.'

They assumed that this implied that a place would be found for Ben and his friend Luke in an Irish medical school, the pair set out for Ireland.

18 The Servicemen's Readjustment Act of 1944, more commonly known as the 'GI Bill', was a US law that provided a range of benefits for returning Second World War veterans. It was signed into law by President Franklin D. Roosevelt on 22 June 1944.

Five days later we got on board a ship, the *Brittanic*, and came over. Landed at Cobh and went up to Dublin. And Fr Senan was lovely and he said, 'My friend, the president of the college, Monsignor Browne, has been away all summer and I haven't had a chance to talk to him. But not to worry.

If the young Americans were at all anxious that they might have made a grave mistake in crossing the Atlantic, they certainly did not show it as they were escorted around Dublin for a couple of days by another friend of Fr Senan's, a senior member of the Garda Siochána:

> Fr Senan picked up the phone ... All he said was, 'I've got some American boys here, I'd like you to show around Dublin.' So for two and a half days he drove us around. And all the time [my friend] is worried. I'm having a wonderful time, but [he] is saying, 'Shouldn't we be going to school?' So finally Fr Senan said, 'Alright, I'll send my driver to take you down to Galway tomorrow.'

Having arrived in style in Galway the young Americans set out to meet the president, Monsignor de Brún.

> We were led upstairs to the President's Office. Now Monsignor Browne was busy translating the Iliad ... from the original into Irish without Latin in the intermediary. And we went into this big room upstairs. And he said, 'Welcome, I haven't done anything about it, but tomorrow we'll ... ' you know? And he said, 'I fancy you should stay at the Banba,' which is a hotel out in Salthill ... which was four guineas a night.

After their costly first night in Galway the young men set out next morning to meet the dean of the Faculty of Medicine, Prof. Stephen Shea.[19]

> We came back the next day and he sent us down to see Dr Shea, down in the Anatomy Department. And Dr Shea said, 'Nice to meet you, but didn't you get our letter?' And we said, 'No.' Our parents at this point are reading the letters, 'We're sorry, we're all full, we can't take you ...'

Understandably dejected by this polite, but firm, rejection by the dean of medicine, Ben and his friend were considering their folly in coming all the way from America when they once again encountered Monsignor de Brún:

> So [my friend] and I walked out, devastated ... Coming down the path is the president, and he said, 'Ah, they forgot what the system is ... they teach, I

19 Shea was professor of anatomy 1921–67, and dean of medicine 1927–67.

admit. Go back in.' We went back, and Dr Shea said, 'Of course, we're glad to have you in our school, welcome aboard.' And … our career began.

Finding suitable digs was the next priority for the young Americans:

> We went out to Salthill. The people who had the house had lived in America, and they had brought all of their lamps and stuff back. Of course they didn't work.[20] So in the living room where we were to study there was one little bulb … And [my friend] and I had to sleep in the same bed. We were both 17 stone at the time, and it wasn't incredibly comfortable.

In spite of the far from ideal conditions Ben and his friend soldiered on for a few months until the opportunity to move to more suitable digs arose:

> Right next door was a house where three fellas from Newfoundland [Canadian ex-servicemen] were in digs. And I guess it's probably the time when they went to Dublin [to do clinical practice], we moved over to their house. So that got us through the year. When we came back then in the fall we decided to take a house on Lower Salthill. We stayed there and we ate either at Wards Hotel or at St Joseph's Guest House.

The American students did so well in Galway that the word spread, and more and more of them began to arrive. In one case, as Dr Corballis recalls, an American student came to study medicine at UCG courtesy of some American students who were already studying medicine there – and a Shannon stopover:

> He was in medical school in Italy. But [he] went to Kennedy Airport to get on the plane to go to Italy, and met two or three of these lads … and on the way over they convinced [him] that he really ought to be in school in Ireland. So he got off the plane at Shannon with them and came up to Galway.

The American students not only added great colour and excitement to the college, but they were also very good students, who worked extremely hard. As ex-servicemen they were generally disciplined, and in most cases were older and more mature than their Irish counterparts, and had already completed a science degree in the States. They were also very focused on completing their medical degrees and going back home to practice. As a result, both they and their Polish counterparts, who were also ex-servicemen, raised the bar considerably in terms of the number of first- and second-class honours degrees being awarded in medicine.[21] Dr Connell

20 This was due to the different electrical voltages in use in Ireland and the United States.   21 Polish medical students began to arrive at UCG when the Polish School of Medicine in Edinburgh closed in 1949.

Cunningham, who graduated in 1955, recalled the unique make-up of his Second Med class:

> At one stage we found ourselves with twelve Irish, fourteen Poles, four English and four Americans in our class. We Irish, just out of boarding school, were inclined to take life easy, the Americans had already got a science degree under their belts and many of the Poles, several years older than us, had been through the war, or at least had been displaced by it and tended to take life much more seriously.[22]

THE IMPACT OF FREE EDUCATION

The introduction of the free-education scheme in 1967 saw a large increase in the numbers attending secondary school, and completing second-level education to Leaving Certificate level. As a natural consequence of this the numbers opting to attend third level increased significantly in the 1970s, and Grace Timlin, who was educated at Salerno in Galway, was one of those for whom going to university was not only possible, but was actively encouraged, as she explains:

> That time, Salerno didn't want to know anything but university … practically all of my class went to college. We were all geared towards university, and the requirements were much lower than they are now. And so I think something like eighteen of my class of twenty-four came to college here in Galway. There was no CAO at that time, you basically had the college of your choice, so everybody picked Galway, being the nearest, because most of us lived in Salthill.

Grace's choice of subjects – history, geography, archaeology and English – was not guided by any particular career path she had planned out:

> I was just here for the social life at the time. Sorry to have to admit that but I wasn't very academic. I went to all my lectures and I did what I was supposed to do, but I didn't spend enough time in the library, looking up references and stuff that we were supposed to do that time.

STUDENT ACCOMMODATION

By the 1970s most students were no longer living in digs, but instead rented flats or houses during term time. The prospect of designated student accommodation was somewhat down the road at that stage, but in the late 1970s the idea was

---

22 Dr Connell Cunningham, 'Life as a medical student, 1949–1955' in 50 Year Club/Cumann Caoga Bliain publication, NUI Galway, 2005, p. 6.

first mooted, as Brendan ('Speedie') Smith, a student-union activist at the time, explains:

> We approached the college with a view to taking over the Rahoon Flats and turning it into a student town. That was modelled on the German thing that you would get in Munich, and we would in turn swap land for houses. But [we were told] absolutely not, not in a million years, you will never have student accommodation on an Irish campus. Even though TCD had, but that was a tradition going back centuries, and Maynooth had, but that was only for the clerics [we were told]. No way would it ever happen. So look how much times have changed.

The learning process

THE 1930S

Budge Clissmann's arrival in 1930 coincided with a particularly volatile period in Irish politics, and the internal politics of UCG at that time reflected this. From a staunchly republican family in Co. Sligo, she came to UCG to study French and Irish, and her parents instructed her to keep her head down, study and stay away from politics. Although she sought to follow her parents' advice, she sometimes found it difficult:

> When I came to college it was still Cumann na nGaedhael, not Fine Gael. And when I was going back to my second year, that would be 1931, I think Cumann na nGaedhael realized that they were on a losing wicket, or that they had the possibility of losing in the election that was coming up in '32, and so the bishops, who of course were very Cumann na nGaedhael anyway, issued a letter, an Episcopal letter, that was to be read off the altar. Anyway, Sligo was at that time a very republican town, and when there would be a letter from the bishops which contained something really objectionable, which wasn't rare, you walked out. And then when I went back to college in my second year, the letter was being read out at Mass. And all the professors and their families went in the front in the Jes for 11 o'clock Mass.[1] So there was a statement that anybody who was in the IRA, or supported or sympathized with the IRA ... of course I was waiting to see what was going to come, and I thought, it'd have to be very, very bad before I could walk out ... so when we got to this thing about they would be excommunicated ... Anyway, I walked out. And to my amazement I was the only one.

Budge's walkout, however, had been witnessed by a large contingent of the academic staff of the university, and there were to be repercussions from her actions:

> The following day, the lady dean of residence said she wanted to talk to me, and that she had been asked to interview me by the Acadmic Council. The chairman of that, he was professor of philosophy,[2] and he had a long white beard, he was in college for donkey's years. And she was to interview me,

───────────

[1] This is a reference to St Ignatius church in Sea Road, which is attached to Coláiste Iognáid, the Jesuit secondary school, known to Galwegians as 'the Jes'. [2] John F. Howley was professor of philosophy 1914–36.

and to enquire had I left the church in an ostentatious manner, on Sunday, because I was ill or upset, and had I come back to Mass afterwards to fulfil my obligation.[3] So, I explained, no I wasn't ill, and I left because I couldn't agree with what was being said on the altar. And I hadn't come back, so I hadn't finished Mass? And I said no, I showed my good intention, I went to Mass, I had every intention of finishing Mass, but unfortunately I wasn't able to because of this statement which I couldn't accept. I just couldn't accept it, because I did sympathize with the IRA, and I would be excommunicated. So she said that she'd have to report that to the council, and she said, 'You know this is very serious, the Academic Council is taking this very seriously.' I said, 'I realize that, but I can't undo the facts.' But I heard then what happened, Liam Ó Briain told me, he was a member of the Academic Council, of course, and we were great friends.

Liam Ó Briain was Budge's professor, and he proved to be a formidable ally to his promising student. Having fought in the Easter Rising, and subsequently been imprisoned in Wandsworth prison and Frongoch internment camp, he was appointed to the chair of Romance languages at UCG in 1917. But his political activism did not end with his academic appointment, as Rosaleen O'Neill recalls:

> The early years of his tenure were interrupted by further periods of imprisonment: three months in Belfast in 1919–20 for organizing the Michael Collins-inspired National Loan in Co. Armagh, where Ó Briain had been a Sinn Féin candidate in 1918, and thirteen months in Galway gaol, Galway Town Hall and the Curragh in 1920–1. In the second instance, shortly after Bloody Sunday (1920), he was taken from the college dining room by a troop of Black and Tans who had surrounded the entire Quadrangle building.[4]

Prof. Pádraig Ó Céidigh, who later became a great friend of Liam Ó Briain's, recalls the professor of Romance languages recounting a story to him of his activities during the 1916 Rising:

> He arrived back from a travelling studentship in time for 1916, and he joined the Citizen Army, and he was under the command of the Countess, and he was up in Stephen's Green. And the first gun he ever had in his hand, he said he was behind the railings and he saw a British soldier coming along on a bicycle and he says, 'I pointed the gun at him and I shut my eyes and I pulled the trigger, and next thing I saw him peddling like mad off down the road'. He shut his eyes!

3 This refers to the obligation on all Catholics at that time to hear Mass on a Sunday.   4 Rosaleen O'Neill, 'Modern languages' in Foley (ed.), *From Queen's College to National University*, p. 377.

Given his own background it is not surprising that Prof. Ó Briain would do whatever he could to support one of his own students, but in the political climate that prevailed in the college at that time he had to be careful as to how he did so. His approach proved to be an extremely clever one, as Budge Clissmann relates:

> Oh he had a great answer! It came up at the council that I should be sent down. It was proposed by this long white beard, the professor of philosophy. Liam apparently, he told me this himself, he sat there reminiscing, and he said, 'Many years ago', he said, 'I think it might have been 1918, there was a Jesuit priest' (who afterwards, of course, became very famous, he wrote a whole lot of books),[5] 'in 1918', he said, 'this Jesuit was preaching the sermon in the same church, where we all had been, this Jesuit said that the war, which was still dragging on, was not a matter of principle, it was purely a matter of commerce. And', he said, 'the now professor of philosophy walked out'. End of story. Isn't that great? That's what saved me. It was a lucky thing that Liam was there, and that he remembered.

Prof. Liam Ó Briain's timely intervention in reminding Prof. Howley of his own principled stand as a young man ensured that the matter was subsequently dropped and Budge Clissmann went on to take a first-class honours degree in French and a second in Irish.

Dr Sheila Mulloy was another student who developed a great admiration for Prof. Ó Briain, and believes that Ó Briain was exceptional in the manner in which he taught French:

> I would think that possibly a few subjects were superior in Galway, and I'd say French was, because we had the famous Professor Liam Ó Briain, who was an entertainment in himself. He made everything very interesting, and when we'd be doing Molière or something like that he'd act all the parts, in the classroom, because he used to act down in the Taibhdhearc. And he'd run into one corner and be the Bourgeois Ancien or something like that, and then he'd run into another corner and act the lady, and he was a marvellous entertainment. And the people next door used to find it rather disturbing. Next door we had Síle Ní Chinneide who was a lecturer in history. And you know you'd hear all these thumps and shouts and things going on next door. But everybody enjoyed it, and we enjoyed him. He had a great sense of humour.

5 The priest in question was E. Boyd-Barrett, who left the Society of Jesus in 1924 after twenty years as a Jesuit. He authored, among other works, *The Jesuit enigma* (New York, 1927) and *While Peter sleeps* (New York, 1929), a book that criticized the Catholic church. Boyd-Barrett later became reconciled with the Catholic church in 1948.

Student numbers in the 1930s were extremely low, and it was not unusual for students to find themselves in a class of one for their particular subject, as was the experience of Jo Burke who came to UCG in 1933:

> There were very few that took the honours physics through Irish course. I was the only one actually in my year, the only one that did honours maths and honours physics through Irish. Lectures by myself with Martin Newell, and with [Cilian] Ó Brolcháin. I had Professor [Eoghan] McKenna my first year. He was brilliant. I was the only one with him, really. There were two boys started with me, but they dropped out, so I was on my own to continue the honours maths through Irish. McKenna was lovely, he was like Pa Hynes, he took a personal interest in the college, and his students' welfare.

IMPACT OF THE SECOND WORLD WAR

Dr Mulloy was one of the students who arrived in October 1939, shortly after the war in Europe had started. She found that the college was taking its responsibilities with regard to the safety of students extremely seriously. In fact, it was the taoiseach's daughter who headed up the preparations deemed necessary to ensure that the college was in a state of readiness should the impact of the war be felt in Galway, as Dr Mulloy explains:

> Máirín de Valera was there at that time,[6] she was lecturing in botany, and she was put in charge of the Red Cross. Straight away a branch of the Red Cross was set up in the college. And we were put drilling, and you were given material to make little bags. There was no talk of making the bandages, but they would tell you how, and how to do your knots and tourniquets and all the rest of it. And also giving blood, we were all lined up for that.

While Dr Mulloy recalls that students, as one would expect, read newspapers and listened avidly to radio reports of events in Europe, the war still seemed to them, as they attended their lectures and labs, far removed from their lives. However, she recalls that the stark reality of what was happening came sharply into focus when a group of Japanese, being repatriated from the United Kingdom to Japan, had a stopover in Galway,[7] and during their time in the city came to visit the college – to the astonishment of some students, as Dr Mulloy recalls:

6 Prof. Máirín de Valera was the eldest daughter of Éamon de Valera. In 1947 she was appointed lecturer in botany at UCG, and proceeded to teach almost the entirety of the B.Sc. in botany through both Irish and English. She was appointed the first professor of botany at UCG in 1962, and held the position until 1977, when she retired.   7 The ship carrying 180 Japanese arrived in Galway on 1 Nov. 1940, and sailed the following Tuesday, 5 Nov. *Irish Examiner*, 2 Nov. 1940.

We were all playing camogie and suddenly in came all these Japanese. And they all went down on their hunkers, and sat in a long line and watched us with amazement, and we watched them, with even greater amazement.

As the war progressed the reality of what was happening in Europe and beyond began to be felt in Ireland. The introduction of rationing, and restrictions on travel due to petrol shortages, were the most obvious indicators of 'the Emergency', but it was not long before the harsh realities of the war were brought home, even to the somewhat insulated students of a small university on the periphery of Europe. Jo Burke recalls how the carefree outlook that she and her fellow students had was cruelly shattered by the death of one of their number:

> I remember there was a lad from Loughrea at college, he was doing medicine, he was only in about second year, Reggie Bowes.[8] He was a very handsome fella, now. And Reggie decided he'd go off to the war, and he went and never came back. He was killed over Germany. He was the nicest lad in college, we were all mad about Reggie Bowes, one of my pals was really in love with him. We got an awful shock when he went off in the war. Ah it was very sad.

Still, the college appears to have operated a policy of 'business as usual' during the war years, as Eibhlín Uí Chionna (née O'Malley) explains:

> I went to college in 1942, right in the middle of the war, and it was really beginning to hit, hitting badly, with shortages and all that kind of stuff. By then they were very, very short of petrol, and it had to be [reserved] completely for my father, because doctors were allowed a small ration of petrol.[9] Therefore we had to cycle in and out from Barna and in the winter time you were just always getting wet. My mother was fed up with my coming home wet and so on. And so my sister Sheila had already established it that she would stay in digs in Galway. You went in for the digs Monday to Saturday, and came home on Saturday.

The two-wheeled exodus from college at the end of the day is described by Prof. Seán Lavelle:

> When the classes would end at half six, there would be a huge drove of people on bicycles going out to Salthill, without lights. And one person would have the light, there were no cars on the road. We hadn't recovered from the war.[10] Rationing was still in effect.

8 Reginald (Reggie) Bowes was the son of a well-known Loughrea business family. An accomplished rugby player, and universially popular, he served as an observer in the RAF, and was reported missing in October 1941. *Connacht Tribune*, 4 Oct. 1941. 9 Eibhlín was the youngest daughter of Michael O'Malley, who was professor of surgery at the university. The family at that time lived in Barna House, Barna. 10 Prof. Lavelle came to UCG in 1946.

Rationing and other difficulties aside, it appears that for students like Eibhlín Uí Chionna college was really the only place to be during Ireland's 'Emergency' and like many of her fellow students she found that she didn't have to apply herself too hard to do well in her exams:

> At the end of first year I did well, I have to admit, but on minimum work. The standards in those days were low. Now the scholarship people, they worked alright. I didn't work much because you go into college and you're having a good time. And you know it's so different to what you did before, all the kind of stuff that goes on in college, all the social life and all the societies and that kind of stuff. But when it came to the exam I got first place in every subject.

Eibhlín's results in First Science came about following a series of moves, where she tried out a number of different classes and lecturers before she found the combination of courses that suited her (and her pocket):

> I decided I was going to do maths through English, and I found myself in with three nuns, and all the engineering students, all male. And we were sitting in the front row and I think it was Ralph Ryan was the lecturer. And he said to me, 'Oh you got honours in the Leaving, you'd better go into the honours class.' And the honours class was Professor Power and he had three male students and me. And you'd be sitting there and he'd be doing something on the blackboard and then he'd turn around and he'd say, 'Is that alright now?' and these three fellas were, 'Oh yes sir, yes sir,' and I said to myself, I'm not up to this, these three fellas seem to know it all. So I decided I'm leaving this class now and I heard that the man lecturing through Irish was grand, so I went over to him and this was the man who eventually became President Newell. He was lecturing through Irish, so after the first lecture I went over to the office and got my pound back.[11] Ah well, students you know are smart people. And I think then that when I went down to Prof. Newell and said, 'I registered with you, I found I couldn't follow Professor Power.' 'Oh', says he, 'come into my honours class'. He had an honours class through Irish and he had four in it, myself and three other girls. And then there were the three boyos left behind in Professor Power's class. And Martin Newell was a fantastic teacher, because he took us into his little tutorial room and we all sat around in a little circle. He had [a small] blackboard, and we were all there near him, and he was a fantastic teacher. And then at the end of the year I think that we all passed that, now whether we all got honours, I know I got the honours, I got the first place, but I didn't

---

11 Eibhlín recalled that it cost £2 to do a subject through English, and £1 to do the same subject through Irish at that time.

get first honours, I only got second honours. But meanwhile the three boyos when it came to the exam, they didn't sit the exam at all, they sat the pass … Well you see they were sitting there, 'Yes sir, yes sir,' like gombeens. The trouble was, you know, they'd been reared to say 'Yes sir' to teachers, maybe Christian Brothers stuff, you know? And they were just not taking it in at all. And I mean *they* had frightened *me* off!

While the war did inflict hardship and shortages on the country, it also afforded opportunities for making a little extra income on the black market that operated at the time. One student who seized an opportunity when it presented itself was Eibhlín Uí Chionna, as she explains:

> We were up to all sorts of tricks in the college. But even though I person-ally was reasonably well off you certainly didn't show any sign of money in Galway, that wasn't done. But Miss X, she knew my family because she was related to people from the county. And Miss X had a sister and the two lived together. Miss X met me one day, I think she had probably retired by then, otherwise she wouldn't have done it, and she said, 'Eibhlín, I think you know an awful lot of people in college. I wonder is there any way you could get some tea?' And she said, 'I don't mind paying extra because my sister just loves her cup of tea and she's not well lately and I'd love to make her some tea.' Because the ration of tea was a couple of ounces per person, which was miserable for anyone who liked tea. My mother had laid in a chest of tea because she knew people who dealt in tea, and she had it put into this particular cupboard in our house, and she kept that tea under lock and key, plus whatever else she had in there. So anyhow I said I'd see what I could do. And I met my friend and I said, 'I wonder now what we could do about this?' And then I said, 'Sure, God almighty, we've more tea than we want back home.' And so I went home and took my mother's keys, no bother at all, unlocked the thing and took out tea and filled it into a nice little bag, and then went and met Miss X, and said I knew somebody who knew some-body. So then I said, the usual price is £1, but 10 shillings is fine.' It would have been £1, probably £2, I don't know how much I gave her. Oh she was so grateful. But ten shillings! And therefore a crowd of us went off up to Lydon's and we'd a great feed for ten shillings, oh gosh we'd a lovely time.[12]

STUDENTS BECOMING ILL

Becoming ill while away from home was something that occurred to most stu-dents from time to time, and access to a doctor was something that would have concerned impecunious students. This was even more pertinent in the 1930s, '40s

12 Lydon's, located in Shop Street, was one of the few coffee shops in Galway.

and '50s, when tuberculosis spread like a 'silent terror' throughout the country. However, as Jo Burke recalls there was one doctor at least in Galway who had a soft spot for students. Coming to Galway in 1933, Jo suffered from an ongoing chest complaint that, by Christmas of her first year, her mother felt needed to be addressed, regardless of the cost:

> My mother said, 'There is a very good doctor in Galway. When you go back, go to Dr O'Malley.' And I went in to Dr O'Malley and he said, 'You're a student aren't you?' He examined me and said, 'No, you have no TB, you'll be alright, you've just got a bit of a throat and a cold.' And I said, 'What do I owe you?' 'Nothing', he said, 'you're a student'. He was very lenient with students.[13]

Prof. Seán Lavelle recalls that in his time as a medical student in the late 1940s at least three students died from TB in the college:

> Of course TB was the biggest killer at the time, and everybody knew it, they were open cases. My first year in the college, a first year died. She got TB meningitis, she was from Achill, she got TB meningitis, and miliary TB. The second lad was in First Med, he got TB meningitis, he was in the Vincent de Paul with me, and I went up to see him, but he was comatose. So he died, miliary TB, he died in six weeks. And the third lad had been discharged from Maynooth, he was a saint if ever I came across one, and he was getting his degree, and he got his degree, and he died that summer. But he was a known case.

The death of a student, or indeed a member of staff, when it happened, was observed as a solemn occasion by the academic staff and students, according to Prof. Lavelle:

> We used to all robe for them and the college and all the professors would come out, and I suppose all the students really. And we went down to the church. At that time you used to go down to the Dominicans here.

The scourge of TB did eventually diminish, but even at its height the TB epidemic does not appear to have unduly curtailed the enjoyment of their college days by students. Much as it had done throughout the Second World War, for most students life went on pretty much as normal on campus.

In the ensuing years, except for the arrival of the Americans, the Poles, and the Aiken scholars things had not changed that much by the time Pat Rabbitte came to study at UCG in the late '60s:

13 Dr Michael George O'Malley was professor of surgery at UCG from 1924 to 1956.

If you were doing medicine and engineering, I think you probably did have to apply yourself. But to be honest the rest of the university was more the old Newman concept of a university, in the sense that strict application to the lecture hall was a phenomenon that only came in later. I mean we were very much students of the world, and if you applied yourself in the last months, you managed to get through the exams and it wasn't really that painful at the time.

FINDING 'HONOURS MATHS'

In the early days of their college lives, students often found themselves wandering around trying to find classes and laboratories – and the professors who were charged with the task of teaching them. Indeed, in the case of Tony Bromell and his fellow students in 1951, finding the professor who was to teach them honours mathematics was something of an ordeal – and that was even before the process of 'natural selection' had begun, as he explains:

> Sa Mhatamaitic Onóracha bhí an tOllamh de Paor, Michael Power, a bhí ina Ollamh, agus bhí Máirtín Ó tNúathail ina Léachtóir, ach ní fhéadfaimis teacht ar an gcúrsa onóracha, agus bhí timpeall tríocha ag gabhail, bhuel i dtosach bhí timpeall tríocha ag gabhailt timpeall le cheile. Smaoineamh anois ar dream caorach ag gabháil timpeall, agus gan fhios againn cen áit a rabhamar ag dul, ag fiosrú cá h-áit ina raibh Michael Power, an dtuigeann tú? Agus daoine á rá 'bain triail as an áit seo', agus 'bain triail as an áit siúd', agus mar sin de. Ach bhíomar ag gabháil timpeall ar feadh seachtaine nó mar sin agus dúradh linn go raibh seomra beag aige ins an seomra mór a bhí ag na h-innealltóirí. So seo slua mór, GIBs mar a thugtar ar lucht na céad bliana, ag dul tríd na h-innealtóirí agus ár ndóigh feadáil ar súil acu. Agus thangadar ar an doras agus bhuail duine éigin cnag ar an doras, agus d'osclaíodar an doras, agus bhí Mícheál de Paor istigh ansin. Agus d'fheach sé amach orainn agus muid ag breathnú isteach air. Agus ar seisean 'cad tá ar siul agaibh?' 'Matamatic Onóracha' a duirt duine. Cé mhéid agaibh atá ann? D'fhéach daoine timpeall agus bhí timpeall tríocha is dócha. Agus ar seisean 'feach cé mhéid suíochán atá agam?' Dúirt duine éigean 'sé shuíochán'. 'No', ar seisean, 'cúig cinn, tá a shuíochán fhéin ag Mac', Mac an madra a bhí aige, agus an madra ina shuí ansin. So do dhún sé an doras. So chuamar amach in aon chor. Cúpla lá ina dhiaidh sin d'imigh ana chuid dos na daoine, ní raibh ach seisear fágtha. So bhuaileamar ar an doras arís agus bhí seisean ann agus dúirt sé 'bhuel, tagaigaí isteach'. Bhí duine amhain ina sheasamh – bhí an madra ina luí, ina chodladh, ar an gcathaoir. Bhí ceathrar buachaillí ann, [cáilín amháin], agus bean rialta, bean d'Ord na Trócaire. So sheas duine dos na buachailli don rang ar fad, agus bhí Mac ina chodladh an t-am ar fad. Chuaigh de Paor suas go dtí an clár dubh agus thosaigh sé

ar teoiric na gcothromóidí. Agus lion sé an clár dubh, agus ghlan sé an clár dubh, agus ní fheadaimis aon rud a thógaint síos. I ndairíre is dócha bhí sé dár tástáil, agus ag an deireadh nuair a fuair sé amach nach rabhamar chun imeachta, shocraíomar sios, a'dtuigeann tú? Bí ag caint ar 'numerus clausus'. Bhí sé i bhfeidhm i nGaillimh ar bhealach an-éifeachtach ina na caogaidí. Um Nollag ansin d'imigh an cailín, agus um Cháisc d'imigh an bhean rialta, so ní raibh ach ceathrar fágtha ag deireadh na bliana. Agus fuaireadh trí Céad Onóracha ceapaim, agus duine amháin Dara Onóracha, onóracha í ar fad ar aon chuma.

In honours mathematics there was Professor Michael Power, who was the professor, and Martin Newell, who was a lecturer, but we couldn't find the honours course. There were around thirty of us going around together. Think in terms of a flock of sheep wandering around and not knowing where we were going, asking where was Michael Power do you know? And people saying, 'Try this place,' and 'Try that place,' and that sort of thing. And we were wandering around for about a week or so and we were told that there was a small room he had in the larger room that was engineering. So here you had a big group of GIBs as they used to call us first years, walking through the engineers, and them whistling at us. And we came to the door, and somebody knocked on the door, and the door opened and Michael Power was there. And he looked out at us, and us all looking in at him. And he said, 'What are you doing?' 'Honours mathematics,' said someone. 'How many are there of you?' and people looked around and there were about thirty of us I suppose. And he said, 'Can you see how many chairs I have?' And somebody said, 'Six chairs.' 'No', he said, 'five chairs, Mac has his own chair'. Mac was his dog, and Mac was there sitting on a chair. So then he closed the door. So we went out anyway. A few days after that an awful lot of the people had gone, there were only six of us left. So we knocked on the door again, and he was there, and he said, 'Come in.' One person had to stand – the dog was asleep on the chair. There were four boys, [one girl] and a nun, one of the Mercy nuns. So one of the boys stood for the whole class, and Mac was asleep the whole time. Power went up to the blackboard, and he cleaned the blackboard, and he started on the theory of equations. And he filled the blackboard, and he cleaned the blackboard, and we couldn't take anything down. In truth I suppose he was testing us, and in the end when he discovered that we weren't going to leave we settled down you see? Talk about *'numerus clausus'*.[14] It was in effect in Galway in a very effective way in the '50s. At Christmas time then [the girl] left, and at Easter the nun left, so there were only four of us left at the end of the year.

14 *Numerus clausus* ('closed number') is one of many methods used to limit the number of students who may study at a university.

And we got three first honours and one person got a second honours, all honours in any case.

WOMEN STUDENTS

The number of female students began to rise considerably in the 1970s, but prior to this, in the previous four decades women had represented approximately one-third of the student population at any given time. What is significant however is the fact that a breakdown of those students attending college on scholarships reveals that although the female students made up only one-third of the student population, they accounted for approximately half of all the scholarships awarded during that time – clearly, in an academic sense, these were extremely able, bright young women. Although what has been termed the 'feminization of the arts', i.e. the increasing preponderance of female students and lecturers in the arts disciplines, had been a developing phenomenon for many years, it is also the case that, increasingly, female students began to take subjects that had previously been entirely male preserves. Prof. Seán Tobin recalls the surprise among his fellow students in the late 1940s when a female student joined the honours maths class:

> We had this group of eight or nine mathematicians doing the honours course, all male, and we stuck together, we all went through, we had no casualties. I think in my third year, a girl turned up in the honours maths class. She was a nice girl, I never knew her name, because she was known all the time as 'Honours Maths'. 'Do you know who was out with Honours Maths last night?' This kind of thing.

Engineering was another field that was an exclusively male preserve until, in 1958, the newly appointed professor of civil engineering, Déaglán Ó Caoimh, began to actively encourage women students to take engineering degrees. Paul Duffy explains how this came about:

> O'Keefe set out to recruit women students into the Engineering School in the late 1950s, visiting many convent schools to persuade them to take up the teaching of honours mathematics at Leaving Certificate level. Finally, almost sixty years after the world's first woman engineering graduate, Alice Perry (BE, 1906), qualified at Galway, the college's second female engineering student, Anne Woods, entered the faculty.[15]

Prof. Ó Caoimh's task in encouraging the nuns to begin teaching honours mathematics in the convent schools was undoubtedly helped by the fact that the increasing numbers of religious pursuing degrees at UCG resulted in some very

---

15 P. Duffy, 'On engineering' in Foley (ed.), *From Queen's College to National University*, p. 139.

good-quality teachers emerging from college, and subsequently producing equally good female students who went on to make their own mark in the university in many faculties, including engineering, but particularly in medicine, as Dr Dympna Horgan, who came to UCG in 1961, explains:

> I went to school in Taylor's Hill, and the nuns were really very progressive, especially for their day, and I did honours maths at school, there were four of us in the class. Imagine, they put on a class for four women. And the four didn't actually do the exam, three ended up doing the exam, and two of us did medicine. In fact, that year from Taylor's Hill four girls did medicine and there were only six women in my year, in a class of ... well we started with seventy. But, you know, they were weeded out by Second Med, so there would be about forty graduated.

ATTENDANCE AT LECTURES

Getting into the routine of attending lectures and taking notes came naturally to some students, but for most there was something of a learning curve. Christy Hannon's experience in the early 1960s was typical of most students' at that time:

> Well for a while one was a little bit at sea, initially. You had to take down notes and we had never used folders in school, now, and so I did get a folder and found it a great educational aid. Because ... if you missed out anything you could always slot the pages into the binder. It's a basic thing, it's an obvious one now, but I'd never used one before. But I'd say after a month or two things fell into place. You got your timetable, you attended your lectures and you took the notes.

Christy Hannon had chosen classics as one of his subjects, and he recalls that other departments (such as English, which he also studied) with limited numbers of staff, and large numbers of students, rarely gave assignments to students. Classics, however, had a high level of written assignments, which, in Christy's view, probably accounted for the fact that it was attracting fewer students, as he explains:

> There were a lot of assignments in classics, an exercise every week. There'd be sentences, English to Latin, Latin to English, and there'd be unseens to translate. There was a lot of work in it. But not many were doing it. I would say there were only about twenty. Well, students didn't like the regime of exercises every week, you know?

The small numbers doing classics meant that the professor, Margaret Heavey, got to know all of her students very well, as Christy recalls: 'Oh Miss Heavey knew you. If you met her in the Archway she'd know you instantly now. And she would always speak to you.'

Dr Séamus Mac Mathúna was another of Prof. Heavey's students and remembers how popular she was with students because of the individual care and attention she gave them: 'Duine íontach a bhí inti siúd, ó thaobh díograise chun oibre, agus a bheith ar fáil dos na mic léinn, agus comhairle agus misneach a thabhairt dóibh.' ('She was a wonderful person, in terms of dedication to her work, and being available to students, and giving them advice and encouragement.')

As we have seen, in some cases, when student numbers were particularly small, classes would have been tiny – in some cases amounting to only one student, as was the case with Bobby Curran in his final year of a maths and maths physics degree. Whatever about the wisdom of putting on a class for one student, there is no doubt but that the student in question benefitted enormously, as he recalls:

> Professor Newell would sit down alongside me. He was a lovely man, an outstanding teacher. And so was Prof. McKenna, an outstanding teacher, and a pure gentleman. Prof. Newell had a way of introducing a very difficult subject to us and making it look easy. 'Twas only when you went back to look at it again afterwards on your own volition that you found out how hard it was, and how did this man exemplify it?

Traditionally gowns were worn by academics while delivering lectures. As well as conferring status, the gowns served the practical purpose of keeping chalk dust off the lecturers' clothes, or providing an extra layer of warm clothing in lecture halls which could often be quite cold. Sr Mairéad Murray recalls that the professor of English, Prof. Murphy, always wore a gown when giving a lecture, and carried a number of 'props', or what today might be called teaching aids, with him:

> He'd come in with a big load of books, and he'd slap the books in front of him on the table, and never open one of them. He taught without them.

Students sometimes whiled away the time in lectures if they were bored or otherwise distracted. One such student was Prof. Seán Lavelle's brother, whose talent for drawing won him an unusual fan, as Prof. Lavelle explains:

> My brother used to cover his books with drawings. He was a very good caricaturist. Máirín Dev was also a very good artist. She was teaching botany to the pre-meds, and she remembered him for years afterwards because his books were so interesting.

CALLING THE ROLL

At UCG, attendance was monitored at lectures and labs, much as it had been at secondary school. This was particularly important for students who were on scholarships, for whom non-attendance was simply not an option. Other students, however, managed to derive some fun from the ritual of calling the roll. The names of religious students also provided some entertainment from time to time, including, as Sr Mairéad Murray recalls, for her English professor, Prof. Murphy:

> He'd call the roll then, he was great fun. He'd have maybe Sister Mary of the Sacred Heart, and he'd say, 'You can call yourself anything you like, I'll say the Litany of the Saints for you.' I was Sister Mercedes.[16]

Not all lecturers called rolls however. Sr Mairéad recalls that her professor of Old Irish, Cáit Ní Maolchróin, opted instead to send around an attendance sheet, with inevitable consequences:

> She'd hand around a sheet of paper. And sure they'd write all sorts of things on it, except their own names obviously. They'd have 'Pangur Bán' now,[17] he'd be one of the old reliables, writing names like that. Well she'd laugh heartily at it. She'd a great sense of humour.

While there were without doubt some very serious and conscientious students, there were others for whom attendance at lectures was something they did when they felt like it, when they particularly liked the specific subject or lecturer, or, as Peadar O'Dowd explains, in relation to one of his professors, when their absence would be noticed:

> We'd watch, he'd be coming up the corridor, to see if he had a roll book. And if he had a roll book, we would always be down in our places, but if he hadn't the roll book, when he opened the door, we'd get out the back door.

Dr Dympna Horgan recalls a rather novel approach to taking attendance that was used by the Chemistry Department during the 1960s:

> The Chemistry Department had it so that you sat on an allocated seat, and obscured your number, all the numbers were visible from the front in the tiered lecture hall. So the porter came in and wrote down all the numbers

---

16 Sr Mairéad went on to describe how she later changed her name. 'I was working with homeless people in Dublin afterwards, and when I'd tell them my name, well they used to laugh heartily, because they'd always think of the car! And I said well I can't cope with this, not with everything, so I reverted to my own name, the Irish version, Mairéad.   17 'Pangur Bán' is an Old Irish poem, written about the ninth century by an Irish monk about his cat, named Pangur Bán ('White Pangur'). *Pangur* means 'a fuller'.

he could see, they were the people whose seats were empty, the occupants hadn't turned up.

Dr John O'Donnell confirmed that this was a practical stratagem in large classes: 'You had to go and sit in your own seat, to save the lecturer the bother of a roll call, with 150 people or whatever it wouldn't have been easy.' Dr O'Donnell also recalled that other departments resorted to other methods to monitor attendance: 'Jimmy Cranny used to go round the anatomy,[18] at a quarter past two, with a sheet. And he knew *everybody*.'

Some professors did not take kindly to students missing lectures, or indeed to any type of student activity that reflected badly on the college, as Bobby Curran recalls:

> People who missed lectures, and did a bit of carousing and what have you, weren't given any sympathy at all. No. It was said being caught coming over the Salmon Weir bridge at 11 o'clock at night fairly drunk and meeting X, Y or Z of the professors was a sure fire sign that you were in trouble.

There was another price to be paid for not attending lectures too, as Maureen Langan-Egan recalls:

> Many of the people who came into college at the time would have been on scholarships. But there was quite a grip held on you because you had to get honours in two of your subjects, in first year, and one honour in second year. And you could lose out as well if your attendance was not right. I can recall a lady, a student from Mayo, who lost her county council scholarship because of non-attendance at lectures.

PERCEPTION OF LECTURERS

In common with the rest of humanity, lecturers came in all shapes and sizes, with some becoming notorious for their casual or eccentric dress, and others display-ing a sartorial elegance and aura of academic distinction that impressed students. Christy Hannon recalls one lecturer in particular whose appearance made him really stand out:

> There's a man I always remember, Hayes-McCoy, professor of history. Impeccably dressed, three piece suit, brolly on arm, and a briefcase. Now I didn't do history, but he always stood out. He was a real distinguished gen-tleman, impeccably tailored.

18 Jimmy Cranny was a technician who worked in the Anatomy Department. In his spare time he also became something of a legend in Galway swimming circles, was one of the founding members of the Galway Swimming Club and for years, voluntarily taught thousands of Galwegians, of all ages, to swim.

Grace Timlin also recalled the sartorial elegance of Prof. Hayes-McCoy:

> He was very distinguished-looking, tall, and he looked like President de
> Gaulle or somebody like that. And he always had a starched white shirt, and
> tie, and lovely tweed jackets, and he was different from most of the other
> professors ... he stood out.

Peadar Ó Fátharta recalls that when he decided to study for a BA degree by night
one of his professors created quite an impression on him as he conducted his
classes in the energetic manner which was so characteristic of his teaching style:

> Professor [Etienne] Rynne, who taught me archaeology, a lovely man, he
> used to wear the gown. He'd be running up and down the steps, if he was in
> the Kirwan,[19] or wherever he was, to fix the projector, because always there
> was trouble with the projector, and the gown would be all over the place.

While some lecturers could afford to dress stylishly, the distinctive style of the '60s
was something most cash-starved students could only aspire to. Things had moved
on from the 1930s and '40s when students were lucky to own more than one coat or
a second pair of trousers, but it was still the case that the latest fashion trends were
only possible for students if they could make them themselves, or adapt clothes
they already had. Maureen Langan-Egan recalls that when she came to college in
1960 practicality and serviceability were the principal requirements of the student
wardrobe – with a bit of colour being the only nod to the newly dawning psychedelic times.

> Duffel coats were coming in. University scarves were popular, particularly
> the Queen's University one, which is a beautiful scarf. You'd get the lads
> going up for the Collingwood ... and these scarves coming back.[20] There
> were a few girls in the place who were like birds of paradise. Not so much
> the variety of the clothes as I think now, as the colours, which were kind of
> daring for the time.

Dress sense aside, some lecturers made an impression on their students which had
an impact on their lives well beyond their college years. Prof. Pádraig Ó Céidigh of
the Zoology Department was one such lecturer. Dr Dympna Horgan was a medical student who found his lectures fascinating: 'Paddy Keady, he was fantastic. And
he never had to call a roll, his lectures were always packed. He just made it so exciting that you'd nearly think you'd like to do zoology, it was that good.'

19 This is a reference to the Kirwan lecture theatre.   20 Founded in 1914, the Collingwood Cup is
an association football cup competition featuring university teams from the Republic of Ireland and
Northern Ireland. Organized by the Irish Universities Football Union, it is the oldest surviving all-
Ireland association football competition.

Dr John O'Donnell has good reason to remember his botany professor, Prof. Máirín de Valera:

> The main thing I remember her teaching us was genetics … DNA had been discovered, but the coding, DNA coding for proteins, wasn't known then. That was discovered in 1961. Oh it was very exciting. To be studying the subject and then this discovery is made …

Students were very much aware of the individual characteristics – and particularly the strong likes or dislikes – of lecturers. Síle Ní Chinnéide was Maureen Langan-Egan's lecturer in history, and Maureen and her fellow history students were left in no doubt as to the personal preferences of their lecturer with regard to specific historical figures, as Maureen recalls: 'She absolutely adored Parnell. And thoroughly disliked Daniel O'Connell, who she regarded as a complete demagogue.'

While students may occasionally have questioned why they had to do certain subjects as part of their degrees, it was sometimes the case that these were the very subjects which stood students in good stead in later years. Maureen Langan-Egan was one such student:

> In first year, if you were doing commerce, you had to do law. We had a lecturer called P.J. Gallagher. And P.J. was a solicitor in town and I think it was 6–7 on a Friday evening was the lecture. P.J. would come into this crowd, they were First Law and First Arts and First Commerce, and most of them starving at that hour of the evening. Now students often talk about the relevance of things … and on a Friday evening you mightn't have seen the relevance of this but I've been extremely glad, at several times in my life, that I had the year's law with P.J. It has proved extremely useful … and God be good to him he was a real gentleman.

The beginning of the 'swinging '60s' saw a whole new world of ideas opening up for people, and students, perhaps more than any other group, were anxious to be a part of every new idea, every new book, every new film that came out at that time. The Ireland of the early 1960s was still a very inward-looking, conservative country, and censorship was still very much in vogue. But there were ways around this, and Maureen Langan-Egan remembers one student who really encapsulated the spirit of the '60s for her:

> She had German … and she would swing from Irish to English to French to German, and she was always in a hurry. '*Schnell*' was one of the key phrases. You had censorship at the time, and it could be very difficult to get books if you wanted them. And she used to take an unholy delight in bypassing the Irish censor by getting things in through the medium of French. When you look back at what went on, I think the book *Hotel* was almost banned

– when you think about it, it was innocuous. Another one that was banned was *The world of Suzie Wong*. Oh people went to the States and brought a few of these back and you see the college was small, and they went from one to another like snuff at a wake.

ATTENDING LABS

For the vast majority of students, attending labs in the science subjects was gruelling but interesting, as students got first-hand experience of their disciplines. For others, however, the labs were the least popular part of their courses, as Bobby Curran explains:

> I found the chemistry and the physics tough going, and I'll tell you why. The practicals were three hours. We had one in chemistry and one in physics in first year, three hours from 3–6. It certainly interfered with my hurling and football. I used to be standing up at the practicals and it used to kill me, so I said, geez I don't want to do practical subjects.

Labs were an essential part of all science and medical courses, and the progress of students was monitored on the basis of their work in labs, as Dr John O'Donnell recalls:

> You had a book of the practicals you had conducted, and that were done at the time, and later they assessed the fact that you turned up, and the end of the practical class would consist of the professor or lecturer coming round to see how you'd got on, and that you understood what you were doing. So that was the continuous assessment. We didn't know it was called a continuous assessment of course, but that's what it worked out to be.

Dissections were an essential part of the training of medical students. It was, understandably, something of a shock initially to some students, as Dr Dympna Horgan explains:

> I found it to be gruesome at the beginning, but you got used to it. And you got to know people on your table very well. It was done alphabetically. The Second Meds. used to do the head and neck, and the First Meds used to do the rest. That was the way.

COMHRÁS

Another distinctive element of life at UCG related to the emphasis which was placed on the Irish language. What were known as *comhrás* (conversations) were mandatory for all students, regardless of faculty, except those studying Irish as a subject. *Comhrás* were usually one hour long and involved students engaging in Irish-language conversation practice, usually with a native Irish speaker who was brought in specifically for the purpose, or alternatively with a lecturer from the Irish department. Attendance at a certain number of *comhrás*, and success-fully passing an exam, was necessary in order to graduate, and this stipulation was something which caught out a number of students. Those who showed a reluc-tance to participate in these Irish-language sessions later found that they could not graduate, and in some cases had to repeat their final year. Dr John O'Donnell recalls knowing some medical students who found themselves in this unfortunate dilemma:

> It wasn't terribly hard to satisfy the requirement, but lots of people didn't, and then they found that they couldn't do their degree. They'd pass all their exams and they'd say, 'What about the *comhrás* certificate?' and they had to go and do it. They tried to avoid it, but they did do it.

The *comhrás* were introduced to improve the standard of spoken Irish in the univer-sity, and also to promote the use of Irish among the student community. *Comhrás* were sometimes taken by lecturers or professors from the Irish Department, but wherever possible a *seanchaí*, a native speaker from the Connemara Gaeltacht, would be employed to speak Irish to the students. Eibhlín Uí Chionna recalls her experiences of the *seanchaí* during her college years, 1942–5:

> As you go in through the Archway you turn right and in the corner there was a little room, the *seanchaí's* room. And he had a little turf fire and he had a nice seat, of the old style as you'd see in cottages, not quite a Windsor chair but a nice chair with a thin cushion, and he sat there and we sat in rows of benches. And everybody was required to attend a course of *comhrá* classes, unless they were native speakers. And when I went to college first, after a year out of school they didn't think my Irish was quite good enough, so off I went for my ten classes in the *comhrá* class. And the girls sat in front and the men sat behind, and that included a lot of the various religious men, the Franciscans, in their skirts. But anyhow the *seanchaí* was there and he was blatherin' away you see and we'd all be listenin' away, and there was not much talk from the benches. And you'd do your hour and he kept the roll by means of a copybook, which was under his cushion, and a pencil. And then when he came in he'd lift the cushion, take out the copybook, get his pencil going, put the date on the top and then he'd put ticks, ticks, ticks. And then he would put this carefully under the cushion again, and we'd go out and he'd lock his door and off we'd go.

But as Dr John O'Donnell has stated, there were those for whom attendance at the *comhrás* were something of an inconvenience, which curtailed their other studies, or, more likely, their social lives. Eibhlín Uí Chionna was one such student:

> I missed many of the *comhrá* classes, and I knew many other people did …
> so I said, 'Oh my God, what'll I do about this?' Now Pat Higgins was the
> Porter in the Archway, and I was looking in there and I spotted that he'd all
> the keys. I said, well here goes. And I went in then and I saw the key for this
> room, so off I sailed down, and into the room at a suitable time, got the wee
> book, and ticked in everybody. And of course lots of people got a pleasant
> surprise, they'd the *comhrás* done, they didn't have to go back. I didn't even
> tell them, I just did it while I was doing my own. I put the book back under
> the cushion, put the key back in, they never caught me. I think I had a lot
> of nerve, and I'm afraid I was partly depending upon the fact that nobody
> would ever do anything against a daughter of Dr O'Malley, and I played up
> on that a bit I'm afraid.

Dr Dympna Horgan was one student who actually enjoyed the *comhrás*, and considered it as yet another part of the great adventure that was college life:

> I used to love the *comhrás*, because I liked Irish. It wasn't that tough, you
> never thought that it was that difficult. I mean people used to whisper and
> giggle and that, you know, well for me it certainly wasn't a big deal. It was so
> exciting being in college you see, you've no idea what it was like.

The stipulation of mandatory *comhrás* ended in the mid-1960s.

WORKING IN THE HOSPITAL

Clinical training in the hospital was an essential part of the training of medical
students. But there were often difficulties with the amount of time hospital staff
could allot to students, as Dr John O'Donnell recalls:

> We were given a surprising amount, given the amount of staff there were.
> But we were taught in big groups, so if you were in the back of the group
> you mightn't see what was going on. The front wasn't popular, you were
> more likely to be asked a question. So you had to balance being out the front
> against not seeing what was going on. The clinical teaching, in the wards,
> they would break up a bit. The registrar would take one group, and the pro-
> fessor would take another, and they might swap around. You might go to the
> Outpatients in turns. And there was a thing called a clinical clerkship, which
> was what you were, a medical student, you were supposed to be there on the
> ward round as the student, which again some people did more than others.

Having to present cases was another task for young student doctors, and, as Dr
O'Donnell recalls, sometimes the same case had a habit of making its way around
a class:

You would notice that a class all had the same case, obviously they'd pass the case around, and this fella came in with a cough and it turned out he had pneumonia, and the X-ray showed pneumonia, he was given penicillin and he got better. And that's the report! But you wouldn't always be surprised by that, because there might not be that many interesting cases around, so it wouldn't be surprising if they all had the same one.

The progression to clinical training in the hospital was a major turning point for medical students, and one they greatly looked forward to, as Dr O'Donnell explains:

I think people who had been three years medical students, who'd never seen a patient, now they had the real thing, and they'd look down on the other students. And they were obviously older, the age difference would be noticeable. The fourth-year medical students looked very old to a 19-year-old, or a 17-year-old just come to college.

The medical students at UCG were extremely fortunate that the college was directly across the road from the main teaching hospital in the region. The result was that the Galway students were able to avail themselves of a great deal more clinical training than their peers in other medical schools in Ireland. According to Prof. Seán Lavelle, this began in Third Med:

We had a very good system here whereby every morning we got a surgical and a medical clinic. The patient was brought down, they hadn't any specific room for it, it used be held in the staff room in the old Galway Central Hospital, or the Central, it was a former workhouse. All through your Third Med you were treated to textbook cases that came in, the nearest thing to a textbook case that came in to the ward. And since the house men knew all the patients, and they knew what had been done and what hadn't been done, they put forward good people for that. And we were very used to talking to the patients as well. And that apparently lasted here for quite a while, because one of my in-laws was in hospital in the south, and he said you could always tell the Galway people because they are so much at home with the patients.

When Prof. Seán Lavelle began his clinical training in the late 1940s post-war shortages of medical supplies were still a problem, and the young student doctors had to make the best of what was available to them:

We used to use syringes, glass syringes, which had to be sterilized every time. And so you'd take your needle, your syringe, and wash it out and put it in the sterilizer, and you'd do the same thing with the needles. And the needles were very hard to get at the time, so we all had our own needle. And my friend had a sharpener, and he used to sharpen his needle with it. And that was still there when I came back in 1960. This mass-produced syringe that you just use and throw away, that is quite new. We kept our own needles. When I went to America it was different. But we kept our needles for about a year or so after I came back. They were steel needles. But the American needles were far better, they were mass-produced.

Given that American (1947 onwards) and Polish (from 1949) medical students had begun their studies at UCG, it was only a matter of time before they began to turn up for their clinical training at the hospital. There seem to have been remarkably few difficulties associated with this. However, one obvious difficulty emerged – in a county with a large Gaeltacht population, not speaking the Irish language did occasionally have its disadvantages, as Dr Ben Corballis explains:

> This one little kid came from Aran, or from 'out the Wesht', he had appendicitis. And he spoke only Irish, and I had to treat him with sign language. But everything was fine, and on the last day, he was getting ready to go home, and he said, 'Thank you very much doctor, I really thank you for all you did.' I said, 'You little so and so, you speak English.' 'Ah well', he said, 'you know we get £14 a month to speak Irish in the house. My mother warned me that if I spoke English in here the inspectors might hear, so … no English.'

THE 'YANKS'

Monsignor de Brún, the college president from 1945–59, was instrumental in bringing American students to UCG and by all accounts he appears to have been well pleased not just with the additional revenue they brought to the college but with their academic and sporting achievements also. According to Dr Ben Corballis: 'He called us "my Americans". Everyone else called us "the Yanks".'

As they were mostly ex-servicemen, along with their Polish colleagues, they were disciplined and extremely hard-working, and consequently the exam results in medicine began to improve steadily, with the Polish and American students often coming top of the class, and securing first-class honours degrees. Understandably, this was not something the Irish students particularly welcomed, as Prof. Seán Lavelle explains: 'The Poles and the Americans worked really hard – they made the rest of us look bad. They raised the bar and we had to raise our game accordingly.'

Well-established as they became within the college itself, the American students and their Polish counterparts were officially 'aliens' and there was therefore a certain amount of official bureaucracy associated with their residence in the country during their medical training at UCG. But, as the following story from Dr Corballis demonstrates, the system of controls was, to say the least, somewhat relaxed in nature:

> In the second year we were living with Miss Cloherty, and about March, Miss Cloherty came upstairs, all of a twitter, 'The police, the police are here.' And I went down and there, in all of his glory, was Detective Sergeant X. 'Where', said he, 'have you been hiding?' Well if he didn't know where we were, he was the only one in Galway who didn't know where we were – we stood out like a sore thumb. We didn't know we were supposed to report in once a year ... all foreigners had to report in once a month, Americans only once a year, because of our obvious affinity. So he said, 'I'll have to take your passport.' And I said, 'Well can you guarantee that I'll have it back by June when I leave?' And he said, 'I can make no commitment for the department.' I said, 'Well okay, what are we going to do?' He said, 'You're coming back are you?' I said, 'I am.' 'Ah', he said, 'I'll see you then'.

Dr Corballis had another humorous run-in with the local Gardaí when, in common with perhaps hundreds of students before him, he found that his bicycle had been stolen, or rather 'borrowed', and not returned:

> An art form was stealing bicycles, but not to steal them, it was to ride home on, you know? And one night they got mine. And I had the only blue and white bicycle in the west of Ireland. Well, my bicycle was gone, so I went into town, to the police station, which was just up from the Town Hall Cinema in Eglinton Street. So I went in and there's my bike sitting there. And I went over to the sergeant and I said, 'They stole my bike and it's right here.' 'Oh', he said, 'describe the vehicle'. So I said, 'Well, you know, it's blue and white,' and I thought that was a pretty good description of it. He said, 'Do you have the serial number?' And I said, 'No.' But Tony Rafferty's [bicycle shop, where I bought the bike] was right across the street, so I went over, I got the serial number, and brought it back, gave him the serial number. He said, 'That's your bike there.' I mean there's nowhere else in the world that you could have the fun, and as long as you were ready to laugh at all times ... because there was always some fun happening.

THE POLES

In common with their American counterparts, the Polish officers came to UCG to study medicine and, in general, did very well. Bobby Curran recalls that they were, in the main, ex-pilots.

There was a big Polish flight unit in the British air force, definitely, and they were fairly hardy, you know? The Canadians had a Polish regiment as well. But there was a big number of those going through UCG up till about '57 or '58.

The impact the Polish students had on their fellow medical students was immediate, as Prof. Seán Lavelle recalls:

> The big cutter-down, for those who didn't work, and there were a lot of temptations at that time, were the Polish students when they came. These were ex-servicemen, and they had a grant that wouldn't be renewed and the British government wouldn't renew it if they didn't study, so they all threw themselves at the books. And all these first-class honours began to emerge and it went from maybe one second to maybe two, three second-class honours, and all the pass, and all the rejects which weren't published. But you'd hear more rejects than you'd hear passes. And then all of a sudden the names became, you know … all these first-class honours with unpronounceable names.

One of the main reasons the Polish students came to Ireland was that it was, like Poland, a Catholic country – but there were still culture clashes. Prof. Lavelle recalls the story of one particularly devout young Polish student:

> There was a girl he was very keen on, when he was pre-med, and she was a step dancer, an Irish dancer, and she appeared in *feiseanna*, and that sort of thing. And he went along to see her, but in any case they had short skirts, they weren't that short I suppose, above the knee, and he appeared outside the Columban Hall, every night, to pray for her, and said the Rosary for her.

Not surprisingly, the budding romance did not survive.

Dr Diarmuid Ó Cearbhaill became friendly with at least one of the Polish medical students, Stan Korzeniowski, and recalls that apart from being distinguished by his good looks, the Pole had a familial relationship with a very famous Polish author:

> Bhí Stan Korzeniowski an-dathúil, réalta scannán d'fhéadfá a rá, agus thuigeas uaidh go raibh gaol aige le Joseph Conrad, sin an sloinne ceannann céanna. D'imríos leadóg le Stan agus duine nó beirt eile de na Polannaigh.

> Stan Korzeniowski was very handsome, like a film star you might say, and I understood from him that he was related to Joseph Conrad, it's the exact same surname.[21] I played tennis with Stan and one or two other of the Poles.

---

21 Conrad was born Józef Teodor Konrad Korzeniowski.

Although they probably were not aware of it, the fact that there were Polish students with, at least to Irish tongues, unpronounceable names was a great source of fun to some of the Irish students, as Tony Bromell recalls:

> Do shíneodh duine éigin isteach, abair, Petrovoski Slovaski, no rud éigin mar sin, agus an céad lá eile b'fheidir do ghlaodh sé an leabhar amach, 'Petrovoski Slovaski, is he here today?' 'No sir.' 'Where is he?' 'He's in hospital sir.' Ní bheadh éinne ann den ainm sin, a' dtuigeann tu? Ansin cupla lá ina dhiaidh sin ghlaodh se arís, 'Petrovoski Slovaski, is he here today?' 'No sir, he died last night.' 'Oh! In the name of the Father, and the Son and the Holy Spirit …' Bhíodh an gas mar sin ins na ranganna sin.

> Someone would sign in, let's say, Petrovoski Slovaski, or something like that, and the next day maybe the attendance book would be read out, 'Petrovoski Slovaski, is he here today?' 'No sir.' 'Where is he?' 'He's in hospital sir.' Of course there would be nobody of that name, you see? Then in a couple of days he would call out again, 'Petrovoski Slovaski, is he here today?' 'No sir, he died last night.' 'Oh! In the name of the Father, and the Son and the Holy Spirit … ' We had great gas like that in those classes.

Whatever about the humour derived from their surnames, the Polish students were held in high regard by the professors who taught them. Prof. Eamon O'Dwyer had a number of Poles in his first final-year medical class, and their maturity and work ethic made quite an impression on him: 'The Poles were perhaps a little bit more mature. They had been demobbed sometime after the Second World War, and there were maybe three or four of them. And they were hard workers.'

THE RELIGIOUS

Another group whose dress and lifestyle distinguished them from the main body of students were the religious who attended UCG, and who made up a sizable subset of the student population. Nuns and brothers were generally sent to university to qualify as teachers, and were subsequently employed in the many new schools established by the religious orders soon after independence, as Budge Clissmann recalls:

> It wasn't just to give them, for their own sake, an education, it was to make them employable. And they'd bring a dowry from the family, which was customary, and then they'd use the dowry or maybe they'd get free places.

In their distinctive habits the religious were easy to pick out as they made their way around campus, almost always in groups. Dr Sheila Mulloy recalled that she knew, in particular, when the Franciscans were coming into college, because they would be heard long before they were seen:

> We'd hear them coming in the gate, because they came in pairs and you'd hear the rosary beads clanking at the side. And they used to be led by An tAth. Felim, who was a professor of philosophy in the college. And he'd come in leading them, and they'd all have a black umbrella each.

Sr Mairéad Murray, from the Gaeltacht of Cúil Aodha in West Cork, had joined the Sisters of Mercy as a 20-year-old, and worked in a variety of roles with the order for a number of years. Having done some part-time teaching at primary-school level, in 1958 she decided to formally qualify as a teacher, but first there was a significant impediment to be overcome:

> Anybody who was in the convent, or entering at that time, they all had their Leaving Cert. I didn't have anything beyond primary school, but still somehow I got chances to do things … Finally somebody decided that I would do the Leaving Cert, which I did, in a year.

Having completed the Leaving Certificate in only one year, never having attended secondary school, Sr Mairéad had one more extraordinary feat to accomplish which saw her on her way to UCG:

> I did six subjects for the Leaving Cert, as was the norm. And that was at the end of June. I had left maths and Latin because they were so difficult and I hadn't ever worked on them before. And they said I'd need another year to do them.[22] But when I finished the Leaving Cert, which was towards the end of June, somebody had the brainwave that the Matriculation was coming up in September – 7 September to be exact – and would it be at all possible to do those two subjects?

Sr Mairéad set herself the task of studying Leaving Cert maths and Latin and passing the Matriculation exam in these subjects, in a little over two months, with, as she says with some degree of understatement, 'other things thrown in between'.

> So anyway, I said no harm, I'd try. And I did. I came down to Galway to do it, on 7 September, I remember it so well, it was the anniversary of my father's death.[23] So I did the Latin quite well. You see our Divine Office now, we said it in Latin at the time, and you learn a whole lot of words through

22 Mathematics and Latin were at that time mandatory subjects for matriculation.   23 Mairéad's mother had died when she was only 2 years old, and her father died when she in her last year of primary school, aged 12.

that. And one thing or another anyway, Roman history was there too and all of that. Maths, now I said there's no way I'm sure I will pass these maths, but somehow I got by. Theorems and geometry, I knew nothing whatsoever about algebra or geometry, and I never missed them.

Her reservations aside Sr Mairéad managed to pass both Latin and maths, and so qualified for university. When Sr Mairéad came to register there were other sisters from her order with her, all of whom were destined for a career in teaching. However, she stresses that she was not put under any great pressure from her order with regard to the subjects she chose:

> I said arts, for want of knowing anything else. We were left very free, I must say, very free. And they never put pressure on you to achieve in any of these things. Not from where I came from. Now, different convents had different attitudes … Where I came from you were never under stress, which was a very good thing, because if you're under stress you're distracted and you're using up energy unnecessarily. Anyway, I signed up for Irish, I picked Irish on account of coming from a Gaeltacht, so Irish was no trouble to me, English and geography, and philosophy course B, through Irish.

Given the intense study that had been required on her part in order to get into university, it is hardly surprising that Sr Mairéad found her first year in college remarkably easy in comparison: 'It was like eating jam compared to doing the Leaving Cert in one year. I mean I had nothing to do I'd say. It was so simple to do. I couldn't compare them.'

There were a number of different orders represented in the college, and in the early 1960s some orders were a lot stricter than others in what they allowed their sisters and brothers to do while on campus. According to Sr Mairéad, her own order, the Mercy Sisters, was among the most liberal:

> The Holy Rosary Sisters were here. The Franciscan Missionaries of Mary were a solely missionary order. The Poor Clares were here – they were called the *rich* Poor Clares. They had the place in Newry and they taught, they were in Kenmare, they had a school there. Presentations of course – the Presentations did nursing – and the Holy Rosary Sisters. Altogether in the college I'd say there were maybe fifty between all of the years.

Sr Mairéad recalls that of all the orders the Redemptorists were the most strict, and the Franciscans perhaps the most distinctive:

> The Redemptorists were frightfully strict. They'd stand in the corner by themselves. If we were waiting to get into a lecture, we'd be all talking to

everyone, and they'd have to stand over, not to talk to anybody. You know it's changed an awful lot since then, but they were frightfully strict. The Franciscans then weren't half so strict, in their brown robes. And every first Friday they used to come in with the tonsure cut freshly.[24] That would be done every first Friday.

Nuns and brothers tended to stick together, and not mix unnecessarily with the other students. Sr Mairéad certainly felt that this tended to set them apart from the general student body:

> In the Greek Hall, where we went for Irish, we'd all file into the front. I don't know why we did, I hated being up the front. And we were all dressed up in this big regalia of robes down to your toes and, and I suppose people thought we were from, I don't know, another planet. I'd safely say that nearly everybody who was attending university had come from the religious, you know, the schools, and so we wouldn't have been anything exotic to them, and they didn't treat us as being exotic either. Except that we didn't have a lot, I suppose, in common. We had our own friends, and they had their own.

As Sr Mairéad has already stated, there seemed to be an unwritten rule that nuns in particular sat at the front of any class, but as Peadar O'Dowd recalls there was sometimes a price to be paid for this, something he experienced in a geology class:

> I'll always remember [the professor] was demonstrating igneous rocks … and pouring acid on them, and the poor old nuns were up the front looking at him, and the acid ran down on one of the nun's shoes, and started burning, and she started jumping around like a frog, you know, so between her and the poor old professor nearly getting heart failure, all I could do was laugh.

According to Sister Mairéad the nuns very much appreciated the special room that had been set aside in the Quadrangle for their specific use.

> Oh they were very good to nuns, we had the Nuns' Room, which was very nice. And the newspapers were left in for our use as well, and that was marvellous. There was a fireplace but we wouldn't have had fires. Just a little long table now, a pokey enough place, they all were pokey because of the small windows. 'Twas grand.

---

24 Tonsure is the practice of the circular cutting or shaving of the hair on the crown of the head, as a sign of religious devotion or humility.

Sr Mairéad was very conscious of the fact that as a nun she was fortunate that things had moved on sufficiently with the religious orders that they were allowed out of the convent to attend college:

> Nuns didn't go out, the Mercy Sisters were the first order to go out on the streets. They were all enclosed, even the Presentation Sisters were enclosed, they wouldn't go out on the street. And of course we couldn't go out except in twos. At least you could go to college, but you had to go in twos.

While the religious students appear to have been were treated with some degree of respect by most academics, there were those who were not afraid to occasionally poke fun at them. Peadar O'Dowd recalls one such academic:

> He didn't have too much time for the clergy I think, because we had an unfortunate Franciscan in the class, who was, I think, 6ft 6in., and every so often the room would get very stuffy, and he'd say, 'Is that long Franciscan there? Get up there and open that window, and let's get *some* use out of the clergy.'

The nuns and brothers were of the student population, but apart from it, as Peadar O'Dowd recalls: 'They were strange in the sense that they just came in, did their lecture, and gone, and that was it. You'd see them at lecture, and that was it, they were gone.' There were, however, occasions when nuns, and brothers, were inadvertently drawn in to the more colourful aspects of student life, as the following story from Peadar O'Dowd recounts:

> There used be terrible snowballing going on … we were like national school kids. And I remember here one Christmas time, you had the commerce and science I think against arts and medicine. And there'd be holy war so there would be, terrible, all over the place. And we used to come in with wellingtons, already prepared for the battles you know? The girls of course got an awful going over, needless to say, but there was one lady you wouldn't fire at, and that was a nun. She was sacrosanct, you couldn't fire at a nun. Except for one day there were two nuns going in, one very oldish lady altogether, but she gave us this look now that would put us to hell and back, and one young nun, a young novice, and they were just going up the steps into the Aula, and they looked around and the young one smiled, gave us a big smile, and next minute the snowballs came flying, and all of a sudden hit the other one.

In at least one case a lay student showed a more than average interest in a nun, as Brendan Smith recalls one of his fellow students confiding in him:

He said to me a few months into college that there was something seriously wrong with him. And I asked him why? And he said, 'The only woman I fancy in this whole college is a nun.' There were quite a few nuns in those days. There was a very pretty nun in our year, but she never came back after the first year, so he got a bit despondent.

Some of the religious who attended UCG went on to very successful careers within the church. Christy Hannon recalls one of his classmates from the early 1960s who achieved worldwide fame: 'Another member of the 1964 BA class was Brother Wilfrid, now Wilfrid, Cardinal Napier.[25] And his name was mentioned at the last papal elections. I knew him, a very nice man.'

While many would have considered the taking of a religious vocation as a somewhat limiting experience for the young men and women concerned, for many religious, it afforded opportunities for learning and further studies that would have been completely beyond their means in their old lives, as Sr Mairéad Murray recalls:

> I would always be grateful to the order for how much they afforded me, how much they allowed me to … allowed me is not the right word, but put in my way that I could have done all of that. Because none of my own family would ever have gone beyond primary school. I was given a great opportunity, and I'll be forever grateful for that.

THE ENGINEERS

'The engineers were different' proved to be an oft-repeated phrase in the course of interviews conducted, the comment coming from both engineers and non-engineers. All the evidence would suggest that the engineers did make up a distinctive group of students on campus, and engineering was always a popular, and well-respected degree among those coming to the university. Joe McGrath, from Clifden, Co. Galway, came to UCG to study engineering in 1945, but began by doing a year of science, as he explains: 'I hadn't honours maths, and you had to have honours maths to get in, or else do a year's science. And I did a year's science and got into the Engineering School then.' Such determination reflects the high esteem in which the engineering degree from UCG was held, and from the outset Joe McGrath was impressed by the professor of engineering, Prof. William Hillary Prendergast:[26]

> He had been working out in Assam in India, and he worked mostly on rail-
> ways. I'd say that's why he was appointed, much to the annoyance of some

---

25 Cardinal Wilfrid Fox Napier, OFM, archbishop of Durban, South Africa, spent three years at UCG acquiring a BA degree in Latin and English.   26 William H. Prendergast was professor of civil engineering 1947–57.

other people that were in the college, because I would say Prendergast was more of a practical engineer than an academic engineer, you know?

A former college president, Prof. James Browne,[27] who came to study engineering in 1970, was conscious of the fact that Galway already had an excellent reputation for producing top-class engineers, which was largely borne of the practical experiences imparted by lecturers who taught there, as he explains:

> I'd say Galway had a reputation, for a long time, as being a good place to do engineering. I think it goes back to well before our time, where many of the people who were professors here were well known internationally, and would have been involved in all kinds of projects outside of Ireland. I think there might have been projects in Egypt and so on, now I'm going back now to the '20s, and that was always the rumour, that Galway had a great reputation for civil engineering. And it was born of a long history of people teaching it who were good practitioners. So Galway had a good name. It was purely teaching activity, there was no research at that stage. There might have been some individuals doing private research, but there was no formal research.

This is probably explained by the fact that at that time there was a great deal of practical coursework, which lecturers were required to supervise, and therefore a high level of contact hours with students, something that inevitably would have curtailed any extensive research. Joe McGrath confirms that engineering as a course of study at UCG involved a great deal of practical work, which kept students extremely busy:

> Our first year we had lectures on Saturdays, six days a week. We had a very full day on Monday, we'd less work on Tuesday, Wednesday we'd a full day again, and Thursday was a little bit like Tuesday, and Friday then we had another long day. Well, you see, we'd have a practical maybe on Friday evenings and on Wednesday evenings, and Monday evenings. Then of course every other day we had to spend a lot of time in the drawing office, because we had to produce twenty-one drawings for our exam the first year. Twenty-one drawings! Various things, like, for instance, I remember one of them was the Baths of Caracalla in Rome. We were given a plan of them, and we had to copy it. And I think we did one on the Coliseum as well. Hubert Delap, who was our lecturer, he was very, very interested in architecture.

A wide range of subjects was taught, some of which were not taught on the engineering courses of other universities at the time, as Joe McGrath recalls:

27 Prof. James J. Browne was president of NUIG 2008–18.

We had Ralph Ryan, who had a consulting office, he taught us maths, and he taught electricity in our second year. We did a very sound electrical course in our second year in Galway, which I don't think they do now at all. And I afterwards worked with an awful lot of electrical engineers, you know, so it was good to have that behind me. It was a very good course. It was one of our principle exams that year. At that time I don't think it was common in Dublin, and I don't know that it was common in Cork, but certainly Galway had a strong electrical content. Hubert Delap then used to do surveying and building construction. Pádraic Ó Lochlainn then, he was doing the physics, and he did soil mechanics as well. Soil mechanics was only introduced before the last year we were there, all about the mechanics of the soil, how to estimate bearings and everything like that.

In common with many other students from the faculties of engineering, science and medicine, Joe studied chemistry with Prof. Dillon, who, according to Joe, had a very subtle way of marking the cards of some of his less diligent students:

He always used to say, 'You'd want to be watching this now, some of you boys aren't so careful,' and he says, 'Well, I'll send ye back to the land when June comes.' There were a lot of farmer's sons there, you know?

The practical work involved in engineering really focused the minds of the student engineers, particularly coming up to exam time, as Joe McGrath recalls:

Of course there was always that cramming before exams, and trying to get practical work done. Each year there was something … twenty-one drawings for first year, in second year we had to do a survey, there was a field somewhere up in Rahoon or somewhere like that, and you'd have to go up and survey it. You'd go down, and plot it, and you'd hand in your drawing and your notes. Then, the third year, we had to design a house. And something like a retaining wall or something like that, something involving reinforced concrete. We were doing all that, and walking everywhere. And then we used to do levels.

Bobby Curran recalls observing the training in surveying given to the budding engineers:

The boys used be out with the theodolites, and you got the same problem every year – they were to estimate the height of the tower. There used to be squads of engineers, three of them around every theodolite, looking up at the tower.[28]

28 The tower referred to is the clock tower of the Quadrangle at UCG.

For Prof. Browne, coming to UCG to study engineering in 1970 was something of an obvious choice:

> I was advised, well you should go and do civil engineering in UCG. The idea was very simple at that time: honours maths equals engineering. I'd honours maths, I also did applied maths, I did physics, but honours maths equals engineering.

Prof. Browne arrived in UCG at a very opportune time in the development of engineering in the college. With forty-five students in his first-year engineering class, a new course in a specific branch of engineering opened up for the class in their second year:

> At the end of our first year Professor O'Kelly was hired here as professor of industrial engineering. And then in second year we did civil engineering still, but he taught some courses. And at the end of second year himself and a man called John Roche, who had been hired as a lecturer in industrial engineering prior to Eddie O'Kelly coming as professor, they created a new programme in industrial engineering. And that class, at the end of second year, when we came back in third year, we were formally asked, and six of us opted for industrial engineering.

Interestingly, of the six students who opted for the industrial-engineering course, Prof. Browne recalls that two were women, out of a total of only three women who began the original degree course in 1970.

The development of a course in endustrial engineering in Galway proved to be an astute move on the part of the university, and the manner in which it came about says a great deal about the 'can do' attitude which began to emerge forcefully in the college in the early 1970s, as Prof. Browne explains:

> At the time Ireland was industrializing, there was a recognition that there was no university producing those industrial engineers, manufacturing engineers. There were complaints to the IDA at the time from the major investors, but there was no engineering course that was relevant to manufacturing. And there was a company called General Electric, who had plants at the time in Shannon and Dundalk. They put pressure on the IDA, and the HEA equivalent at the time said what did people think, and Declan O'Keefe put his hand up and said, 'Galway will do industrial engineering'.[29] That's how it came to Galway. His argument was very simple. Other universities had two courses, Cork would have had civil and I believe food at the time,

29 John Declan O'Keefe (Deaglán Ó Caoimh) succeeded William H. Prendergast as professor of civil engineering at UCG in 1958.

they certainly had two. UCD would have had civil and mech. elec., a combination of electrical and mechanical. He felt that Galway should have more than one string to its bow. So he put up his hand, and Galway got it. And we were the very first class.

This placed UCG at the cutting edge of this new discipline, something which was to benefit both the university and the industrial development of Galway and its hinterland in the decades to come.

The course proved to be an excellent one, incorporating elements that made Galway industrial-engineering graduates sought-after. Prof. Browne recalls that within weeks of graduating he had three job offers, like most of his fellow industrial-engineering graduates:

> It wasn't a traditional engineering course. First of all, it was third and fourth year only. Secondly, it was a mix of business, engineering, mathematics and computing, and also psychology and sociology. Because industry required people who understood psychology, and management. But probably its strongest point was computing and mathematics, and at the time that was very, very new. The university had just installed its first computer, which was in the civil-engineering building, and we were the big users of it. The machine took up a whole room on the ground floor in civil engineering. There were no tapes, you punched your cards and you brought your box of cards up to the machine. The machine had, I think, 32K of memory. There's a lot more on a mobile phone today.

Although they studied more than two decades apart, Prof. Browne echoed what Joe McGrath had to say about studying engineering in the 1940s, particularly with regard to the fact that the engineers had very full days, and struck up very close relationships because they spent so much time working together:

> You had almost a nine-to-six day, and we also had lectures on Saturday morning. Saturday morning you were lectured, certainly from 10 if not 9, until 12. Wednesday afternoon was off, for sports, so you had a five-day week, but the fifth day was the half Saturday. Every hour was filled, apart from Wednesday afternoon, with 26, 27 hours contact a week. Because, particularly in first year, you had to do ... I think it might have been twelve drawings, all done by hand, and some of them double-sided. And that meant that you worked as groups all the time. So the Drawing Office was the afternoon, four days a week. Everybody had a locker, and a desk, a T-square, and they had a full board, a drawing board, it was all set up in civil engineering. Now, later that became automated, in the sense that people do a little bit of drawing now, and a lot of computer work. But at that time it was all by hand. I'd say it was slightly boring, slightly over the top in terms of the

effort that was required to do it, but one great effect, it created a great spirit. The class became very united. Because engineers kind of moved in packs. Moved to lectures, moved back to the drawing room, went to lunch, the whole lot, moved around the campus, this group of engineering students, they were all together, which built character into the system. But essentially great camaraderie built up around the drawing office, and that carried us through the four years.

THE LIBRARY

The original college library, which was located in the north wing of the Quad, held many special memories. Prof. Seán Tobin recalled his impressions of it when he arrived in 1947:

> There was a great atmosphere in the library, because it looked like a library, you know? It was the top floor of the right-hand side of the Quadrangle, the north side of the Quadrangle, and it was almost the whole top of that. It had these bookcases between each pair of windows, there was a big bookcase, and then extending out there was something like a five- or six-foot-wide corridor right down the middle, but in every bay then there was a big table, a big heavy table, and big heavy chairs, and you could sit there in the kind of monastic atmosphere. It was hard to see, especially for a lot of the day, because the sun would be coming in from the south. There were glass doors on all the cases, the books were all behind glass. Mr Fahy, the librarian, would march down with the keys dangling … I never heard him utter a single syllable I think.

There were a number of places to study on campus, and while some chose to study in the library, the limited amount of space there made it sometimes difficult to find a place to work, and the peace and quiet to do so. Christy Hannon was one of those who found the Aula Maxima a better place to study, as he explains:

> Students always seemed to be moving up and down the library, exchanging books, you know, there was a very narrow passageway, and the resultant noise didn't make for a good study situation. I suppose that depended on the student too. If you were that focused you wouldn't be distracted maybe.

But Christy Hannon has one very special memory of the old college library, and of its librarian, Christy Townley, as he explains:

> The chief librarian was Mr Christy Townley, who had been working in UCG since his graduation in 1939, I think. He was a very kind, courteous, helpful person. One particular meeting I had, I had come to the library

early with the intention of getting *Cré na Cille* by Máirtín Ó Cadhain. I think the library had only one, at most two, copies in stock, and a question on the BA Gaeilge paper on *Cré na Cille* was always a cert. Christy met me on the stairs, and informed me that President John F. Kennedy had been assassinated. The date was 22 November 1963. It is said that anybody living at that time can remember what they were doing when President Kennedy was assassinated. I was on my way up the stairs to the library in UCG, so I can remember what I was doing at that momentous time in history.

PREPARING FOR EXAMS

Socializing was some students' primary objective, and the only thing that motivated them to any degree of serious study was the prospect of exams looming after Easter. When Jo Burke came to UCG in 1933 she naturally believed that study was obligatory from day one – but some of her fellow students disabused her of that notion pretty quickly:

> I took out my books my first year in college, the week after I came, and I was laughed at and scorned – 'Nobody opens a book till Ash Wednesday! Put away the books!' Ash Wednesday, that was the time to open the books.

Studying and preparing for exams was always stressful for students, particularly those whose study time had been curtailed by social or sporting activities. There was, however, an acknowledgement that lecturers were fair, and if the work had been done, students would be rewarded. Sr Mairéad Murray came to study English in 1959 and had a great regard for Prof. Jeremiah Murphy and the work ethic for English students which he had established, as she recalls:

> Well I tell you, he set a most wonderful paper. You know, you really had to do the work. It was very broad for the degree. He put on about thirty-five plays, I'd say now. That was an awful lot of work. A lot more work went into English now than Irish. And he set a brilliant paper, and if you did the work you got rewarded for it.

Prof. Murphy had a very long career in the college, from 1934 until 1965, along with Sr Mairéad, he was one of the professors who most impressed Maureen Langan-Egan when she came to study for a BA/B.Comm. in 1960. She remembers one incident in particular relating to Prof. Murphy, which was both completely out of character, and yet very revealing of the man's character:

> Jeremiah Murphy forced you to think … You'd get these snippets of wisdom from him, you know? He would have been going back, even back to the troubled times in Ireland. Because I can remember the only time I ever

saw him annoyed was once where it had come on the news – he was always a Corkman, would never be anything else – where somebody had desecrated the graves of the old IRA down in Cork. And he thought that this was such … not as an IRA supporter or anything, but this was such disrespect for the dead. He was very cross at the lecture. He talked about a whole lot of things that day, and it stuck with me.

Another lecturer who similarly impressed Maureen Langan-Egan was her history professor, Síle Ní Chinnéide:

> Síle was a very, very fair professor and lecturer and she'd the greatest way of rewarding people who had done their reading. You'd perhaps answer one part of an examination question on doing the notes, but there is no way you'd be able to answer the other stuff she'd set unless you did the specified reading she asked. She'd a lovely way of doing things. You had to do the reading if you wanted to do well with her.

For many, the socializing and fun, which was so much a part of college life, ended abruptly once April arrived, as Peadar O'Dowd explains: 'All of a sudden, coming up to April you suddenly realized there'd be exams to get, and there'd be a mad, mad rush then for books … and of course there was mayhem in the library.' Mayhem, and some degree of subterfuge when it came to 'borrowing' books, surreptitiously, from the library, as Peadar recalls:

> Well, it was very simple. You'd get the book, and you'd walk down, we'll say, looking at it, and then you threw it out the window, and you'd collect it, you see. You'd go in and somebody sat outside, and you'd throw the book, and your man would collect the book, and that's it. But at least we gave 'em back. We always brought them back.

Joe McGrath, who graduated in engineering in 1949, found the experience of sitting his final engineering exams particularly gruelling:

> We did the final in two halves. We did geology and maths physics in June and we did the balance in September. About seven of us failed part one, which meant you had to do the whole lot in September. So I was the only one to pass the whole lot in September. And some of those who had got part one failed part two, and had to repeat. So I didn't lose any time on it, I got it from May to September. And I remember well when he came to my name, 'Joe McGrath, awaiting the arrival of the extern in respect of Geology' my heart was in my mouth. But anyway, sometime later I went into Mitchell and said, 'Professor Mitchell', I said, 'how do you think this is going to go?' 'Oh', he says, 'I wouldn't worry too much, go home. Ring me on such a day.'

So I rang on the following Friday and I could hear him, 'Hold on …', and I could hear him walking across his office, 'oh you're alright, you've passed', he said.

For Joe, anxious to begin the search for paid employment, the incentive to complete his finals successfully in one go was compelling. But, as he points out, his own efforts were matched by at least one of his lecturers, who went above and beyond the call of duty to prepare him and his colleagues for the exams:

> I concentrated on the maths physics, I never did a better maths physics paper in all my life. And McKenna had to give us a few lectures before the exam. He did us well, he gave us a number of lectures, yes.

Joe McGrath's admiration for Prof. McKenna appears to have been the norm among students. But while most cite his kindness, and his efforts to save students who might have run into trouble in exams, Joe saw what he considers to have been the heart of the man, as he explains:

> He was a beautiful man, a beautiful man, a man that was reared in the country and he never left it. He never lost his roots. And he was a practical kind of a man, and he'd say, 'Well you know when I was a young lad long ago and I used to see them wheeling a cartwheel down to put a tyre on it, I often wondered what kept that wheel so vertical.' And that was his way, he was interested in things like that.

Sr Mairéad Murray recalls that one of her Irish lecturers, Tomás Ó Broin, was extremely popular with his students, particularly due to the fact that he made a point to try and calm their nerves, and reassure them, during the sitting of their exams:

> We loved him. He'd come around when you'd be doing the exam, to see how you'd be getting on. And you know he'd nudge you if he could, well he'd say, '*Tá fhios agat* [You know it], *tá fhios agat*,' that's what he'd say, '*Tá fhios agat*.'

The tactic of cramming in the weeks leading up to exams worked quite well for some. As Brendan Smith remembers, by the time he came to college in the 1970s the Ash Wednesday deadline for commencement of serious study, which Jo Burke had been advised of in the 1930s, had shifted somewhat: 'For a lot of us we didn't switch on to books until after College Week, that was the cut-off time.' For others, their plans sometimes went awry, as Brendan Smith recalls:

> There was one famous individual, 'the Doggy Man', and he only ever studied in College Week. All the rest of the year he partied, or … he was known

as the Doggy Man because he used to spend all his time betting, particularly on the dogs, you know? And as far as he was concerned he had all the college papers wrapped up. And he did, right through till the final year. I met him the day before he did the history exam, we were doing modern Irish history, and I asked him how did he feel? 'No problem', he said, 'I've looked through the exam papers, as I always do, from previous years and as long as you know Éamon de Valera, Michael Collins and Charles Stewart Parnell', he says, 'it's a walkover'. And I said, 'They changed the course this year, it's social history, not political history.' That was with less than twenty-four hours to go, you know? Ah he got it on the repeat, he didn't get it that time, not at all.

Anticipating what was going to come up on exam papers was a constant occupation of students in the run-up to exams. Sometimes they got it right, and sometimes they got it wrong, as Dr Ben Corballis recalls:

When I took the Second Med exam, you know, students have a wisdom about everything. Well, the wisdom was they could not ask you about the clotting mechanism, it was too complicated. So I sat down and the professor said, 'Tell me what you know about the clotting mechanism.' And I say, 'Aw jeez, I mean I don't know!' He said, 'Do you know anything about bleeding diseases in cows?' And I said, 'Sir, I'm from New York, till I came over here I never saw a cow. I don't know the first thing about them'. And they all laughed and passed it off, and it was okay, they let me go.

Michael Ryan, who studied science in the late '50s/early '60s, recalls having a practical exam he was repeating cancelled for a very unusual reason – the arrival of Hurricane Debbie, which hit Ireland on Saturday 16 September 1961, and brought a trail of destruction in its wake:

I can remember going down Eyre Square and the trees shaking. And I think we had the exam that afternoon, it was a chemistry exam, a practical, in the Model School. And I remember there were three or four things you had to do. You'd to do melting point and you'd to do identification of a compound, and you might have had to do a titration for establishing, say, whatever it was, sulphur content or something, of a particular substance, and I remember the big thing was the electricity for the melting point, would that go off? I remember that the noise was ferocious. Anyway it was cancelled, and then we did it the following day.

GETTING EXAM RESULTS

Having endured the tension of the exam hall, the next phase in the process was the anxious waiting for results, and the manner in which these were announced was a source of tremendous stress, sometimes great distress, and occasionally euphoria, for students. One student, Ben Corballis, described the experience of waiting for superintendent of exams to emerge from the Exams Office to announce the result as like standing 'at the door of death'.

The results were firstly read aloud in the Quad. Once read out they were not repeated, no matter what manner of pleading from the student concerned. If a student missed his or her name and result, they had to wait to check the written results broadsheets, which were posted some time afterwards on the Archway noticeboard. The results of final-year degree students were also published in the local paper, the *Connacht Tribune*. Perhaps the most striking aspect of the reading aloud of the exam results was that a student who would have failed would have his or her name read out, followed by one word: 'REJECT'. It is hardly surprising, therefore, that students approached the annual reading out of results with trepidation.

For some, the tension of the occasion was simply unbearable, and Sr Mairéad Murray recalls how grateful she was for the architecture of the Quadrangle on these occasions: 'I always made a point to stand up beside a pillar, for fear I'd fall over.'

In Sr Mairéad's time at college, in the early 1960s, the results were read out by Prof. Eoghan McKenna, who retired in 1962 and was replaced as *maor na scrúdaithe* (supervisor of examinations) by Paddy McDermott. Bobby Curran recalls the differing styles of the two men:

> McKenna used to come out and he'd say, 'Ah poor oul Bobby Curran, great Sigerson player, but in fact he didn't do as well now in his exams at all.' He'd always say something nice about you. And he'd say 'REJECT' in a very nice voice, albeit a Cork accent.

Paddy McDermott, who succeeded him, chose not to engage in such banter, and reverted to the formality that had characterized these occasions of old. Peadar Ó Fátharta recalls Paddy coming out to read the result and the manner in which he was greeted by the students:

> Paddy would stand in the Quadrangle, outside where the Accounts Office is now, that was the Exams Office. He'd come out, stand there on the steps, and the big hurrah would go up, Paddy would be like the pope coming out to give the blessing, but it wasn't a blessing of course for some of them.

The tension of the results day could end in crushing disappointment for some, and a pleasant surprise for others. Peadar O'Dowd recalls his own somewhat stressful experience of the process:

> I remember when I got my B.Comm. degree, I was working in CIÉ at the time, and they were supposed to be read out at 2 o'clock. And I couldn't get

off till 2. So I ran all the way from the railway station to find it was over, our results were read out. And this fella with me … I said, 'How did I do, how did I do?' 'Oh, I don't think you did well,' he says. I said, 'Oh Jesus, no!' So I ran up anyway, and Paddy McDermott was reading them out, but he wouldn't read them out again. And I was in an awful way, because I thought I had done okay. So I came out anyway, I was so sad, and I was so mad because: a) I didn't get the results, and b) your man had said I'd done badly, because it's tense you know? Anyway they put up the results then outside, and I saw the results and I looked, no name, and I says, 'Jeez, I have to go home and say that I failed it.' And then this guy came over to me and I got a wallop, I was put flying, and I said, 'What are you going on like that for?' and sure I'd got honours! I didn't realize, I was hoping for a pass. Well, I just looked down and I got the fright of my life.

Sr Mairéad Murray's first-year results threw up a similar surprise:

They posted up the results in the Archway. There was this list of our First Arts year, and I said, in fear and trembling, I wonder am I on this at all? And I started down, I'm small anyway, and I started at the bottom, and I said, 'Oh God I'm not in it at all, I'm not in it!' And I nearly gave up. And my name was the second from the top! First-class honours.

The dreaded word 'REJECT' was something students never wanted to hear. But, as Dr John O'Donnell explains, there were other ways of giving bad news to students, which did not, at first glance, appear to be an indication of failure:

I remember the first time I read the results in the *Connacht Tribune*. I thought there were some of the brighter students who had been 'exempted for further examination in the following subjects'. Do you understand what that means? It means they'd failed the other one. It means that you have to repeat Third Med, but you don't have to repeat this subject in it. But the casual reader wouldn't notice this, they thought this meant, 'He's a master of the art, and he doesn't have to be examined again.' So there were different phrases that meant you could conceal the result, I suppose, by doing it that way.

The practice of reading aloud the exam results ended in the mid-1970s, and Dr Séamus Mac Mathúna explains how this came about:

Nuair a tháinig mé ar ais ansin i 1972, ag obair, is in Oifig na Scrúduithe a bhí an chéad phost agam, agus bhí orm féin bheith ag léamh amach roinnt des na torthaí freisin nuair a bhí Maoirseoir na Scrúduithe, Pádraig Mac Diarmada, as láthair. Is de bharr go raibh a fhios ag na mic léinn go raibh

an Bord Scrúdaithe ar siúl ar an lá áirithe sin, agus gur chruinnigh siad
thart sa Chearnóg ar bís lena dtorthaí a fháil, gur fhás an traidisiún go léifí
na torthaí os ard ó dhoras Oifig na Scrúduithe díreach tar éis an Bhord
Scrúdaithe, mar áis dos na mic léinn. Mar a tharla, laistigh de bhliain nó
dhó nuair a d'imigh Pádraig Mac Diarmada le bheith mar chéad Stiúrthóir
ar an NCEA, is ina dhiaidh sin, go luath ina dhiaidh sin, a fuaireamar réidh
leis sin agus ina áit thugamar fógra go mbeadh na torthaí crochta san Áirse
ar lá áirithe. Cé gur chruthaigh sé sin moill bhreise, bhí sé níos daonna agus
freisin lig sé dúinn cruinneas na dtorthaí a chinntiú sula gcrochfaí iad.

When I came back then in 1972, to work, my first post was in the Exams
Office and I had to read out some of the exam results also when the supervisor of examinations, Paddy McDermott, was absent. It was because the
students knew that the Exam Board was going on that particular day and
gathered in the Quadrangle, anxious to get their results, that the tradition
of reading the results aloud from the door of the Exams Office, immediately
after the Exam Board, grew, as a facility for the students. As it happens,
within a year or two, when Paddy McDermott left to become the first director of the NCEA,[30] it was after that, shortly after that, that we got rid of it
and instead gave notice that the results would be put up in the Archway on
a specific day. While that created an extra delay, it was more humane and it
also allowed us to verify the accuracy of the results before they were put up.

WORKING ABROAD DURING THE SUMMER

Once exams were out of the way, for a great many students the summer holidays were a time to go abroad – initially to England, and then, with the advent
of cheaper airfares, to places like mainland Europe and the US – in order to earn
next year's fees and living expenses. Lack of employment in Ireland meant that in
the 1950s and '60s England was the only real option for getting work and making
some money during the summer, as the only initial outlay was the cost of the boat
to England, and some spending money to cover the first few weeks before the student began earning. Christy Hannon was one of those who spent all their summers
while at college working in England:

After exams you'd go home for a few weeks, and you'd go to England then.
There was no work here, none, and you would get something in England.
And it was relatively well paid – I think I was getting £20 a week. The wage
was higher than you would be getting in your professional work many years
later. I used to work in England every year, even a few years after I'd started

---

30 Paddy McDermott became the first director of the National Council for Educational Awards
(NCEA), now the Higher Education and Training Awards Council (HETAC), in 1973.

teaching. The initial salary was very bad at second level, £400 a year, £200 from the school and £200 from the department. So I was earning more money in England, doing, you know, manual work, than when I was teaching. I used to work with United Dairies, and they used to hold the job for me every year. I worked in Walls as well – steak and kidney pies! They had an ice cream factory as well, and a refrigeration plant. But I worked in the steak and kidney pie factory in Hayes, Middlesex. You'd go when the exams would be over in end of May, early June, so you could go from June to September. There was no communication, there were no phones, you know? My mother used to write, and I'd write back.

As well as making enough money to pay his fees (which he recalled in the early 1960s were £24 for arts), Christy was also careful not to squander the little extra money he made while in England:

I remember one year I bought all the books [for the next year] in Foyles Bookshop, in Charing Cross Road, it's the biggest bookshop in the world. So I bought all the books over there because I had the list.

Michael Ryan's experience is typical of that of many of his fellow UCG students at that time:

We went over on the *Princess Maud*. That was a flat boat, and we were all sitting in steerage. Steerage was the basic, and you got in to Holyhead and then you got the train right down to London, and then you all looked for work … I remember one time walking the whole length of the Edgeware Road looking for a job in the '60s.

Like Christy Hannon, Michael Ryan was one of those who went to England every year to earn the money to cover fees and living expenses. Over time certain employers became a regular source of employment for the Galway students, as he explains:

Everybody went to England for the summer, to the Walls factories. You see Walls had two factories. Walls Ice Cream was in North Acton, and Walls Meats was in Willesden, so if you didn't get in to Acton you could get in to Willesden. But the two were separate. In Acton they did all the ice pops and the confectionary, ice cream, and then in the other place in Willesden they did the pies, the sausages. I went there in 1960, and I worked with the lads on the sausage line which was weighing out sausages, 2lbs, sitting down, from 8 o'clock in the morning until 4 o'clock, and then you took the overtime as well. And music while you were working used to come out on BBC. 'Lipstick on your collar' was the big song that time. And then they moved me upstairs to make the great Grosvenor pies … which had all this pork, and a lovely crisp crust. I did that as well.

As if working with pies all day wasn't enough, the students also found that with money scarce, buying pies at a reduced rate from the pie factory meant that they literally brought their work home with them – to eat in their somewhat basic accommodation, Michael recalls:

> We lived in a flat. And it was a big room, three of us, myself and two broth-ers, and you shared the cooker outside, it was on the landing. And you had to wait for whoever was in that room, he came out and put on whatever, and then you got a chance to cook and you brought it back in and ate it on the bed. Well, mostly we had the pies you see. Well, we had to buy them, but we knew what we were buying, you know, and you could heat them.

Michael then got promoted to the killing line, where the pigs were slaughtered.

> They just brought you in and you did it. They just told you how to do it, there was no training programme as such, and I did that for a while. So I was watching all this and then the following year I was doing second-year chemistry, and I wrote to them and I asked them would there be a vacancy in the lab? And they gave me the vacancy in the lab. And of course the lads … I was going 'round in the white coat, and the lads were zapping pigs. But then it ended up I hadn't as much money as they had, you see you didn't get the overtime, so I started working in a bar as well.

At the end of the summer the students returned to Ireland, spent what they needed to spend on essentials, and waited for the arrival of an envelope in the post, as Michael recalls:

> You came back then, and you got yourself a set of clothes, redeemed your ring,[31] did all that type of things, and then the tax came. Up on the board, the envelope with the crown on it. And once that came in, it was coming and the tax was paid back.[32] And England, I've a lot of affection for England, because they did provide a lot for us at that time, employment, at a critical time really.

In the 1970s, with the advent of the J1 working visa programme, and particularly with the establishment of USIT, the specialist student travel agency, increasing numbers of UCG students opted to travel to the United States to work during the summer holidays. Brendan Smith went in the late '70s:

31 This is a reference to pawning a ring in a pawn shop, for cash, and redeeming it later on with the money earned during the summer.   32 The tax paid by Irish students working in the UK during the summer months would be refunded in a lump sum.

The lucky ones went to America and because of the Irish-American connection we'd get jobs in the bars in New York and that. I remember my
first night was spent in what I discovered was gay New York, that was
Greenwich Village, and it was an eye-opener. The Greenwich Village that I
thought existed was the Bob Dylan, Joanie Mitchell, the coffee house, that
had well and truly gone by then. I came just at the end of the '70s, when
it was disco, John Travolta and the Bee Gees doing their stuff. A lot of the
students at that time would have gone to places like Chicago, Boston and
Atlantic City. A lot of the others would have gone to work in construction sites in London and in places like Munich. And then you had enough
money to spend a month going around Europe on Interrail, which I did,
like most of us did.

GRADUATION

For many final-year students their graduation was the culmination of their
college career, and an enjoyable and proud day to be spent with family and
friends. However, Jo Burke, who graduated in 1936, recalls that with three siblings studying at teacher-training college, her attendance at graduation was not
an option:

> I wasn't here for my graduation. I couldn't afford to come up, I graduated
> in absentia. I was disappointed at the time. I wanted my photograph to show
> my grandchildren. Ah well, that's that. You see my mother was struggling
> to keep us all there, and I just couldn't ask for extras. I mean there she was,
> making sacrifices for me.

The religious graduates, similarly, were conferred in absentia, as Sr Mairéad
Murray recalls: 'We never went to the conferring of the degrees, none of the religious got conferred at that time, it wasn't even contemplated.' The reason for this
was also financial, as Dr Séamus Mac Mathúna explains:

> An rud a tharlaíodh ag an am sin, de réir mar a chualas ó Christy Townley
> é, ní hé go raibh bac orthu teacht chuig Bronnadh na gCéimeanna, ach bhí
> ar an gcéimí £5 a íoc le hOllscoil na hÉireann mar tháille bhronnta, agus ar
> ndóigh mheas na hOird Rialta féin go bhféadfaidís an £5 sin a chaitheamh
> ar bhealach i bhfad níos fearr agus níos éifeachtaí – ar na misiúin nó rud
> éicínt mar sin. Ach timpeall deich mbliana nó mar sin ó shin, bhí searmanas
> speisialta againn leis an bpár céime a bhronnadh go pearsanta ar na daoine
> sin.

> What happened in those days, as I heard from Christy Townley, is not that
> they were prevented from coming to the conferring of degrees, but that the

graduate had to pay a conferral fee of £5 to the NUI, and of course the religious orders themselves felt that there were far better and more effective ways to spend £5 – on the missions or something else like that. But about ten years or so ago, we had a special ceremony to confer the degree parchment personally on those people.

Sr Mairéad was fortunate in being one of those conferred at that particular conferring ceremony, something she greatly appreciated.

For Dr Ben Corballis, attendance at his graduation was complicated by the fact that he and some of his American colleagues had already booked their passage back to the United States. To his astonishment, however, the professor of medicine went to extraordinary lengths to ensure that the matter was resolved satisfactorily:

> They set up graduation, and they announced the date, and it was after we were supposed to sail. I went into Dr Shea and I said, 'Can you help us?' 'Well', he said, 'you know the problem is we only have one set of caps and gowns, and they're scheduled in such a way that they can be used, cleaned and sent to the next university'. He said, 'Let's see if [University College] Cork will switch with us.' Imagine that! And they did. And we were able to go to the graduation and make the ship. And go back and start the rest of our lives.

The graduation ceremony in itself proved to be a memorable occasion for Dr Corballis, and one he still recalls with great fondness:

> In the first place I didn't know that graduation was going to be in Irish, and people say to me, 'Did you graduate?' and I say, 'I have no idea, I didn't know what the hell they were talking about!' But I said to Dr Shea, 'Are we going to take the Hippocratic Oath?' He said, 'My God, have you learned nothing?' He said, 'That's a pagan oath, we don't take pagan oaths in Ireland.' And so when people say to me, 'You took the Hippocratic Oath,' I say, 'Not me, never did that.'

Going to such lengths to facilitate a group of students gives some indication of how great an impression the American students had made at the college, particularly in the Faculty of Medicine, and they were to become a regular feature at conferring ceremonies for many years to come.

Setting students on their way with some good advice was often a part of post-graduation functions, but the following story, recounted by Dr Corballis, recalls how Prof. Michael O'Malley, professor of surgery, decided that brevity was the key, and he kept his advice short and to the point: 'I'll always remember the night we graduated, and we had the party, and his parting speech to the students was, "I hope you all make as much money as I did."'

Students who graduated in 1959 had the distinction of being conferred by Éamon de Valera, at that time the president of Ireland, acting in his capacity as chancellor of the National University. This came about as a result of the retirement of Monsignor de Brún in 1959, and the interregnum before his successor, Prof. Martin Newell, was appointed. The degree parchments signed by one of the most formidable figures in Irish history must be particularly valued by those who received them.

FINDING EMPLOYMENT

For many students, the initial period of elation upon graduation was followed by anxiety as to where they were likely to find employment (if they did not intend to go on to further study), as Budge Clissmann relates:

> In those days [the 1930s] you know employment was very hard to get and most graduates, women graduates, who did arts or something, they would inevitably be teachers, and if they weren't teachers they might go for nursing if they had a poor degree, and that was it, more or less.

With a first-class honours degree in French and second in Irish, and postgraduate studies at the Sorbonne in Paris, Budge Clissmann was a particularly well-qualified graduate, for whom other options should have been available, as she recalls:

> Academics went into the civil service, they went for the Junior Ex in Foreign Affairs. And I would say there would have been about 150 women who sat that exam, as well as the same number of men maybe. And there were three jobs. And there was an interview and you had to have a degree in Irish and you had to have an interview in Irish. And I had been at the Sorbonne in Paris, and I felt very competent. Well anyway, I failed, and they don't tell you why you failed, I just failed. So I had a very good friend, in Dublin, and when I met her somewhere in Dublin I told her what I'd been doing, and she said, 'Oh I wish I'd known you were going to do that, I could have stopped you.' I said, 'How could you stop me?' You see she was a god-daughter of de Valera, and she used to go to the de Valeras sometimes on a Sunday for lunch, and she had been also a republican extremist, and she had been sacked out of the civil service in 1923, and she was therefore due, under de Valera's regime, for reinstatement, and de Valera had asked her at the table had she applied for reinstatement. ... so she said well there was really practically nothing in the civil service that would interest her. 'Well', he said, 'anything within reason, you know you're very experienced now, and you could apply for it'. 'Well', she said, 'one of the things that would interest me really would be Foreign Affairs', External Affairs it was called. And he was minister, not alone taoiseach, but he was also minister. And he said to her

'Well, that's the one thing I really can't do.' And she said, 'Why can't you do it?' and he said, 'Well, you see, the British haven't appointed any women to their foreign service yet, they probably will but they haven't done it, and we really can't go ahead on our own and start appointing women.' Now, he said that no women would be appointed. And they took an entrance fee of I don't know how much money from about 150 or 200 women to sit the exam and those women had to come and stay in Dublin to do the exam, and they sweated, and they couldn't get it. Appalling. You see he probably was told that by his civil servants.

Clearly there was still some way to go before the fledgling Irish Free State was confident enough to step out of the shadow of the British civil service mentality – and a long way to go before women were afforded the same employment opportunities as men.[33]

Some exceptional female students came through UCG over the years, many of whom went on to very successful careers in academic and non-academic life. However, Jo Burke recalls how her own career, initially supported and indeed mentored by her former mathematics professor, Martin Newell, took a turn over which she had very little control:

> Martin Newell, after I got my degree, got me an application form for a training college in England. 'They want a maths teacher, I'm recommending you.' It was in London. So I went home and told my mother, 'I'm thinking of going to take up a job in London.' 'What are you going to London for?' she asked, 'Can't you stay at home?' 'Well, this job', I said, 'was in a training college, and I'll be a professor there, of mathematics'. And she wouldn't hear of it. She said, 'Go down to your uncle, Fr Eddie.' I had an uncle, a priest, he spent a lot of years in England. Fr Eddie said, 'Listen, for God's sake stay in Ireland, whatever you do. When I was over there, the girls … !' He said, 'They used to go for recreation in the evenings down to Essex. 'Twas terrible. They were accepted into clubs and everything in England.' It was a different time. He said, 'You'd be totally lost over there.'

The result, unsurprisingly, was that Jo Burke stayed in Ireland, and, thanks to the generosity of the then college president, Monsignor Hynes, she was given an assistant post in the Department of Physics. But in difficult times unemployment affected all sections of society equally, regardless of gender. Donal Taheny recalled that:

33 Josephine McNeill became the first Irish woman diplomat abroad when she was appointed to Luxembourg in 1949 and Mary Tinney Ireland's first woman ambassador in 1973 when she was appointed to Sweden and Finland.   34 Donal Taheny graduated in 1940 with a BA and H.Dip. in education.

Most of my class emigrated to England during the war years,[34] as there was little or no employment at home. One of my class, I remember, got a post teaching in one English public school, I think Marlborough, a prestigious school. He had very interesting experiences to tell ... he taught there for many years.

Over a decade later, Tony Bromell, who completed the H.Dip. in education in 1955, recalls the post-graduation feeling of elation, and dejection in a difficult economic climate, all too well:

> Tar éis na scrúdaithe i mí Méan Fomhair, an cúpla seachtain a bhí fágtha, bhíodar ar fheabhas ar fad, mí Dheireadh Fomhar. Bhí deireadh leis na scrúdaithe, bhí an chéim fáighte agat, bhí tú ar mhuin na muice, an saol ag oscailt amach romhat. Ach maidir leis an saol ag oscailt amach, ba chuma cén chéim a bhí agat, ní raibh tú ró-chinnte go bhfaighféa post ins na caogadaí, mar bhí an-dífhostaíocht, bhí an dífhostaíocht úafásach ag an am. Céad míle dífhostaithe ins na caogadaí.

> After the exams in September, the few weeks that were left, in October, they were fantastic. The exams were over, you had your degree, you were on the pig's back, and life opening up before you. But with regard to life opening up for you, it didn't matter what degree you had, you weren't sure that you would get a job in the '50s, because there was a lot of unemployment, unemployment was dreadful at the time – 100,000 were unemployed in the '50s.

STUDENTS GRADUATING IN THE 1960S – THE SPECTRE OF VIETNAM

For students graduating in the 1960s – particularly medical students – the traditional appeal of emigrating to find work, and further training, in the United States was undermined by wider events, which made Canada a much more attractive option, as Dr John O'Donnell explains:

> When people were going to get training abroad in my time, if you went to the United States you'd be drafted to Vietnam, especially doctors. You had a more than 50 per cent chance of being drafted if you went as an emigrant. And it did happen to a number of people. Now an awful lot of the people that I knew very well, either went to Canada, if they wanted to have the option of staying and wanted that kind of visa, which I did, or they took a student visa so that they could go to do a fellowship [in the US] for a year and come back, or maybe two years, whatever the visa would allow.

There was a considerable expat community of doctors trained in Galway who tended to keep in touch with one another, as Dr O'Donnell confirms: 'People would find each other alright. And not only people in your own year, you'd get to know all the other Galway graduates, or Irish graduates.'

DOING THE H.DIP. IN EDUCATION

In the days before MAs and PhDs became more readily available options, the most common postgraduate qualification pursued was the higher diploma in education, which prepared students to teach at second-level schools. In common with most of her fellow religious who were destined for teaching, Sr Mairéad Murray proceeded straight from her degree year to do the H.Dip. in education in 1962. She opted to do it through Irish, and recalls her professor, a priest called An tAth. Eric Mac Fhinn. 'He was quaint. He'd have brought his notes, they were all tied together in bundles, tied with twine, and he'd pick out the relevant topic, and he'd just unleash it all on us.'

Most students would concur that the H.Dip. year – combining, as it does, formal lectures and projects with teaching practice, preparation of lesson plans and correction of class work – is one of the toughest years one can spend at college. Sr Mairéad, however, with the extraordinary work ethic and intellect that had characterized her entire academic career at university, was undaunted:

> I hadn't enough to do at all, I was bored to my wits. I got an interest then in Italian, so I took it up as a study for the dip. year. I did it mostly on my own … but I did First Arts in it, and I don't know should I have! I was there anyway, and I did it. I taught it then … I taught it up to Leaving Cert.

Donal Taheny recalls studying for the H.Dip. in 1940: 'I did the H.Dip. under Prof. Patrick Larkin, and I have very pleasant memories of his classes. A very instructive and a caring man. I liked him very much.'

Some of Prof. Larkin's teaching methods were innovative yet effective, as Adrian Ryder, who did the H.Dip. in 1964, recalls:

> He had a thing that in class every so often he would ask somebody a question, and if somebody answered he'd pick out a lollipop and give the person a lollipop. He did. Penny lollipops, lovely little things, if you got one of those, oh you were … I never got one. But he was putting over a point without stating it, which is that small rewards are good.

One of the first priorities of all H.Dip. students was to find a school willing to give them a class for teaching practice. This was an essential part of the course, and Donal Taheny recalls that he was almost caught out in this regard:

I fear I was too casual, and left it too late, and so I could not get a practice class anywhere. Eventually I got one in the old Monastery School in Lombard Street. Brother Anselm Fogarty was the principal and he kindly gave me hours. He asked me to give a sample lesson first, and then accepted me. There were eighty pupils on the roll; roughly sixty regulars. I taught every class from infants to sixth, seventh, and it was a great experience. My most difficult task was to call the roll in infants; it seemed an easy task, but as their names were called out in Irish many did not respond and with a huge roll call it took ages to achieve.

Donal Taheny's long and distinguished career as a teacher had begun.

The experience Donal Taheny had in finding a school in which to do his teaching practice was mirrored over twenty years later when another young teacher – who, like Donal Taheny, went on to become an eminent Galway historian, Peadar O'Dowd – also went to the Old Mons to look for teaching hours:

I left it till the last moment, and I was very lucky. The best school at the time was the Mons, as we called it, the Monastery Christian Brothers. So I went down and the guy in charge started roaring laughing at me, and said, 'Sure, all the classes are gone weeks ago.' And I was walking out the gate of the schoolyard, and didn't he come running after me. A phone call came through that this guy wasn't taking his class. And that was the best class of the whole lot, fourth class.

Like Donal Taheny before him, Peadar was unfazed by the large class that faced him: 'There were fifty-four in the class. There was no problem at all. I took to it like a duck to water … I knew that I was fine.'

PSYCHOLOGY AND MARINE BIOLOGY

The 1970s was a time of great change at UCG, with an influx of new staff, the physical expansion of the university, and new courses coming on stream. The subject choices made by students sometimes reflected a particular interest at certain times in specific areas, and more often than not reflected changes in society in general. Engineering, and later information technology, experienced surges in student numbers. Another subject which became extremely popular in the 1970s was psychology. Eamon Gilmore was one of the first students to study for the degree when he came to the college in 1972:

The professor was Professor Martin McHugh, who was from Belfast, a lovely man, and the first day that we turned up for lectures – then, I suppose, departments and lecturers didn't know who was coming in until the first day – So huge numbers turned up to do psychology, this was the first year it was going to be offered. And obviously it was a really, really interesting subject, and everybody wanted to study the mind, it was kind of trendy. And I remember Martin McHugh went to the blackboard and he wrote up this massive big statistical equation on the blackboard, and that solved the problem. He gave a lecture on statistics, the very first day, all of the different coefficients, and so on. And that shook it out. The second day it was down to those who were really serious about it, who really wanted to do it, not just wanted something trendy to study. It was very academic, very strongly based on experimentation and on research, so you had to be good at maths in order to do it, and you had to get, whatever it was, the honour, in your first year in order to progress to second year. I think twenty of us got through to the second-year stage.

Eamon Gilmore was to discover that Prof. McHugh's introduction to the subject gave him skills and knowledge that would be useful when he entered political life, as he explains:

Actually the biggest help that I got from my degree was understanding surveying and the techniques of research, social research, which I learned. I mean things that I find useful as a political leader is that I know how sampling is done, and I know how questionnaires are constructed, and how things can be skewed, and so on. And where there's bias in question, and so on. So I find that end of it probably more useful. So Professor McHugh was right, absolutely, drive all the trendies out, just keep the mathematicians.

Prof. Maria Byrne came to Galway in 1975 with one objective in mind,[35] to study marine biology in the university that was considered the best in this field in Ireland at the time:

I came here as a second-year science student, because I did First Science in Maynooth. But I wanted to do marine biology, so myself, and there were others as well, came across in 1975 to do Second Science. Zoology, botany and microbiology were my three subjects, and it was quite clear then I was going to specialize in zoology for honours in 1978. And anyone in Ireland, you asked them, you wanted to do marine biology, Galway was always the one. I mean obviously as a 19-year-old I wouldn't have been expert at which place was the best, but that was where I was advised to come to. And I came to Galway and of course fell in love with it. Who wouldn't? It's a great place.

Much though she later came to love Galway, Prof. Byrne's initial experience of student digs wasn't exactly promising:

35 Byrne is professor of developmental and marine biology, anatomy and histology, at the School of Medical Sciences Bosch Institute, University of Sydney.

At that time there was no student accommodation, you had to find what you could. And so my sister joined me, and we looked for a place together. My sister and I had digs with this family in Highfield. And there was a grand-mother, a daughter and a mother, so it was like all three generations. And there wasn't a man in the house … so it was a funny situation. She'd lock the kitchen though at night. She wouldn't necessarily count out the number of pieces of toast per head, but she wasn't totally generous. And there was always that notion that you didn't have a complete freedom to come and go as you pleased.

Prof. Byrne and her sister decided to move on after the Christmas vacation:

When we came back from Christmas we had found another place on Fr Griffin Road, and this was a little chalet … well it wasn't, it was a garage, with a roller door, and a little door beside. Freezing! So, by the end of January everything we had was covered in mould. And my sister … she had the allergy gene. So with the mould, she was sick as a dog from January … We stayed there, finished out the year there, January to May/June, but couldn't live there.

The girls decided to look for a house along with some other students, and found what they were looking for in Snipe Lawn:

For about a year and a half we were in Snipe Lawn. Eleven girls in the house. Each of us paid £3 each for the rent … and I think the kitty was just a few pounds a week, so it was cheap living. I was fortunate that I had my sister with me, so we didn't mind sharing a bed because we were familiar. But there were beds everywhere.

As if eleven girls in the one house wasn't enough, Prof. Byrne recalls that their hospitality often had to extend to putting up homeless engineering students at the end of the academic year:

Very often for the exams the engineering students would either have given up their digs or have run out of money, and so we'd often have fellas on the couch, during the exams … At any one time you'd have fifteen people in the house.

With the atmosphere in Snipe Lawn not exactly conducive to study, other alterna-tives had to be found, as Prof. Byrne explains:

We had to go to the library. And there used to be a little study room, it was hot, it was this hot box. There was the library, and then on the bottom floor of the library, or of the old biochemistry block, there was a room, which was a long room, just a room for study. And it would be hot and smelly and the stress … by May people were getting stressed, they hadn't studied, they hadn't applied themselves, so you studied where you could. And if the weather was fine you were absolutely frustrated. Half the time you'd want to go up the Corrib for a row or go up to Salthill with your books, and fall asleep instead of studying.

Fending for oneself as opposed to living in digs meant that shopping became an issue, as Prof. Byrne vividly recalls:

> Doing the shopping on the bicycle – try and do it with the bags of potatoes, and everything, in your backpack. And if the potatoes fell off the back of the carrier, there were potatoes all over the road, mashed potatoes on the road, cars running over them, you know? So, typical student life, more or less … and in fact you see the students nowadays doing pretty much the same thing.

Prof. Byrne's memory of the 1970s was that there were still quite a few male students living in digs because of the difficulty male students had in renting houses. Many of the digs left quite a bit to be desired, as the experience of her husband testifies:

> I have a very funny story from my husband, because he did engineering at UCG. And he was in a house, with an elderly lady. They had no heat in the house and the window of their bedroom was jammed open by paint, so the wind was coming in all the time. And she grew her own cabbages and had a sycamore tree. She was almost blind, so she used to feed the boys the burgers with the plastic on either side. The plastic would be still on the burgers, and they'd have cabbage from the garden – with sycamore leaves in it. They'd spend half the time picking out the sycamore leaves, and they were just so miserable. But the girls used to manage to get reasonable houses, if you could get enough girls to get together to make the rent.

Every student has their own story of the 'housemate from hell', and very often it was the sharing of cooking duties that was the problem. Brendan Smith shared a house with a group of other male students and recalls how things were organized in the house he shared in the late '70s and early '80s:

> We had a great system. There were six of us in that house, and each day we took a turn at cooking … I cooked a meal on a Monday, I bought the food, prepared the food, served the food and washed up afterwards, and it meant

for the next five days I'd nothing to do. And Sunday was a day of rest, a lot of us went home anyway. But it worked out I must say.

That was until one of the housemates began to shirk his cooking duties:

> He prepared the food, and I had come back a bit late and the lads said, 'He has to go.' And he served the food, it was sausage and beans, which is not what most people would expect – it's not a lasagne or a spaghetti bolognaise – but the problem was when we looked at the sausages they were black on one side and white on the other, he didn't turn them! So he had to be given the boot.

OUT WITH THE OLD, IN WITH THE NEW

The 1970s was a time of a great changeover in staff, with a lot of lecturers and professors from the 'old school' retiring. Prof. Maria Byrne recalls that she was fortunate in being taught by one of the greats before she retired:

> I was very lucky because we were one of the last classes to have Máirín Dev. She would have been an old lady when she was lecturing us. And I remember we were down in Finavarra, at the field station, where she did a lot of her work, and there she'd be, with the wellingtons and the skirt, and the buckets, out on the shore. For us, as young students, we thought, oh, you know, she was just this odd old dear, but looking back on it, as an older person myself, the fact that she was so dedicated, so passionate, about her seaweeds … we all got a buzz from her excitement from what she did … by my third year Máirín de Valera was gone, so her last year then would have been 1976.

Prof. Byrne acknowledges that having a woman professor was quite unusual, and she has great respect for one of the younger women lecturers who taught her in zoology:

> The other female lecturer we had, whom I really hold in high regard, was Julie Fives, she was terrific. She was a good role model. She was younger than Máirín, so we could relate to her. And then she was having children, you know, she'd come in, give her lecture pregnant, you know the message to the young girls, that it was possible to have a family, and to be a scientist.

Practicals in zoology were something Prof. Byrne remembers vividly – but perhaps less the detail of what went on than the smell, as she recalls:

> We used to do seven dissections of the dogfish, and you'd have your own dogfish, and after you'd done the cranial nerves, they would go into the vat of formalin, and they'd be pulled out again, and you'd do another body

system. You'd go back into the vat again, and you'd do that for seven weeks. But by the end they were absolutely reeking.

Some of the lecturers who came to teach in the 1970s represented something of the youth culture that existed at the time, given that many were quite young themselves when they arrived. Brendan Smith, who was studying arts, was a particular fan of one lecturer who in fact taught in another faculty:

> I used to go to his lectures to watch him lecturing because there'd be signs up 'No Smoking', [and he] had his Jesus sandals on him, the long hair, and he'd have the fag. He was really anti-establishment, you know?

With such young lecturers on staff the relationship between the students and their teachers was a great deal more relaxed than it had been in previous decades. On occasion when students had a lecturer whom they knew had a sense of humour, there was also the opportunity of playing the odd prank, as a harmless way of livening up the daily routine of lectures and labs. Brendan 'Speedie' Smith recalls that one lecturer who was particularly popular with students, and went on to become the college president, Prof. Iognáid Ó Muircheartaigh, was someone the students felt they could play the odd practical joke on – with engineering students apparently the main culprits:

> I remember he had a lecture up in the Concourse, and just before he came, the eng. students, there was kind of an accordion barrier between the two rooms, they opened it, they got all the seats, threw them into the next room, closed it, and they were all sitting on the floor when he came in. And he got really upset and tore into the Buildings Office. Another time he had a lecture over past the library, in Block H, they were old terrapins, where the Arts Millenium is now,[36] and I remember him telling me he was walking past, and he saw the class, all the eng. students, just standing at the library looking at him. He was saying, 'Jeez, I'm supposed to be lecturing them now,' and he walked on and they all stood behind him and they sang, 'Hi ho, hi ho, it's off to work we go!' the whole walk up. He said, 'What could I do? I just smiled and walked as these guys were doing the Seven Dwarfs behind me.'

STUDENT ACTIVISM

Student unrest and student activism had begun in the late 1960s and had become an integral part of college life by the 1970s, as Pat Rabbitte, who came to UCG in 1967, explains:

36 The term 'terrapin building' was used to describe modular or prefabricated buildings erected on campus at UCG at a time when the college was expanding rapidly. These temporary structures were put up to accommodate lecture rooms, but also served other purposes, such as recreation rooms and the college shop. The Arts Millenium building was erected on the site of the old terrapins.

It was an extraordinary time of student unrest and turmoil, right across from Berkeley in California, Paris '68, across all the way to Galway, and we thought we were hugely significant and we were going to change the world. So yes, it was a busy time.

The minister for education, in response to student agitation at the time, acceded to the demands of students that there be student representatives on the governing bodies of UCG, UCD and UCC. Pat Rabbitte made history when he was the first student appointed to the governing body of a university in Ireland in 1971, as he recalls:

> There were six bishops on it. And Bishop Michael Browne was the chief whip and dominant figure, and accustomed to everybody doing what he told them to do. And apparently I didn't conform to that. There were some remarkable rounds … He was very powerful. I mean the rest of the bishops were very much playing second fiddle. He was the dominant figure, and his writ ran. And the academics often used me, in the sense that they would furnish me with information that they weren't prepared to contest themselves at the meeting, they would give me the information and let me do it. And the battles were memorable.

3

The student life: socializing on and off campus

In an open letter to first-year students published in the October 1965 edition of *UNITY*, the college magazine, the then president of Comhairle Teachta na Mic Léinn, the student representative body, set out to advise students as to how best to employ their time while at university:

> Academic distinction is, and seems likely to remain, the prime purpose of most of the first-year students who have joined us. Whether this purpose answers to the classic definitions of a 'university education', or not, is rather doubtful. One thing, however, is all too clear: should the pursuit of this purpose be made the exclusive occupation of students during their years at college, then, whatever be the feathers in their caps, they cannot make any claims to having received a 'university education' which answers any definition whatever.
>
> The pursuit of academic distinction must be complemented by an exploration of those channels through which alone the intellectual and 'social' development of the student can come to fruition. Consequently each student should show a healthy interest in those college societies which he finds most congenial to his particular disposition.
>
> I make no apology for the restatement of these perennial truisms, since, despite all the warnings concerning 'all work and no play', the number of Jacks who turn out to be 'dull boys' is still on the increase.

The letter is signed by 'M.A.G. Ó Tuathaigh, Uachtarán C.T.M.', and given the subsequent illustrious career of its author, Prof. Gearóid Ó Tuathaigh, it may be seen that taking his own advice certainly did no harm in the case of this young history student.

The advice given was eminently sensible, but it was probably not needed. For most students, getting a good degree and beginning a professional life was obviously important, and they were certainly prepared to work hard when the occasion demanded. But, first and foremost, college was a place where they could escape from parental supervision, mix socially with the opposite sex, for perhaps the first time in some cases, and have a good time.

The various societies in college were not just important social outlets for students – they also provided an opportunity for students to spend some time away from their cramped digs. With no TVs or radios – certainly in the 1930s, '40s and '50s – students were forced to make their own entertainment, or there simply wasn't any. Having spent his first year, by his own admission, just 'dancing', Prof. Seán Lavelle was one of those who, in his second year, decided that he needed to broaden his horizons somewhat:

> The second year I joined the Boxing Club, the Boat Club and the Drama Society. And so did most of the people, because there was something on in college every night, and we usually went down to it. You mightn't stay there but we would start there, nearly every night. I think we all had keys [to the various society rooms], and we could come and go as we liked. Oh the night-life was the main reason for coming to college.

For many students, second year was the year they really got into their stride in terms of developing their social life, as for many the pressure of exams was much less of a factor than it had been in first year, as Dr Séamus Mac Mathúna explains:

> Ag an am sin bhí ceithre ábhar agat sa Chéad Bhliain den BA agus trí cinn díobh sin sa Dara Bliain. Ní raibh aon scrúdú de chuid Ollscoil na hÉireann ann sa Dara Bliain, ach amháin do lucht BA (Onóracha) – bhí orthu siúd an scrúdú BA (subsidiary) a sheasamh agus pas a fháil (ní raibh onóracha i gceist) in ábhar amháin (an mionábhar) díobh sin, agus b'in deireadh ansin leis an ábhar sin. I gcás lucht BA (Ginearálta), ní raibh scrúdú ar bith acu sa Dara Bliain. Mar sin, bhí an Dara Bliain fágtha réasúnta saor ó scrúduithe go ginearálta.

> At that time you had four subjects in the first year of the BA and three of those in second year. There was no NUI examination in second year, except for BA (honours) students – they had to sit the BA (subsidiary) exam in one of those subjects (the subsidiary subject) and pass it (honours were not available), and that was then the end of that subject. In the case of BA (general) students, they didn't have any exams at all in second year. So second year was left reasonably free of exams generally.

With whatever time they had on their hands, students had the choice of where to socialize, depending on the extent of their budget (which in most cases was extremely limited). The college societies, which provided a wealth – and unending variety – of free entertainment, were an obvious place for most students to start.

THE DRAMA SOCIETY

The arrival of Prof. Jeremiah Murphy to UCG to take up the professorship of English was a major boon to the college, particularly with respect to the promotion of drama.[1] Donal Taheny recalls that 'he started the Dramatic Society in College.

---

1 Jeremiah Murphy was professor of English language and literature 1934–65.

And he started the plays in college and he was very accessible, and he was a real Cork man. He was involved in setting up the Taibhdhearc'.

Among the young students who took an active role in the Drama Society was the daughter of Prof. Eoghan McKenna, Siobhán, who went on to find world-wide acclaim as an actress of exceptional skill. Having an actress of the calibre of Siobhán McKenna gave the Drama Society, and by extension the Taibhdhearc Theatre, a significant boost. But Siobhán McKenna's abilities were not confined to the stage alone, as Dr Sheila Mulloy recalls:

> Siobhán McKenna was translating plays for the Taibhdhearc. And she communicated with Bernard Shaw, and he communicated in postcards. And she wrote to say she wanted to translate his *Saint Joan* [into Irish], and he wrote and said he'd be delighted, and that was it, you know, he didn't go into any further details. And she did a lovely job of it, and she acted very well in it.

Dr Mulloy recalled that the postcard reply from Shaw, which consisted of two lines, advising McKenna to go ahead with the translation, and wishing them luck with the production, was pinned to the noticeboard outside the porter's lodge in the Archway for some time, before being eventually collected by McKenna.

While the Drama Society continued to operate very successfully and performed plays throughout the '50s and '60s, without actors of the calibre of Siobhán McKenna it was not to achieve the dizzy heights of the 1940s for another twenty years, when a new group of raw talent came to the college and transformed DramSoc, and the Galway art scene, forever. The '70s and '80s were a time of great creativity in the college, and much of the creative talent that emerged at that time was channelled through the Drama Society. Before student politics became the more dominant force in his life, Eamon Gilmore recalls being very much involved in the Drama Society in his first year at college, and being in very good company:

> I'd been in plays and various things in school, and some of my friends were involved in it. Garry Hynes was the Auditor, and Marie Mullan and Patsy McGarry – Patsy and I were, and still are, very good friends – were involved. Ollie Jennings actually was in the first play that I was in, which was *The bespoke overcoat*. And the reason I think Ollie was in it was because he had a good overcoat. And he subsequently withdrew from the play, decided he didn't want to go on, acting wasn't for him, the stage wasn't for him … and the director let him out of the play on condition that he left the coat! And then there was a subsequent play that we were in, and I remember Mick Lally was in it, and Máirtín Jaimsie Ó Flaherty was in it, and they had an arrangement between them that they would hold a collection, one of them was a priest, I think Máirtín Jaimsie was the priest in the play, and at an appropriate time Máirtín Jaimsie would pull the plate out, and say, 'Time now for the collection,' and he would go down into the audience, and hold

a collection. And I think the lads had an arrangement that whatever was gathered in the collection, they would adjourn to Murty Rabbitte's and ... it would be dispensed with.[2] So I have a recollection of one night in the play, Máirtín Jaimsie is down doing the collection, and Mick Lally standing at the edge of the stage looking down to see how he's getting on, and Máirtín said, 'They're a bit tight tonight Father.'

THE LIT AND DEB

The Literary and Debating Society, or the Lit and Deb as it was more commonly known, was extremely popular. It served the important dual purpose of providing a major source of entertainment for students, who were enthusiastic audience members, and in some cases almost semi-professional hecklers, and a platform for some of the brightest, wittiest students to practice and hone their public-speaking skills. Over the years the Lit and Deb benefited from the talents of some exceptional individuals, many of whom have gone on to successful careers. But the intellectual jousting that so characterized the debates was always underpinned with what the society was really all about – having fun.

The Lit and Deb of the 1960s was fortunate in having some outstanding speakers – and the odd consummate showman. Seán Mac Iomhair recalls one incident when a speaker made what could only be described as a spectacular entrance to a debate:

> Oíche amháin ag tús díospóireachta tháinig X isteach ar bhealach an-difriúl ar fad. hOsclaíodh an doras i Physiology, a bhí ag bun an Greek Hall, agus brú isteach cónra, ar truck, agus osclaíoeadh an cónra, agus shiúl X amach as.

> One night, at the beginning of a debate, X came in, in a very unusual manner. The door opened in physiology, which was at the bottom of the Greek Hall, and a coffin was pushed in, on a truck, and the coffin opened, and X climbed out of it.

Dr John O'Donnell recalled another leading light of the debating scene at that time, whose quick wit shone through:

> I remember the motion was about Cardinal Newman's essay, 'The idea of a university'. We covered it I think on the Leaving Cert English [course], so I knew about it. But the motion was that the idea of a university was to produce gentlemen. So they debated this, good-o, and the other side, Trinity I think, said that 'Cardinal Newman would turn in his grave if he saw you

---

2 Murty Rabbitte's was a local pub, popular with students.

fellas doing ...', whatever it was. So heckling must have been allowed and X said, 'He turned before he died.'[3]

Dr Séamus Mac Mathúna recalls the high standard of debating that was a feature of college life when he was a student in the 1960s:

> Daoine ar nós Gearóid Ó Tuathaigh, Póilín Ní Chiaráin agus Seán Ó hUig-inn, a bhí ina dhiaidh sin mar Ambasadóir na hÉireann in áiteacha éagsúla, agus ar ndóigh Mícheál D. Ó hUiginn, a sheasann amach im chuimhne. Go háirithe bhí údarás nádúrtha, líofacht agus smaointeoireacht de chineál éagsúil ag Seán Ó hUiginn. Go leor cainte agus díospóireachta ar leibhéal an-ard a bhí eatarthu siúd agus le daoine eile, agus Halla na Gréigise ag cur thar maoil agus, ar ndóigh, trasnaíl de shíor ó na cúlbhinsí.

> People like Gearóid Ó Tuathaigh, Póilín Ní Chiaráin and Seán Ó hUiginn, who later went on to be Irish ambassador in various places, and of course Michael D. Higgins, are the names which stand out in my memory. In particular there was an easy authority, fluency and different kind of thinking from Seán Ó hUiginn. There was much talk and debate at a very high level between them and others, with the Greek Hall packed to capacity and, of course, continual heckling from the back benches.

CUMANN ÉIGSE AGUS SEANCHAIS

The other college society that organized debates was the Cumann Éigse agus Seanchais. This Irish-speaking society was charged, along with its promotion of Irish language and cultural pursuits, with the organization of the annual Seachtain na Gaeilge (Irish Week) in college. Tony Bromell was a young arts student in the 1950s and was astonished when his request that de Valera come to the university to chair a debate was accepted:

> Toghadh mé i mo Reachtaire ar an gCumann Éigse agus Seanchais don bhliain 1954/5 ... agus shocraigh mé le hoifigigh airm an Chéad Chatha[4] go mbeadh díospóireacht idir iad agus foireann ón gCumann Éigse agus Seanchais le tús a chur le himeachtaí na seachtaine. Roghnaíomar an t-ábhar 'Go bhfuil claonadh chun na barbarthachta i meon na Fichiú hAoise', de bhrí go raibh sraith airteagal faoin ábhar sin san 'Sunday Press' ag an am. Bhí Cathaoirleach mór le rá ag teastáil uaim agus scríobh mé chuig Éamon de Valera, a bhí mar Cheannaire ar an bhfreasúra i ndiaidh an olltoghcháin

---

3 The reference relates to the fact that Cardinal John Henry Newman had converted to Catholicism, having been born and raised a Protestant.   4 An Chéad Cath, the First Battalion of the Irish army, is the only Irish speaking battalion in the armed forces, and was transferred to Renmore Barracks Galway in 1925.

i 1954. Cad é mar ghliondar a bhí orm nuair a fuair mé freagra uaidh go mbeadh áthas air bheith linn. Bheartaíomar go mbeadh dinnéar againn roimh an díospóireacht sa 'Great Southern', agus go gcaithfimis éadach foirmiúil.

Chuaigh mé go dtí an tUachtarán, an Mons. Pádraig de Brún (Pa), chun cuireadh a thabhairt dó bheith i láthair. Ba bheag aithne a bhí aige ar na mic léinn, ná acusan air, ach thosaigh sé ag comhrá liom faoin stair, agus d'inis sé dom faoin oíche a chaith sé le Seán Mac Diarmada sular maraíodh é i 1916. Bhí mé dhá uair an chloig leis agus ní chreidfeadh aon duine mé.

Faoi dheireadh tháinig an oíche mhór. Bhí tuairim agus tríocha ar an dinnéar, lucht an airm, coiste an Chumainn agus Ollúna agus Léachtóirí a chuidigh linn i rith na bliana. Bhí mé féin ansin ag ceann an bhoird, Dev ar mo dheis, agus Pa ar mo chlé. Bhí sé an-éasca labhairt le Dev. Bhí sé fiosrach faoi na mic léinn agus faoi staid na Gaeilge sa Choláiste. Baineadh siar asam nuair a rinne sé comhghairdeas liom as Scoláireacht Theach an Ard-Mhéara a bhuachan. Cé go raibh sé ina Sheansailéir ar an Ollscoil, ní fhéadfainn a chreidiúint go smaoineodh sé ar a leithéid, ach ba é sin an cineál duine a bhí ann.

I was appointed as auditor of the Cumann Éigse agus Seanchais in 1954/5 and … I arranged with the officers of the First Battalion that we would have a debate between them and a team from the Cumann Éigse agus Seanchais to kick off the week's activities. We chose the topic 'That there is a tendancy towards barbarism in the spirit of the 20th century', because there had been a series of articles on this topic in the *Sunday Press* at the time. We needed a major chairman to speak at the event, and I wrote to Éamon de Valera … You can imagine how overjoyed I was when I got a reply from him saying he would be happy to come. We arranged that there would be a dinner before the debate in the Great Southern.

I went to the president, Monsignor de Brún (Pa), to invite him to attend. He didn't really know the students much, nor us him, but he started talking to me about history, and he told me about the night he had spent with Seán Mac Diarmada before he was killed in 1916. I was two hours with him, and no one would believe me.

Eventually the big night came. There were around thirty at the dinner, the army, the committee of the *cumann*, and professors and lecturers who had helped us throughout the year. I was there at the head of the table, Dev on my right and Pa on my left. It was very easy to talk to Dev. He enquired about the students and about the status of Irish in the college. I was really taken aback when he congratulated me on having won the Mansion House Scholarship. Even though he was chancellor of the university, I could not believe that he would even have remembered that, but that was the kind of person he was.

The reunion with Monsignor de Brún was doubtless a pleasant one for both men, for they were great friends, as de Valera had taught the young Pádraig de Brún mathematics at Rockwell College.[5]

According to Tony Bromell another remarkable reunion also took place that night in the president's residence, where a reception had been organized following the debate. Prof. Liam Ó Briain, himself a veteran of 1916, but who had taken the pro-Treaty side in the Civil War, walked up to de Valera, greeted him with a '*Seo dhuit a Dev, agus ní hé an céad uair dom deoch a thabhairt duit* [Here you are Dev, and it's not the first time I've given you a drink],' and presented him with a glass of whiskey, which de Valera accepted. The young students present were told that this was the first time the two men, former comrades in arms, had spoken to one another since the Civil War.

FINDING THE MONEY TO SOCIALIZE

With money hard to come by, students had to do whatever was necessary to find the cash to pay for digs, buy essentials such as books, or merely to socialize, as Prof. Seán Lavelle explains: 'It was very common at the time, when people came back at the start of a term they pawned their overcoats, or whatever else was pawnable, a bicycle maybe, and then they redeemed them just before they went home.'

Michael Ryan, who came to college in 1958 to study science, was one student who became very familiar with the pawnshop in High Street, near where Kenny's Bookshop used to be: 'Most of us had nice rings, and you'd pawn the ring for say four or five quid, and you'd redeem it then when you'd come back from England. Everybody went to England to work for the summer.'

One major advantage UCG had was the rowboats that were available on loan from the college Boat Club, which could be taken up the Corrib. Joe McGrath for one found it a very useful addition to his socializing options, as he explains. 'The boats in the summertime were great. The odd time now if you had a date you might go up, you'd take a lady up the river. You wouldn't have the money to take her anywhere else.'

During the 1930s and '40s, for those staying in hostels, socializing in the evenings was allowed, but students were required to observe a curfew – which was strictly enforced. However, there were occasions when students were tempted to break the rules, and for Budge Clissmann, at that stage staying in the hostel in Shantalla, such an event brought her to the attention of the college president himself, as she recalls:

---

5 Tony Bromell also recalls having been told that the relationship between the two men was such that when Fianna Fáil were in power Monsignor de Brún was loath to apply for funding for the college for fear of embarrassing the great man if it were the case that the application had to be rejected, and that when Fine Gael were in power, 'He wouldn't give them the satisfaction of asking.'

I was an established student, it was in my third year, and there was a nice Reverend Mother. Anyway, they were holding the Galway Blazers Hunt Ball [in Loughrea], and some of the students were mad keen to go. And I said, 'No, I'm not going.' So we all went to bed in the hostel. And then there was gravel against the window. And I stuck my head out and there were my friends down below, saying, 'We can't go because they won't rent us a car unless we've a licence, and you're the only one who has a driving licence. You have to come.' So I succumbed. I mean I wasn't tempted, but I was pushed. And I got out the window, which was on the first floor, but some-body held my feet, and I got out the window, threw out my evening clothes and then off we went to Loughrea.

And it was a wonderful ball, wonderful. But then they all scattered, that was my undoing, I should have organized them strictly beforehand, before the thing finished, but I didn't. It didn't occur to me that they wouldn't all come flocking and say where did you put the car? But they didn't. So they had disappeared into this blank, which was an Irish pub, at 3 o'clock in the morning, and there's no way that they'd answer the door or answer anything, because they'd think it's the guards. So anyway, I hunted them out eventually, as soon as I got two I got the other two, so we started off and we got back, and it was daylight, which was very bad from my point of view, because I had to put the car outside the garage, otherwise I would have had to pay another day. So I put the car where it should be and I still had to get back to the hostel. And I got in unseen, and I was in bed and one of the very nice young lay sisters came along and said would she bring me up my breakfast, she said, 'You're very tired.' She didn't know!

But others had seen Budge walking in her evening dress through the town in the early morning, and eventually word of her exploits filtered through to the college, and reached the ears of the president, Monsignor Hynes:

The word got out to Pa Hynes, because people in the town had seen me, at half past seven in the morning. And funny enough I was noticeable because I was tall. I'd been seen, and so it might have been two, three weeks later, and I remember him, he said, 'You know Budge, I'm very fond of you, and I'm very fond of the Reverend Mother, and she thinks the sun, moon and stars shine out of you.' ... And I knew she [did]. If some of the other students in the hostel wanted to get the AC [all clear] for a dance she'd say, 'Well is Budge going?' and if I was going 'twas okay. We had a great opinion of one another. And so he said, 'You know it'd be a pity to disappoint her. She has really a great opinion of you. So I said, 'Well, I know that, and I usually don't.' ... I won't get out the window again, in other words. Because there was no talk about how I got out the window, he never mentioned about the window, oh no no, only about upsetting the Revd Mother. She never knew, never brought it up.

Up until the 1980s male students always significantly outnumbered female students – which gave the female students a distinct advantage, particularly in the 1930s and 1940s, as Jo Burke recalls: 'We used to love going up to the hops in college. You'd certainly never be waiting for a partner.' In the 1930s, Budge Clissmann recalled that female students did not tend to attend dances or hops with a male partner who paid in for them, for financial, as well as other reasons:

> The Skeffington, they had a hop every Friday, or on a regular night, and the main thing was you paid for yourself, because then you didn't have to commit yourself to anyone. You were an independent woman. So you paid for yourself, and then you were independent.

As one of the few tall female students, Budge's prospective partners at these hops were often limited:

> I remember going in to those hops and I'd stand on my toes and count the heads that stuck up, and there'd only be about four or so. There were some, I remember there was a very nice boy and he was about the size that I was and he was a wonderful dancer, and he was a student also.

Since secondary schools in those days were single-sex, for many students college was the first time they had the opportunity to socialize formally with the opposite sex. Jo Burke had been educated with the Louis nuns in Kiltimagh, Co. Mayo:

> I hadn't any brothers, so that was a disadvantage. I didn't know the second sex so well. Prof. Ó Brolcháin used to say, 'Don't tell me you had to come to college to learn that there was a second sex in the world!' to some of the girls coming in.

Prof. Seán Lavelle was one of the students in the 1940s who revelled in the opportunity to fraternize with his female fellow students:

> Well, the first year we just danced, because girls were … we were totally separated, these were new creatures. And there were dances three, four times a week. Monday in the Aula, Wednesday down near the docks, the Astoria ballroom.[6] All the good dancers used to hang out there. And there

---

6 Tony Bromell recalls that by the time he came to Galway in 1951 the letter 'i' had disappeared from the word 'Astoria' at the front of the building, and it was known thereafter to him and his contemporaries as 'The Astora.'

was the Hangar in Salthill, and that had dances I think about twice a week. And then there was always a dance on Sunday night.

Joe McGrath was a contemporary of Prof. Lavelle and having done one year of a science degree in 1945, he went on to do engineering for the remainder of his time in UCG. Joe recalls that the dances in the college were usually organized by college societies:

> Every Friday night all the faculties had their night, and the best of the whole lot would be the engineers and the medical, they would be the main ones. Why? I don't know, they were better organizers, and maybe there were more students in that particular faculty, you know? Oh the Aula was a great night on the Friday night. And then beforehand there'd be all sorts of posters drawn by the engineers, mostly by the engineers, they made very good posters.

With so much socializing going on it was inevitable that the constant late nights would eventually catch up on students. Eibhlín Uí Chionna recalls that occasionally her attendance at lectures was more in body than in spirit:

> All my botany lectures were at 9 o'clock, and I used to sit towards the front, and my lecturer was Máirín Dev ... and she told me afterwards that she used to see me sitting there in the front and half the time I'd be fast asleep. Well, you see you'd be out the night before. I got on great with her, she was very nice and had a great sense of humour.

The price of admission to a dance was sometimes a problem for students, but as the saying goes, where there's a will, there's a way, as Prof. Lavelle explains:

> They were nearly always 8–12, and the fellas would come in when the pubs closed, and there might be bargaining at the gate to see how much you could get in for. And if you couldn't get in there would be various stratagems by which you could climb up a drainpipe and that sort of thing. You could get into places anyway.

Joe McGrath recalls very deftly employing one of the 'stratagems' referred to by Prof. Lavelle in attempting to get into a dance in the Hangar in Salthill:

> There were three of us going out one night, and I hadn't a ha'penny in my pocket, and neither did the other two fellas much either. But anyway we were there for a while and someone said to me, 'You know, if you went in there now as a taxi driver, you'd get in free.' And one of the lads had a taxi driver's badge, because his father had taxis, and when he was on holidays

he used to drive it. Anyway, I put up my badge, and I went up and I said, 'Do taxi drivers get in here?' 'They do. Did you bring in a crowd?' 'I did.' 'Where did you bring them from?' 'Oh I brought them from Athenry.' 'Have you a badge?' 'I have.' 'Oh certainly,' says he. I hadn't even tuppence in my pocket to put in my coat. Ah there was all sorts of tricks ... it was all very innocent, everybody was in the same boat.

Joe recalls having less success, however, with the college dances, which were usually run by the college societies. 'Of course we always used to do our best to crash them, but it wasn't easy to crash in the Aula. Oh they were shrewd enough. The crowd that were looking after it knew all the loopholes as regards crashing.'

CATERING FOR HOPS

During the war years, with pretty much everything in short supply, catering for college events became something of a problem for the students organizing them. Dr Sheila Mulloy recalls one Sigerson Cup event vividly:

There were supposed to be three hundred and about a thousand came. And we could only laugh, because we'd made a thousand sandwiches with Miss Kirwan that morning.[7] And we didn't have sliced bread remember, and we had one jar of fish paste, there was very little available, and a little bit of ham, and we had to stretch that to make a thousand sandwiches, we did. Well ham was extremely limited and there was very little available, we might just butter one side of the bread, you know? Now this supper was supposed to be at 11 o'clock, but within half an hour it was all gone, and they all went in and sat at the table and started banging the cups and banging the tables, there was complete chaos, and we sat and laughed, you couldn't do a thing about it. And they sat there until they saw there was nothing else coming.

Dances or hops off campus were probably preferable to those held on campus in the Aula, due to the constant presence, at college hops, of the lady superintendent. The position of lady superintendent came about in the early 1900s when the numbers of female students coming to college began to increase, and it was deemed necessary to have a designated member of the college staff to ensure that the needs of women students were being sufficiently met – and, perhaps more importantly, that their personal conduct and moral well-being were closely monitored.

Miss Rosalie Kirwan was appointed as the first lady superintendent in 1914, and she retired in 1944. Ms Kirwan was replaced in this position by Miss Sarah Keane.

7 Rosalie Kirwan was the lady superintendent.

Mrs Keane died in 1948 and the position of lady superintendent was taken up by Mrs Mary O'Driscoll, who served in this capacity for many years thereafter. Prof. Seán Tobin recalls her presence at college dances in the late 1940s:

> She had to turn up at dances and chaperone them, and see if everything went well. I remember being on a thing called the Science Society one time, arranging a dance, and practically all the dances were held in the Aula. And they were supposed to be strictly for students, but we were always glad to admit nurses. But poor Mrs O'Driscoll would have to turn up for any college society that was running a dance like that and the organizing committee would have to see about having a box of chocolates to bring in to the lady superintendent. And furthermore, it was de rigeur, you'd have to make sure she got a dance.

Prof. Seán Lavelle makes the point that the music and dancing that were the norm in the 1940s – before the advent of rock 'n' roll – were more sedate: 'In the dances you could talk to your partner, that was very sociable, much more so than now.' But the spectre of Little Richard, Buddy Holly and the rest of the rock 'n' roll generation wasn't too far away, as Prof. Lavelle recalls: 'There were some jitterbugs around, and they didn't dance, well they spent a fair amount of time whirling round, but they came back together every so often.'

Christy Hannon recalled that there was a special inaugural dance for first years:

> I think the social function that we attended was what was called the GIBs Dance. It was for the first years, and that was held at Seapoint. All student dances were held in Seapoint. And I think the admission was 4s. 6d.

Dr John O'Donnell recalls that the move to Salthill had happened just prior to his arrival at college in 1959, due in the main to the increasing numbers of students, who could no longer be accommodated at functions in the Aula. But although much had changed, some things had not, as he explains:

> There had been a transition where the college dances, which in times before ours had been held in the Aula, were held at Seapoint now. And they were supposedly only private functions, that only students were supposed to go to. This wasn't observed, especially for girls, who were needed!

As we have seen, the watchful eyes of the lady superintendent and the college chaplain were ever-present at college dances, as Dr Dympna Horgan recalls: 'Would you believe Mrs O'Driscoll and Fr Kyne used to sit at the side of the dance floor, observing, and Mrs O'Driscoll would wag her finger if you were dancing cheek to cheek. Honestly!'

The late 1960s in particular proved something of a challenge to the lady super-intendent and Fr Kyne, largely on account of a new fashion trend, as Seán Mac Iomhair explains: 'An tAthair Ó Cadhain agus Ma O'Driscoll, bhíodh iad siúd ag breathnú ar na damhsaí, agus cur na mini skirts go mór astu.' ('Fr Kyne and Ma O'Driscoll would be watching at the dances, and the miniskirts upset them greatly.') But there were other changes coming in the '60s and '70s, including a more open attitude to issues like homosexuality, and Seán Mac Iomhair recalls one incident when the days of finger wagging at couples dancing cheek to cheek must have felt like a distant memory to the chaplain and the lady superintendent:

> Bhí fear áiraithe a raibh clú air amach ansin, agus mar a deir lucht an Bhéarla, 'He preferred his pal to his lassie,' agus céard a rinne sé? Thog sé innealtóir a bhí ina dteannta amach ag damhsa leis i gcomhar slow waltz, díreach os comhar an bhord ag a raibh an sagart agus an lady superinten-dent. Cur sé sin as do dhaoine.

> There was a certain gentleman, who afterwards became quite famous, and as they say in English, 'He preferred his pal to his lassie,' and what did he do? He took an engineer, who was in his company, out dancing for a slow waltz, right in front of the table where the priest and the lady superinten-dent were sitting. That put people out.

GOING TO THE PICTURES

At one time Galway had three cinemas, all of which offered special discounts to students. In the mid-1940s, when Joe McGrath came to UCG, going to the cinema was, along with the hops, a favourite pastime for him and his fellow students:

> Pictures then were cheap. We'd get into the second night for one and sixpence, for ninepence. It would be one and six normally, and students after the first night in the Savoy in Galway we'd get half-price ... but in the Astoria in Salthill, the last night of the performance you'd get for half-price. And the Town Hall also showed pictures and you'd get in there on the last night for half-price. So we always went on the half-price night.

Even with the discount it was often difficult for students to find the price of a ticket, let alone take a girl out on a date to the cinema. When they did find both the girl and the money, there were other obstacles to overcome, as Eibhlín Uí Chionna explains:

> Girls didn't expect to be taken out on a Saturday night, the big night was Friday. Students got in half-price and that meant you could sit in the

ninepenny seats for fourpence and you could sit in the one and fourpenny
seats for ninepence. So you see you'd hope that if you were taken out on a
date that they would rise to the one and fourpenny seats for ninepence. It
was a cheap date to take you for fourpence you see. And some poor divils
couldn't afford to take anybody out, and some poor divils were too nervous
anyhow. They'd have come from Christian Brothers schools, or would have
come from boarding schools … they were very immature, and they were
nervous fellas.

Prof. Seán Tobin recalls that, in common with most of the country in the late
1940s, Galway was still suffering the effects of wartime shortages, and to provide
employment to Irish musicians and entertainers a new law was introduced, which
enhanced the entertainment prospects of those students who had even a little
money to spare on socializing:

After the war had ended, things were still a bit tough and scarce and the
government introduced a law requiring a certain proportion of all entertainments to be home-produced. The Town Hall Cinema used give us the best
possible value I would say for a night's entertainment because, for I think it
was a shilling on a Saturday night, you could go in there at about 7 o'clock
and they'd have a band playing, they'd bring on some kind of an act, like
jugglers or clowns or whatever it might be, singers not with the band, and
then you'd have a short film and then you'd have the main film, and it was
really good value.

Another consequence of food and fuel shortages was that when students were out
socializing, or working late in the library, the landlady would save on fuel by not
lighting fires in the digs, as Dr Diarmuid Ó Cearbhaill recalls:

Ní raibh aon teas lárnach ann, agus b'fhéidir go mbeadh tine sa lóistín, agus
an cheist a bheadh ag bean an tí, an dtuigeann tú: 'An bhfuil sibh ar fad ag
dul chuig an leabharlann nó chuig na pictiúirí?' Mura mbeadh daoine ann,
b'olc an rud é sin dá rachaimis amach agus an tine lasta mar bhí gual nó
móin gann go leor.

There was no central heating, and maybe there would be a fire in the digs,
and the question the landlady would ask you was: 'Are you going to the
library or to the pictures?' If there was nobody going to be there it would be
a terrible waste to have a fire on, because coal, or turf, were scarce enough.

The advent of the Hammer horror films, from the mid-1950s to the 1970s, proved
an unexpected boon to male students, as Seán Mac Iomhair explains: 'An cleas, ar
ndóigh, a bhí ann ná cailín a thabhairt chuig ceann de na scannáin sin agus nuair a

thagadh eagla uirthi bhí deis agat barróg a bhreith uirthi!' ('The trick at the time was to take a girl to one of these kind of films and when she got scared you got your chance to give her a hug!')

COLLEGE ROMANCES

With such a large number of young men and women mixing and socializing on a regular basis, it was inevitable that romances would blossom between students. Joe McGrath recalled that although some of these led on to marriage, most college romances ended as soon as the students graduated:

> Very few college lines ended up in marriage.[8] Well, I suppose I could well understand it because you're in a different life there, student life is a very artificial life. You're out in the real world afterwards and things are different.

Some romances that began in college did survive, though, and Jo Burke recalls one couple she knew well from her own college days in the mid-1930s, Des and Maureen Kenny, of Galway's well-known Kenny's Bookshop and Art Gallery.

> Maureen and Des were at college with me, they were doing arts. They met in college … they were a twosome. Ah they were part of one another. There was a party one night, and she arrived with someone else, but anyway Des got after her, and kept pursuing her from there on. He was a wise man, she was a good wife to him. A lovely person.[9]

Budge Clissmann, who came to UCG in 1931, recalls the president of the college addressing the newly arrived students on the subject of college romances – although he was careful to avoid the use of the term itself:

> When we came to college first Monsignor Hynes said to us, 'Now, you are probably wondering what I think about friendships between boys and girls. Well now, I would advise you to have lots of different friendships with lots of boys and girls, but no one special friendship with no one boy or girl.' That was the advice he gave us.

But all the sensible advice in the world was of no use when impressionable young men and women came to college and found themselves mixing socially with the opposite sex for perhaps the first time. Prof. Seán Ó Cinnéide was one young

8 The expression 'doing a line' meant having an exclusive dating relationship.   9 An obituary on the death of Maureen Kenny stated that she won a scholarship to UCG in 1936 'and on her first day there she met Des Kenny. As Des often said later, 'That was that.' *Irish Times*, 29 Mar. 2008.

student who enjoyed many casual romances with his fellow students during his college days. However, he remembers well the first occasion, when the college heart-throb at the time, Donogh O'Malley,[10] who later became a government minister, stole his girlfriend from under his nose and caused Prof. Ó Cinnéide to become a kindred spirit with one of Ireland's greatest poets:

> Ní raibh mé ach dhá mhí anseo, agus thit mé i ngrá le cáilín. Chuamar go dtí damhsa san Astoria Ballroom i Merchants Road. Tuairaim is a deich a chlog chuas síos cun buidéal lemonade a fháil don cailín seo. Agus nuair a thaining mé aníos leis ní raibh sí le feiscint. Dúirt duine éigin liom go raibh sí imithe, go ndeachaigh sí amach, gur imigh sí le Donncha. Agus bhí aithne agama ar Donncha alright, bhí sé sin ag déanamh an bhliain dheireanach den Innealtóireacht. Agus gan dabht, mar a deirfeá, bhíodh 'ball seirce', an rud a bhí ag Diarmuid Ó Duibhne, ag Donncha, agus ní raibh aon fhadhb aige le mná, ní raibh ionam ach spriosán i súile na mban i gcomparáid le sin. D'imigh sé léi. An áit a bhfuil an gáire ar fad ná, ní raibh mise, ni rabhas ar mo chumas filiochta chomh maith faoin ócáid ná 'on Merchants Road, on an autumn day, I saw her first and knew ...' ach an fear bocht eile, Paddy Kavanagh, chum sé fhein dán faoi Hilda, Hilda Moriarty, a phós Donncha, on Grafton Street a bhí Paddy, i Merchants Road a bhí mise.

I was only two months here when I fell in love with a girl. We went to a dance in the Astoria Ballroom in Merchants Road. Around 10 o'clock I went down to buy this girl a bottle of lemonade. And when I came back up with it she wasn't to be seen. Someone said to me that she had gone, that she went out, that she left with Donogh. And I knew Donogh alright, he was in his final year of engineering. And without a doubt, as they say, Donogh had the 'love spot', the same thing that Diarmuid Ó Duibhne had,[11] and he had no problem attracting women, I was just a nonentity in the eyes of the women in comparison with him. He went away with her ... and the funny thing was that I wasn't really able to compose any really good poetry about the occasion, only 'On Merchants Road, on an autumn day, I saw her first, and knew ...' But the other poor man, Paddy Kavanagh, he wrote a poem about Hilda Moriarty, who married Donogh. Paddy was on Grafton Street, I was on Merchants Road.[12]

10 Donogh Brendan O'Malley (1921–68) was a Fianna Fáil politician, a TD for Limerick East from 1954 until 1968, and subsequently served as minster for health and minister for education. 11 Diarmuid Ó Duibhne was the hero of the Fianna in the Fenian Cycle of Irish mythology. Famous as the lover of Gráinne, he was reputed to have had a *'ball seirce'*, or 'love spot' in the middle of his forehead, which made him irresistible to women. 12 The reference is to Patrick Kavanagh's poem 'On Raglan Road', in which he recalls the early days of his courtship of Dr Hilda Moriarty, who married Donogh O'Malley in 1947.

PARTIES

Compared to the more raucous affairs that house parties were to become in the 1970s and 1980s, Jo Burke's account of a party in a vacant house in the 1930s is quaint and almost childlike in its innocence:

> People were away on holidays, and they left the key of the house over in the digs where the lads stayed. The lads, when the [landladies] were gone to bed, they went in and got the key. Candles they had, the lights were switched off. About six lads and five girls … we started playing forfeits. I got a forfeit to go upstairs with this lad, and he got a candle to go upstairs. And what did he do only blow out the candle. I screamed and fled. 'Twas very innocent. We were very harmless really.

Another party involving furtively entering a premises after dark took place in the mid-1940s – except on this occasion the party was in the college itself. Eibhlín Uí Chionna recalls what happened:

> We'd always be looking for a place to have a party. Now you couldn't in your digs mostly, you wouldn't be allowed, so I think it was coming towards the end of the year, and we examined the situation and the Ladies Room was this lovely room, lovely armchairs, and a beautiful turf fire going all the time. Only a small number of people used it, you used to be in the Ladies Room between lectures. I'm afraid it might have been my idea too for that reason. So there was a window into the Quadrangle, and it would be very easy to leave that one window open. And last thing in the evening, before I went home to my digs, I could put a few bits of turf into the ashes of the fire. And I said, 'I'll go home and then we'll meet about 8 o'clock on the Newcastle side of the college on the boundary wall,' which we did, a few of us. And then you'd boot over the wall, creep along, get in the window into the Quadrangle, no bother at all, then up the stairs. Now I think Monsignor de Brún would have been there, but he was in the other corner.[13] Then up the stairs, get the fire on in no time, and we had a right party around the fire there. Well, I mean, who was going to catch us? In those times Galway was a sleepy town.

The social lives of nuns and brothers attending university were even more restricted than those of their fellow students who were in digs. Sr Mairéad Murray recalls the efforts made by some of the sisters to save a little money to have the odd party for themselves.

> We'd have parties out in Seamount, ourselves now, and we thought we'd get stuff for it, but we hadn't the money, the convent didn't give you money, we

---

13 The president's quarters were at that time located in the opposite corner of the Quadrangle.

had very little. And we'd do anything to save the bus fare. So that time you'd get money for empty biscuit tins, you'd get money sometimes for empty jam pots as well. We brought in a pile of old biscuit tins that we had used up. We got half a crown, or something big, for each of them, sure we had a great party altogether.

WINTER WONDERLAND

Winter, and the snow it brought, provided a rich source of new entertainment for the student population – or at least the male students. Prof. Seán Lavelle recalls that in his second year at UCG, in 1947, there was a particularly severe winter. Far from being obstacles, the heavy snow and iced-over canals became yet another source of fun and entertainment for students:

> There was a very bad winter, and the snow was on the ground for six weeks. We built a big wheel, St Mary's was opposite us,[14] and we went into that and we made up one of these wheels where you roll the wheel over the snow and it catches on, and it was as high as we could reach. And it didn't melt until May as I recall. That year the river iced over, and a chap I knew later on, Tom Kelly, he skated up to Oughterard – he did. Alone … if he had gone through the ice … The Canal down here was frozen as well, and coming home one night I stepped onto it, onto the ice, and it held me up and I stepped another step, and it let me down. The fellas were above me, and I was young and athletic at that time so I got out easily enough.

The fun continued on campus, as Prof. Lavelle recalls:

> The winter that the snow lay, 1947, it snowed all day, or the early part of the day, and there was a Governing Body meeting this same day. And the girls were mainly in the Arts Faculty, and the engineers then would gather outside and snowball them. Síle Ní Chinnéide was a lecturer in history through Irish, and she came out and she said, 'Go way outta that, leave the girls alone!' Somebody threw a snowball and a volley came, so she had to beat a hasty retreat.

But the playful antics of the students were in danger, at one point, of earning the displeasure of the most powerful man on campus, as Prof. Lavelle recalls:

> The archbishop of Tuam came in his car to the front gates, and the fellas had put a roll of snow against the front gate so it couldn't be opened. So the chauffeur got out, and came over to reason with the boys and they snowballed him.

14 St Mary's College is a secondary school located on St Mary's Road, Galway.

Then the archbishop got out and he was snowballed too. And he went down to the Great Southern[15] and phoned the president,[16] and the president came out, he was a very big man, and he had a huge head, and he walked down, and nobody DARED to fire a snowball. So he said, 'Clear out that snow so the gates may be opened, and the governors can get in.' And it was done.

MA CREAVEN'S COFFEE SHOP

Mrs Creaven's coffee shop, or Ma Creaven's as it was more affectionately known by generations of students, was something of an institution on campus. Established in the early 1950s by Mrs Creaven, a Galway native, and for many years the only catering facility for both students and staff until the establishment of Smokey Joe's in the mid-'70s, Ma Creaven's was the social hub of the college, and provided both companionship and much-needed shelter from the cold and rain.

Prior to the establishment of Ma Creaven's, in a distinctive, though tiny, structure, students had nowhere to go on campus to relax and drink a much-needed cup of coffee between lectures, as Prof. Seán Tobin recalled:

> When I was a student here you couldn't get a cup of coffee in the college, there was nothing. You couldn't get a drink of water even. You had breakfast, you came down to the college, probably got wet, went back for lunch, and then came down again. And then you'd be down, possibly, often enough, sopping wet for three hours, dripping water in the Physics Lab, or the Chemistry Lab.

But for students in the '30s and '40s, the lack of facilities was only part of the problem, as Sr Mairead Murray recalls: 'There was no coffee shop, and even if there was we hadn't the price of it. Lydon's was really the only place.' (And Lydon's wasn't on campus, it was in town.) The establishment of an on-campus coffee shop was therefore a real boon to the students and staff when Mrs Creaven set up her operation in 1953/4. Right from the start, she set the tone as to the sort of operation she intended to run – as Christy Hannon put it, 'she ran a tight ship'. One of the truly great characters of the college, Mrs Creaven, fondly known as 'Ma', quickly became a legend on campus, and as Peadar Ó Fátharta recalls: 'Students and staff were always on their best behaviour while having their coffee in Ma's house.' David Burke (BA, 1969; MA, 1974), writing in *Cois Coiribe*, recalls that:

> Mrs Creaven was never referred to by students as anything but Ma Creaven. 'Ma' in UCG did not have the connotations of disrespect the word would imply to an outsider. It was a title conferred on a few distinguished ladies,

15 The Great Southern Hotel, now the Hotel Meyrick, is located on Eyre Square, Galway.   16 The president in 1947 was Monsignor Pádraig de Brún, who had taken up office in 1945.

among them a professor, who had by their qualities of fairness or learning, or strength of character, or sheer personality, earned the respect of even the irreverent. Perhaps 'Ma' meant just that, a subconscious mother image to a crew of would-be adults.

The coffee shop provided a social outlet, especially for students, for many of whom college life was their first opportunity to socialize with their peers without parental supervision. Dr Dympna Horgan recalls:

> It was so exciting being in college you see, you've no idea what it was like. My parents would have been fairly strict, and, you know, the freedom of going to college. And the fun of it, going to the coffee shop.

The shop was an instant success, due almost entirely to the hard work and efficiency of Mrs Creaven and her staff. Mrs Creaven quickly put her own unmistakable stamp on what was to become her own small empire within the college. There are many colourful stories told about Mrs Creaven and her operation, but what is clear from them all is that, with a very small space and limited facilities at her disposal, she did an extraordinary job of servicing the refreshment needs of an entire college, embracing academic staff and students, and did it with good humour and no small degree of efficient management. According to Bobby Curran:

> Ma Creaven, she'd look down at you and if you had gone beyond your allotted time, you know, drink your coffee and have a bit of a conversation, she'd call you out. 'Curran, you've been here since 11 o'clock?' 'Twas easy to know us all by name. There was a thousand students maximum, and I suppose the coffee shop was frequented by three or four hundred we'll say, or whatever, and you'd have to go.

Even those who didn't frequent the coffee shop, such as grounds supervisor Brian Finan, who was, as he says, 'more or less always outside', were nonetheless very aware of, and admired, Mrs Creaven's undoubted skills: 'Mrs Creaven, Ma Creaven she was called, she was a good disciplinarian, she had good control over students. I think there were more characters hanging around college at the time, maybe more messers.'

Whether that was or wasn't the case, there is no doubt that one of the greatest characters of them all was Mrs Creaven herself – and any 'characters' or 'messers' who crossed her path had more than met their match. J.T. O'Brien (BE, 1957), in recording his own college memoirs, which are now in the college archive, gives us a wonderful account of the institution which was Ma Creaven's:

> UCG had a family feel to it. On cold mornings the members of the family attempted the occupation of the only available hothouse in UCG, the coffee

shop, run by a no-nonsense lady with the sharpest tongue in the West and a heart of gold. Such was Mrs Creaven, who in times of snow had to be linked home and safely delivered. The reward for this charitable act was a free coffee. The many had to share some fifty square metres with steaming dispensers, a countertop and a reserve space behind, into which the shivering professors and lecturers would cram, warming their hands on hot coffee mugs. It was standing room only for them. I never saw a single undergraduate invade the august space behind the counter. Only the little man, one Jimmy Cranny, who managed the building hidden in the trees (where medical students furtively pursued the anatomical secrets of the human form), was allowed to stand tall with the learned group behind the counter.

The coffee shop played host to both academic staff and students in the early days. Prof. Tom O'Connor recalls:

The only staff facilities for coffee and so on were in the back, behind the counter in Ma Creaven's little kitchen there. And you used to have people in there, piled one on top of the other … They eventually got a staff room over in what is now Séamus Mac Mathúna's office, over in the Quad, for a while.

Teresa O'Hanlon (née Ward), a student here from 1954–8, in her memoirs, recalled that:

Frequent visits to the campus coffee shop were interrupted only by Mrs Creaven's peremptory admonition to 'Get up out of that and go to your lecture!' That wonderful woman knew where every student ought to be at any particular time, and the coffee only cost sixpence.

This was especially true of Galway students, whose parents she inevitably knew, as Dr Dympna Horgan recalled: 'She always knew … and she used to throw people out, you know, say, "Your poor father, your poor mother, is working there trying to put you through, and there you are lounging!" You know, she knew everybody.'

As Maureen Langan-Egan recalls, the most important thing about the coffee shop was that it facilitated communication between students, and provided a welcome break between lectures:

You could have great old chats in the coffee shop around Ma's time if it wasn't too busy, provided she liked you of course. But she didn't want people to be hanging around indefinitely in the coffee shop. She would feel that well, if you were there, you were there to work. You see this was the point – if you went to your lectures, if you were off at 11 o'clock and you'd a lecture at 12, you didn't clown around.

Dr Séamus Mac Mathúna was another student who appreciated the task facing Mrs Creaven in operating in such a small space, and also her determination that students would not idle away their time when they should be working:

> Bhí an áit ana-bheag, ar ndóigh, ag an am, agus mar sin bhí uirthi custaiméirí a choinneáil ag gluaiseacht. Agus freisin, ní hamháin sin ach is dóigh go raibh, mar a déarfá, coinsias aici ar a son siúd, nár chóir dóibh a bheith ag cur ama amú trí bheith ag ól caifé nuair ba chóir dóibh bheith ag léacht nó ag staidéar nó rud éigin mar sin.

> The place was very small at the time and therefore she had to keep the customers moving. And not alone that, but I suppose she had a conscience on their behalf, that it wasn't right for them to be wasting time by maybe drinking coffee when they should have been at a lecture or studying, or something like that.

Dr Mac Mathúna recalls that Mrs Creaven was also keen that no one would be under any illusion as to who was in charge in her shop: 'Ar ndóigh, cuid den chur chuige sin, ní bheadh aon ró-mheas aici uaireanta ach oiread ar an lucht acadúil. Bhí sise ina máistreás ar an áit, agus ba chuma cén seasamh a bheadh ag éinne eile.' ('Of course, consistent with that approach, she would on occasion show no great regard for academics. She was mistress of the place, and it didn't matter what status anybody else had.')

Dr Dympna Horgan believes that medical students were treated somewhat differently (and in some cases more benignly) than students from other faculties, because of the significantly longer time they spent in college: 'She got to know you, you were there that long.' But there were other, more compassionate, grounds for her toleration of the more prolonged loitering of medical students, according to Bobby Curran:

> There was one exception to Mrs Creaven's rule of telling you to go, and I'll tell you who they were. The medicos, you see, the guys in Third, Fourth and Final Med, they would have had clinics all morning from 8 o'clock, and they used to come down at 11, and they used to have white faces on them, because they had seen terrible things up in the hospital. And they'd come in and sit down. And they were exempt from this rule.

Maths student Bobby was quick to capitalize on this fact:

> The cute fellas around, like the fellas from Waterford, we'd infiltrate a table … And she'd look down and she wouldn't see you, and we'd be all fine, and often we'd be sat with a group of medicos from 11 until 1.

But Mrs Creaven's tolerance of medical students did not extend to those whom she considered might be 'getting notions' about themselves having completed their degree, as George Deacy recalls:[17]

> Oh, she used to give the doctors an awful time! You know if one came up and the other sat down, you know, to get the coffees, two coffees, she'd say, 'Oh, he's being served today, he's got his degree, and will we call you "doctor" now? Bring up that cup that's down there! No good walking out of here and leaving your cup! Who did you think is going to clean up after you!' Oh, she'd give them an awful slagging, 'Oh, you're a *doctor* now!'

As Prof. O'Connor recalls, the only concession made to staff was that they were permitted to take their coffee behind the counter, while the students occupied the remainder of the confined space. The fact that academic staff were given no real extra privileges other than being allowed to stand behind the counter in the tiny coffee shop was something one visiting academic was particularly struck by, as Prof. Jim Flavin recalls:

> Bhí Liam Ó Buachalla istigh taobh thiar den counter. Bhí Eamon Nash[18] ann agus bhí cúirteoir aige ó Shasana, agus cur sé an cúirteoir in aithne do Liam Ó Buachalla. Agus dúirt Eamon, 'Liam Ó Buachalla, chairman of the Senate,' agus ina dhiaidh sin dúirt an cúirteoir le Eamon, 'That was a very nice man, and what position did you say he has?' 'Well', says Eamon, 'he's Cathaoirleach of the Senate, in other words he's the equivalent of your Lord Chancellor'. 'Oh', arsa an cúirteoir 'this is a very democratic country'.

> Liam Ó Buachalla was in behind the counter. Eamon Nash was there and he had a visitor from England, and he introduced the visitor to Liam Ó Buachalla. And Eamon said, 'Liam Ó Buachalla, chairman of the Senate,' and afterwards the visitor said to Eamon, 'That was a very nice man, and what position did you say he has?' 'Well', says Eamon, 'he's Cathaoirleach of the Senate, in other words he's the equivalent of your Lord Chancellor'. 'Oh', said the visitor, 'this is a very democratic country'.

For those students away from home for the first time Ma Creaven's was a wonderful 'home from home', complete with an 'Irish mammy' substitute. Roscommon native Christy Hannon was one of those with very fond memories of Ma Creaven's:

17 George Deacy had a 49-year career in the college, arriving as a 15-year-old in 1956 and retiring as computer services operations manager in 2005. 18 Prof. J.E. (Eamon) Nash founded the Department of Engineering Hydrology at UCG in the 1970s.

She ran a very good show, with good humour, but kept great control. I suppose there were students jumping queues and you know ... but she kept
great control. It was a lovely haunt really, and she used to have lovely biscuits ... the kind of coffee biscuits, with a kind of sugary brown crust on
them. It was a lovely place really, you'd go once a day, for a coffee and a chat.
It was small, very small. But she ran a tight ship, well she had to, but she
was good humoured.

The importance of the coffee shop as a major meeting place on campus is evidenced by the fact that it was here that notices about sporting and other events
were placed. According to Dr John O'Donnell:

It was the other centre of the college, like the Archway, even more so. The
rugby team, for the match at the weekend, would be posted in the window
of the coffee shop ... The noticeboards were outside it, or whatever else was
running, the college dance, but that's where they were, the noticeboards
were all around the outside of the coffee shop.

Given its popularity, and limited size, at certain times it might be impossible to
even get in. Dr John O'Donnell and his wife Dr Dympna Horgan met during
their student days and Dr O'Donnell recalled their own efforts to socialize in Ma
Creaven's:

You wouldn't always get a seat, you wouldn't always get in. But people
would be working, not everybody would be there at the same time. It was
fourpence for a cup of coffee, I remember that well, that's 4*d*. now.

When Mrs Creaven retired, her coffee shop was taken over by Peggy Jordan, and
thereafter became known as 'Peggy's', but it retained much of its original character, and it continued to provide both sustenance and a much-needed social facility
on campus for yet another generation of students. In time other facilities came on
stream – The Staff Club, Smokey Joe's, and the main college restaurant – but Ma
Creaven's was the first, and is perhaps the one remembered with the most affection
by the generations of students and staff who frequented it.

LYDON'S CAFÉ

Before the establishment of Mrs Creaven's on campus, Lydon's Restaurant in Shop
Street had offered another place for those students who could afford it to socialize. Teresa O'Hanlon, a student from 1954–8, recalls in her memoir: 'Saturday
afternoons were spent in Lydon's café on Shop Street, more for the gossip and
to eye up the talent than for any need of sustenance.' Lydon's was also one of the
few places to eat out in Galway that would have been affordable to an impecunious

student trying to impress a young lady, as Prof. Tobin recalls: 'Well it was the only game in town, that was it – Lydon's Restaurant. And if you were bringing a lady out you would take her to Lydon's, because the food was alright and it wasn't over expensive.'

The popularity of Lydon's and its cakes was such that the company was often asked to supply various functions organized by the college. Eibhlín Uí Chionna, who came to college in 1942, recalls one occasion when the cakes supplied for a particular function eventually found their way back to the restaurant – and afforded a group of audacious students the opportunity for yet another scam:

> We were at a hop down in the Commercial Rowing Club, somebody was running this in aid of something, and therefore [it was] a little bit pricier than the usual, because they were going to give you supper. And supper meant that they'd give you cakes and tea. So we all went along, and it wasn't very well supported, because of the price, and therefore there was far more cakes than people could eat. And … somebody found a bag somewhere and they took the cakes, it wasn't me this time, it was some of the fellas. They put them into a bag, a dozen or so cakes, Lydon's cakes. And then the next day we all met, about eight of us, up in Lydon's, and ordered coffee and cakes. And the cakes arrived and then the waitress went off and we looked at the cakes. And there were two we liked, there were always two, and there would be the less nice ones. So we ate the two nice ones, and we replaced them with the substitutes, two or three, from the bag. And then after a little while called the waitress over and we said, 'Really, you've given us a very dull selection, could you bring us another selection?' So then the next one came along, and she put a different selection, we took five or six that we wanted, and we replaced them, and she was back again. Can you imagine this? And so they did it a second time, and if she really looked … I mean she couldn't work it out. And then they came out with more. It ended up with five cakes eaten, a total of eight people and all having tea and coffee. I felt ashamed, but the fellas were delighted with themselves. I always think of the poor people who got the stale cakes with the bit of icing fixed up with a bit of handiwork. Well that was students, you know? It wasn't meanness, it was completely the devilment of the thing, absolute devilment.

NORA CRÚB'S

Nora Crúb's in Quay Street was yet another Galway institution, much frequented by students, largely because the crubeens served there were filling – and cheap.[19] Maureen Langan-Egan remembers the place well, and the colourful lady who ran it.

19 Crubeens, otherwise known as 'pig's trotters', are a dish made of boiled pigs' feet, which are then battered and fried.

She was a small woman. And I can remember hearing a story … about her giving out some change for somebody one night, and she gave a sovereign or some very valuable coin as change, and this girl said, 'You've given me the wrong change, you've handed me over very valuable stuff.' And she said, 'No, what I handed to you, you keep it.' She was that kind of a generous type of person.

Owen Callan, who in the 1950s dated one of the assistants working in Nora Crúbs, recalls waiting inside the shop for his girlfriend to finish work, and witnessing the mayhem which would result when the pubs closed and hungry customers – including students – made their way to the Quay Street establishment:

She would see the crowds coming, and when it got too busy she would shut the door. And there would be dozens of fairly drunk individuals pleading through the letterbox, 'Please Nora, please, give us a crubeen, ah go on, please!' And if she knew them well enough she would do it, she would give them the crubeen – but she'd shove it through the letterbox. She would! And the fat would be running down the door. But they were just so hungry after the few pints they didn't mind.[20]

Maureen Langan-Egan recalls that Nora Crúb's generosity also extended to giving impecunious students the bones left over from the crubeens, which the students boiled up to make soup. According to Maureen: 'She fed half the students of Galway that way.'

Another favourite haunt of students in the 1960s, according to Maureen Langan-Egan, was Thornton's chip shop on Henry Street: 'It was a great place to get chips on a Friday night.'

STUDENT POLITICS

The involvement of students in politics – both national and international – has long been a feature of college life. In the 1930s in particular, the tensions between the two main political parties at the time – Cumann na nGaedhael and Fianna Fáil – manifested themselves in college politics also, bringing some students into conflict with the college authorities. Budge Clissmann recalls one such incident, which involved Prof. Tommy Dillon and the then college president, Monsignor Hynes:

Prof. Dillon was very Free State, of course, and so Prof. Dillon also was

---

20 Owen Callan, interviewed by the author, 23 Dec. 2009.

very Free State. Cumann na nGaedhael … had a monster meeting in Eyre Square. There was a hotel facing the square, and, facing the open square where the people could gather, they had the first-floor window open. It was one of these nice old-fashioned windows that open out, and so the speakers spoke from this window on the first floor to this meeting. And I, and others as well, we went to this meeting to disrupt it as much as possible. So we got into the middle of the crowd, there was a big crowd, and there was a man called Hogan,[21] who was minister for agriculture and he was very clever, because I remember one little episode where one of the boo-ers was saying, 'Well what do you know about agriculture? … You don't know anything about agriculture,' he says, heckling … and then Hogan says, 'Well I know as much as you,' or something like that back, you know, an ordinary answer, and your man shouts back, 'Well, how many toes has a pig?' and the answer comes back, 'Take off your boot and count.' Hogan was very quick, and very witty.

But I was heckling away like mad of course too. The window was very large and you could see Dillon was in the window, prominent, a professor, you see Cumann na nGaedhael was the only respectable place to be if you wanted to be interested at all in politics, and you see his brother you must remember was a TD. But then I could see that there was a guard behind, there was three or four people together, but I could see there was a guard, and I could see Dillon pointing me out. So I didn't take any notice, and I stayed where I was and then eventually after about 10 minutes … there was a little tap on my shoulder, and [the guard] said, 'I'm afraid you have to come with me.' So I said okay, not to make a big scene there and then, so I went with him, and he wanted to get me out of the meeting, that was all. He said, 'Don't go back into that.' I said, 'Okay,' and went on. He was under instruction from Professor Dillon, or from whoever else was in that window, to get me out of there, because I was a kind of a ring leader and this beautiful monster meeting was getting disturbed. Anyway I didn't mind, I had done my bit, and you see he would have had to bring me to the barracks if I'd gone on.

News of Budge's antics at the meeting that morning quickly spread to the college, she recalls:

So that afternoon I was coming into college and I met Pa Hynes, coming out of college and going down the footpath, and he said, 'Well there you are Budge, I was on me way down to the jail to visit you!'

21 Patrick J. Hogan (1891–1936) was an Irish farmer, solicitor and Cumann na nGaedheal politician. He served as minister for labour and minister for agriculture during the first independent Irish government between 1922 and 1932.

A MINOR REVOLUTION – WOMEN WEARING THE TROUSERS

While the miniskirts, psychedelic fashions and haircuts of the 1960s certainly caused a stir on campus, there was one particular event that perhaps created the most impact among both academic staff and students, as Prof. Seán Tobin recalls:

> I don't know what year I was in the college when there was a kind of a hush all over the college, and then the word went round that a girl had appeared in the college wearing trousers. Of course, up till then that was either frowned on officially, or just believed to be frowned on.

As Pat Rabbitte remembers, this happened during the very first College Week, in the late 1960s:

> Ralph O'Gorman organized the first College Week, and there wasn't anything ever to compare to it again, because it was a remarkable event, with a huge participation. I remember [a female student] arriving, wearing slacks, and it was the first time a woman ever wore trousers onto the campus, in rebellion, during College Week, and Mrs O'Driscoll acknowledged that she had to surrender.[22]

With so many changes happening in the 1960s, on both the political and social front, it is sometimes the little details that mark the way Irish society was changing at the time that people remember. One such relatively minor event is recalled by Peadar O'Dowd:

> The '60s were expanding, the world was exploding, and we were part of that. I remember once, a new strange phenomenon, an actual drink was coming into the college. And it was a thing called Coca Cola. And I'll never forget it, it was in the Greek Hall, in the Quad, and we thought this Coca Cola was an alcoholic drink, and sure it wasn't. So these big crates were there and this poor idiot was up and he was expounding on the virtues of Coca Cola. And what were we doing? We were 'baptizing' everyone coming in.[23]

COLLEGE CHARACTERS

Every new crop of students seemed to throw up the odd 'character', who distinguished themselves by their quirkiness or individual talents. Prof. Seán Tobin recalls one such character who attended college with him in the late 1940s:

22 Mrs O'Driscoll was the college's lady superintendent from 1948 until she retired in 1981. She was succeeded in the role of lady superintendent by Mrs Margaret Fletcher-Egan. 23 'Baptizing' infers that the students were dousing those entering the building in Coca Cola.

Paddy ... he was from down somewhere in the country, and he affected, for some reason, he thought it was kind of characteristic of his upbringing and everything else, he had the trousers tied with binder twine, as you might in the country ...

Then there was the agricultural science student, who, according to Prof. Tobin, came up with a novel – and somewhat audacious – scheme to earn some extra cash:

We had some students of agricultural science, and one of those as I recall, liked to 'sell' seats in the library to unsuspecting first years. I don't know if he ever got his comeuppence, if he sold one to the wrong person, but there was a story that he was successful from time to time, selling a library seat.[24]

SOCIALIZING IN THE 1970S

Although student numbers were on the increase, they were still relatively small in the 1970s. The focal point of socializing among students had moved out of town by the '70s, as Grace Timlin recalls:

All our craic at that time was in the Cellar and the Skeff up town ... and all the action was in Salthill, not in the town, at weekends. All the societies would have their parties in Salthill. The Beach Hotel, which is no longer there, had a huge amount of parties ... Straight across from Mortons there's a little road which actually brings you onto the Prom ... That was the Beach Hotel. Tracey's used to run that and a lot of the college societies had their parties there. And then there was another place on Salthill proper, across from the church, the Holiday Hotel, which is no longer there, that used to have a lot of college parties. And the Oslo was used for dances, and there was a band called The Archway in existence that time. And they used to do a lot of the college dances. And then Seapoint was used for college dances, when I started first, and there was a band called The Philosophers, I'm sure a lot of people remember them, they were quite popular. And Andrew Strong, he was in The Commitments, well his father Rob Strong, and the Plattermen, they played a lot for the college dances. And they had something called the GIBs Ball, I think it was for first years, your first dance of the year was called the GIBs Ball. And when I started here it was held in Seapoint, so you'd have 3,000 people or so packed in to Seapoint, it was incredible.

24 One of those interviewed for the project confided to the author that they had, as a naive first year, been duped and 'bought' a library seat from the said agricultural science student.

1. Porters Martin Joyce and Pat O'Reilly. Source: An Teanglann (Patsy Clancy).

2. Students at the boat club, summer 1965. Front: Pádhraic Dochartaigh, Harry Connolly. Back: Seamus Ó Cinneide, and two unidentified people. Source: An Teanglann (Patsy Clancy).

3. Prof. Elizabeth 'Nellie' Lee, Assoc. Prof. Seamus Cahill and Mary O'Driscoll in 1981, on the occasion of Mrs O'Driscoll's retirement as lady superintendent, a position she had held for thirty-four years. Source: UCG Archive.

4. Gordon Young, systems manager, at the DEC 20 system terminal, and Bobby Curran, director of computer services, in 1978. The DEC 20 system was a mainframe computer supporting up to 120 terminals. Source: UCG Archive.

5. Mrs Creaven, known to all as Ma Creaven, standing outside the college's first coffee shop. Note the noticeboard, advising of all college-related social and sporting fixtures. Source: Mrs Susan Courtney.

6. Diarmuid Ó Cearbhaill, dean of the faculty of commerce, at the time of his arrival at UCG in 1947 as one of the first Aiken Scholars. Source: Mrs Helen Ó Cearbhaill.

7. Professor Máirín de Valera and Dr Maurice McDonald of the Botany Department.
Source: UCG Archive.

8. Seamus Mac Mathúna, Runaí Um Gnothaí Acadiúla sa Ceathrú Rua, *c.* 1980. Source: An
Teanglann (Patsy Clancy).

9. UCG Boxing Club 1962. Winners of the Sir Harry Preston Trophy for British and Irish Universities and Hospitals Championships at Coventry. Standing: Malcolm Little (hon. sec.), Vincent Daly (light middle), Kevin Gill (middle), Frank Kerrane (light heavy), Luke Murtagh (welter) and C. Townley (president and hon. treas.). Sitting: George Glynn (heavy), Senen O'Loghlen (feather), Rory Cazabon (capt. and trainer), Terry Kavanagh (fly) and Pat Donohue (bantam). Source: UCG Archive.

10. UCG hurling team, Fitzgibbon Cup winners, 1968. Back: Sean Burke, Michael Keane, Richard Walsh, Niall McInerney, Gus Costello, Eamon Corcoran, Tom Cloonan, Peter Cosgrave. Front: Sean Broudar, Paul McNamee, Seamus Hogan, Terry Crowe (capt.), Jim Goulding, Colm O'Flaherty. Source: UCG Archive.

11. The UCG basketball team, intervarsity champions 1950–3, which was almost entirely comprised of American students who came to Galway to study medicine – the only exception being John Kennedy, who was from Liverpool. Back: John Hession, Tom Santacroce, Ben Corballis. Front: Luke O'Connor, Don Roach, John Kennedy, Michael McLoughlin.

12. Like father like son: Padraic Ó Fatharta, porter 1959–88, on the day of his retirement, with his son, Peadar, who worked as a porter from 1973, and became head porter in 1977. Source: UCG Archive.

13. Susan Ansell, secretary to the director of computer services, and George Deacy, operations manager at the DEC 20 system terminal, observed by Gordon Young, systems manager, in 1978. Source: UCG Archive.

14. Catherine Lyons, Registrar's Office; Bríd Walsh, Library; Bríd Carr, Academic Office; Tony Lyons; and Mary Cooke, Health Promotion, attending the second annual graduates' reunion, which was held at UCG Aula Maxima in September 1985. Source: UCG Archive.

15. Brendan 'Speedie' Smith. Source: UCG Archive.

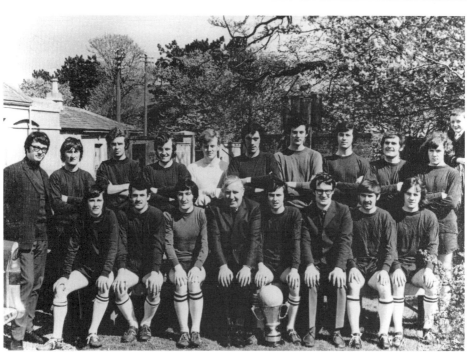

16. UCG Collingwood Cup winners, 1971. Front: D. Doherty, N. McCann, D. Cooke, A. Corcoran (pres.), J. McDaid, Prof. P. Fottrell (treas.), B. Park, J. MacMahon. Back: P. Grant (sec.), N. Burke, J. Fahy, L. Cunningham, C. Keyes, D. Lillis, G. Brennan, K. Fahy, A. Molloy, M. Henderson. Source: UCG Archive.

17. UCG camogie team, Ashbourne Cup winners, 1968. Back: Prof. E. Lee, Ollie Hanniffy, Bernadine Ottara, Ann Nestor, Eileen Naughton, Grace Divilly, Rita Hanniffy, Kathleen Pyne, Mrs Mary O'Driscoll. Front: Jane Murphy, Mary Canavan, Kay McMahon, Barbara Glynn, Bridie Carr, Bernie Clarke. Source: UCG Archive.

18. The Wallace brothers, Willie and Peter, both worked in Buildings. Willie (right) served on the Governing Body. Source: UCG Archive.

19. Peter Curran, caretaker-in-residence at the Men's Club.

20. Eibhlín Uí Chionna (née O'Malley), B.Sc. (hons.) 1945. Source: Ó Cionna family archive.

21. A commerce lecture with Professor MacBryan, 1939.

22. Peggy's coffee shop, the successor to Mrs Creaven's coffee shop, run by Peggy Jordan.

23. The Aula Maxima at UCG, laid out for an examination. It was one of the first places students encountered when they came to UCG, as they went to the Aula to register, and it was also one of the last, as conferrings were also held there.

24. Comhairle Teachta na Macléinn, 1964–5. Ag seasamh ó chlé: Liam Kelleher (Fó-Rúnaí), Ger Cloherty, John McCarrick, Ralph Ryan (Cisteoir), Paddy Kerr, Patsy Griffith, Mick Reynolds. Suite ó chlé: Sheila O'Regan, Briain Mac Eoghagáin (Rúnaí), Mícheál D. Ó hUiginn (Uachtarán), Luke Clancy (Leas Uacht.), Mena O'Donnell. As láthair: Donogh Ó Donnchadha, Gearóid Ó Tuathaigh, John Purcell.

25. The actress Siobhán McKenna with her father, Eoin McKenna, professor of mathematics at UCG, in 1966.

26. First-year engineering students at drawing class, 1939.

27. Tony Bromell pictured with his family outside the Aula on the occasion of his graduation. The entire family travelled from Limerick in a taxi for the occasion.

28. Christy Hannon, BA, H.Dip. Ed. Source: Hannon Family Archive.

29. Christy Townly, UCG librarian 1960–82. Christy joined the staff of the library in the early 1930s and acted as an agent both of progress and continuity in his work as a librarian and in his involvement in numerous college clubs and societies.

30. Pádraig Ó Céidigh, professor of zoology at UCG 1962–99. He became professor at the age of 28, making him one of the youngest NUI professors ever. His department was instrumental in establishing the shellfish and aquaculture industries in Ireland in the early 1970s.

31. Thomas Walsh, professor of pathology, hygiene and medical jurisprudence, giving a lecture on the heart to fourth-year medical students. Facing camera: Sissy Keogh, unknown, Gertie Noonan, Paddy Fitzgerald, unknown, Robbie Simmons, Billy Donovan. Source: UCG Archive.

32. The BA/B.Comm. class of 1946. Source: UCG Archive.

Brendan Smith, who came to college in 1975, is happy to admit that when it came to the party life of the college, he was at the very heart of it, in spite of the fact that he was a very diligent student, and was heavily involved in student politics too:

> We had loads of parties. I used to live in Hazel Park, it was *the* party house in Galway. We'd have toga parties, and fancy-dress parties of all types. So you'd go to the pub, then you'd go to the disco, then you'd all go back to the house, and we turned the lights off for an hour until all the taxis had settled down and people who had been invited had found the place, and then we turned the lights on and we'd party till five, six in the morning. But it was very open because a lot of those areas had rented houses, and the people in them that owned their own house were young, so they'd come to the parties, or the nurses would come to the parties, so it was very much 'open the doors to everybody'. They were a very young, neighbour-friendly society.

Brendan Smith also recalls some of the discos and nightclubs, both in town itself and in Salthill, which students attended in the 1970s and early '80s:

> There was the International, which was probably the smallest and it was underground – I worked there as well as a student serving drink. There was the Beach, which was very popular … Seapoint, that was only for the really big gigs. The Beach and the International, they were the big two probably out in Salthill, and the Lenaboy came later, C.J.'s came in a little bit later as well. But Rivelinos, it became the Castle, that was probably the number-one place, and that was run by Bridie O'Flaherty, the mayor. Rivelinos was upstairs, it was very popular, and served drink late. They were not hotels, they didn't have a hotel licence, they had to serve food. And you got this thing called 'smash'. Remember that? It was mash … and it was chemical. Out of a packet and you put water into it. And half-cooked burgers. None of us ever ate them, but they were just there, for the food. And afterwards you'd fall into Wimpy for your curried chips. And then you went to a house party after getting your curried chips. But normally we didn't go out a lot during the week because we had no money, it was fairly tight. Thursday night was *the* big night, and maybe Friday if you had a little bit more. But we always went to the Aula and there was no drink there. You know money was very tight and people like me, lots of us, we'd work during college, because the grants were very small.

THE COLLEGE BAR

On-campus socializing changed forever in 1980 with the opening of the college bar. According to Brendan Smith it was a collaborative effort:

When I opened up the college bar in September 1980, we got the money from the previous year – £2,000 was put together from Smokey Joe's, that was the students union canteen. Gráinne McMurrough was president there, she was very involved in that, and I continued that, and we got it open on 19 September. The bar facilities and so on were supplied, and the carpentry work was all done by the college.

The bar was welcomed by students, but there were others who reacted far less favourably to its establishment, as Brendan recalls:

We were raided constantly by the guards, because all the pubs downtown blew a fuse because they felt this was the end of their business. That students would leave the library, go straight into the college bar, and that was the end of life as they knew it. And in those days, I still have my membership card, you had to have a membership card if you were a student, because it was a club, it was a membership club, like a rugby club, or any sporting club, and anybody who wasn't a student had to be signed in by somebody. So we were constantly raided, at least once a week, to make sure no one was there who shouldn't be there, because of the pressure from the vintners downtown. But that has died a death now, it's even forgotten about.

Dr John O'Donnell, a student in the 1960s, said that students who developed problems with alcohol were few and far between right up until the 1980s – for a very practical reason:

When I see students drinking now, it wasn't that students were abstaining in my time, nobody had the price of a pint. Not even one, never mind ten pints or whatever they claim they have drunk when they've done something wrong, they want an excuse. They just couldn't afford it. That's not to say that nobody went out for a drink, but you couldn't afford to get drunk.

Some students did, however, get into difficulties, either due to their having a relatively wealthy family, and thereby sufficient funds to socialize on a more lavish scale than their fellow students, or a scholarship that they squandered. Joe McGrath recalled one student during his time at college in the mid-1940s who developed a problem with alcohol:

I remember there was one fella in particular, he was doing medicine, and I was horrified afterwards when I went to Dublin, he was on O'Connell Street, he was a real wino. Oh that was sad, very, very sad, I felt very sad that day.

A few pubs became firm favourites among students. Peter Michael's, opposite what was then the Central Hospital, and later became the Regional Hospital, was popular with students. Because of its proximity to the hospital, it had a special licence to open earlier than most other public houses at the time – it was one of the so-called 'early houses'. Prof. Seán Ó Cinnéide recalls that during his time in college, in the 1940s, the refrain from the barman at the end of the evening would be, 'Time gentlemen please, you may call again at seven in the morning.'

However, for most students drinking was something that was strictly limited by the funds at their disposal.

THE COMMON ROOM AND SMOKEY JOE'S

Throughout the 1970s facilities on campus began to improve for students, with more and more new buildings coming on stream. One welcome development was the establishment of the student Common Room in one of several terrapin build-ings that dotted the campus in those days. Although there was no official college shop on campus in the 1970s, the availability of the Common Room meant that there was a place where students could buy some basic items, as Grace Timlin recalls:

> There was a Common Room, behind Ma Creaven's coffee shop, another terrapin building, which is long gone. But Mrs Lardener had a little section of the Common Room where she used to sell things like college scarves, which you never see any more, and college rings. I had a beautiful ring with a big red stone in it, a gold ring, and I bought mine from her, Mrs Lardener, and she used to sell things like newspapers, and all that kind of stuff at this little shop. There were supplies likes pens and notebooks, and maybe she sold tickets for various events or something, and then the other side of the room they served food, you could buy soup and sandwiches.

Basic and all as they may have been, in advance of more permanent structures, the terrapin buildings proved to be extremely important in the evolution of student facilities on campus. Smokey Joe's was one such facility, which is remembered with great fondness by Brendan Smith:

> Smokey Joe's was a great place. It was in Terrapin 5. The terrapins were run-down places, where the sweat would be rolling off into your pint from the ceiling, but they were great places where the Boomtown Rats would play, or where Christy Moore would play, Planxty would play, or Clannad and all the rest of it. I remember Christy Moore having his pints down in the Cellar, and working his way up towards Smokey's to play the gig.

Catherine Lyons recalls the culinary delights of Smokey Joe's, which was operated under the watchful eye of Ollie Jennings: 'I used to have my lunch over there. He'd have big doorsteps of white bread and big chunks of cheddar cheese, and that was your sandwich.'

The new ideas and experiences that occupied students at UCG in the '70s were symptomatic of the changes taking place elsewhere in society at that time. For Brendan Smith, college served a much wider purpose than simply providing an education in specific subjects, as he explains:

> It was definitely where you learnt about life outside of your subjects, even though the subjects were great. And the great thing is we were all thrown together and for a lot of us we were the first generation of our families ever to go to college. So we broke the cord with the land, with the family business, or with the factory. We were the first people, and our parents were proud of us. It was really a great liberation time. And I remember, outside of college life, sometimes if people would go home, you'd have a friend home with you that was a girl, but she wasn't your girlfriend, she was a friend that was a girl. And it was very much a melting pot, and people palled around with each other as friends rather than for anything else, and that was great. And people partied together as a group rather than just as individuals. And because we were the first generation we didn't have older brothers and sisters to tell us about it, we learnt by living.

STUDENTS OWNING CARS

For most students, the only form of transport available was their bicycle, and, if they could avoid their bicycles being 'borrowed' from time to time, they found that this was sufficient to get them where they wanted to go: to and from college, or to the odd hop or party out in Salthill. Owning and running a car, right up until the 1980s, would have been practically impossible for the majority of students. However, there were cases of students who were given, or loaned, a car by their parents when the family lived a distance from Galway and when two or more of the family were attending college at the same time. Prof. Seán Lavelle recalls, for example, one student who commuted from Athenry: 'He drove in every morning, he had two sisters going to college as well.'

Those rare students who had cars found themselves wonderfully popular, as having transport significantly opened up the possibilities for socializing. Prof. Lavelle recalls a student friend who had a car that he was just about able to keep on the road:

> [He] had an old car, he was mechanically gifted, that he kept alive. And the professor of anatomy said to him one time, 'I suppose it costs you a lot for oil, it uses a lot of oil?' And [he] says, 'She would, if she got it!' And that passed into the folklore.

THE ARMY LADS

The army began sending its cadets to the college in 1971 and from then on the presence of students in army uniform on campus and attending lectures became a regular feature of college life. Dr Pádraig Lenihan was one of those army personnel who came to the college in 1977: 'I was a cadet, although people in college used to refer to all army people as cadets indiscriminately, but after first year they were all commissioned officers, commissioned lieutenants.'

Understandably, army students did not live in digs or flats like other students, but rather, at least during the early years, stayed in Ryan's and Flannery's hotels on the Dublin road, until the University Students Administration Complex (USAC) had been built in Renmore, adjacent to the army barracks. This was a three-storey accommodation and dining block built specifically to cater for the needs of student cadets and officers.

The army students were afforded a great deal of freedom in choosing the subjects they wished to study for their degrees. Dr Pádraig Lenihan recalls:

> You had pretty much free choice, though latterly some subjects that were perceived to be of less relevance, like Latin in my case, were discouraged, that didn't stop me. For final degree I had history and legal science, subsidiary Latin.

For Dr Lenihan, and many of his colleagues, it could probably be said that the fact that they were able to look forward to a career in the army, and still were able to pursue a degree, rendered them extremely fortunate young men, something Dr Lenihan in particular was very conscious of, as he explains:

> I loved it, loved it. Why did I love it? I loved the books, I was a swot, studying, the library, there was a lively social life, the parties, student societies. I found my first year there particularly liberating and particularly exciting having come from the pressurized and physically quite demanding cadet school. I can remember with my mackintosh raincoat and my briefcase tucked under my arm, walking in the line across Lough Atalia and thinking how lucky I was, and how happy I was.[25]

A formal dress code was in operation for the army students: 'You wore your uniform to college during normal working hours, 9 to 5, when you were an officer, jumper and pants, for cadets it was the full tunic.' But wearing their uniform on campus did not make the army officers feel awkward, or feel they stood out in any way, as Dr Lenihan recalls:

25 Dr Lenihan is referring to the section of railway line over Lough Atalia bridge, which was a popular shortcut for students coming into the city centre from Renmore.

We felt conspicuous initially, yes, but then there were so many cadets and officers on campus when I was there, about 120 to 130 altogether, in what you must remember was a much smaller student body. My cadet class had about 80 in it, including air corps and navy and army, and of those about 40 went to college.

While the cadets and officers generally played a full part in all aspects of college – including the social activities, sports and societies – there were certain aspects of college life they avoided. Smokey Joe's was one such place:

> I wouldn't have gone there, not in uniform, not during normal hours – the only time I would have been in Smokey's was in the eveningtime in civvies.[26] I don't remember any absolute prohibition, but it was generally understood that it was a bit grotty to be seen there in uniform.

The fact that 'the army lads', as most of their fellow students called them, were earning a salary while they were studying somewhat set them apart from their fellow students, as Brendan Smith recalls:

> A lot of us lads used to hate the army lads because by the second year in college they had the car or the motorbike, they had the money and they had the dolly birds. There was a particular type of [glamorous] woman that used to hang around with the rugby or the army lads, they'd be always down the Skeff.

As an 'army lad', Dr Pádraig Lenihan would not dispute the cachet that having a car and a uniform gave him: 'I think I would have been in second year in college before I got the car, though not the girlfriend, that other part of the young officer's image.' Although Dr Lenihan was involved in the Sub-Aqua Society, most of his colleagues, as he recalls, were involved in more conventional sporting activities: 'They were disproportionately involved, as you can imagine, in football, hurling, rugby and of course rowing.'

STUDENT POLITICS IN THE 1970S

A political force that developed in the early 1970s was the Maoist movement, and as Pat Rabbitte recalls, they created quite a stir on campus:

> They used to sell Mao's Little Red Book and I think they were opposed to all the power structures of the existing society. And that Irish society were pawns of American imperialism, and that the power structures in

26 Civilian clothing.

the university were to serve the elite in society, and so on. So they had a very, very far-left political philosophy, but they created quite a lot of colour around UCG at the time.

Grace Timlin recalls UCG's committed Maoists:

A medical student who was very prominent at the time … he was our Maoist representative. I remember him getting up on a kind of a soapbox and spouting all this political stuff. He was very serious, but then of course, as happens a lot of people, when they get the taste of money, you know, the principles go out the window.

Grace Timlin was a contemporary of both Pat Rabbitte and Eamon Gilmore, and recalls that both showed early promise of the political and oratorical skills they were to use to such good effect in their subsequent political careers:

Pat Rabbitte was our students union president my first year in college, and I think Eamon was president probably my BA year. But Pat was huge into all that side of college, he was always a marvellous speaker. And you know, very much into socialism and that. Well at that time that was the thing for students, people used go round with Che Guevara T-shirts and all this stuff.

Like many others Pat Rabbitte came to college in 1967 with no particular interest in politics. However, the spirit of the times, and the extraordinary events which were taking place around the world, soon politicized him in a way that he could never have imagined, as he explains:

I wouldn't have had a particular political anchor before going to college. But remember, I went to college in the most extraordinary of times. I mean the anti-war movement was very big, the Vietnam War was a huge issue. The explosion of the civil-rights movement in the United States transferred into Northern Ireland. The explosion in Northern Ireland in '68, '69 was something that would have been unknown completely in the Republic … Plus the Lemass/Whitaker era had dragged us, begun to drag us, out of the dreadful last years of Mr de Valera's reign, when of course the country haemorrhaged emigration, and was a failed economic entity. Because emigration was the norm from Galway, and Mayo, and the western counties in particular during those years.

I mean Mr de Valera might well have retired in 1948, he didn't, he didn't retire until '59, and those eleven years were a lifetime in the history of young people. And Lemass would have been a younger man. So therefore that's where the politics came from. I also began to learn in university that you could only be in university if you could afford it, and that's where the campaigns started in terms of the grants.

You had a very strong, very well organized Union of Students, and two Galway alumni preceded me as president of the National Union of Students in Ireland, that was, immediately, Frank Flannery, and before him Richard O'Toole. And, Ralph O'Gorman was president in Galway and Seamus Brennan was a member of that executive. Pat 'The Cope' Gallagher was there in those years too. Michael D., of course. Jim McDaid was in my year, entirely apolitical and uninvolved. Jim was a good soccer player, he was involved in the soccer, not at all in politics.

In common with Pat Rabbitte, Eamon Gilmore recalls that some of the new wave of students who came to college in the 1970s came from backgrounds where access to third-level education would have been seen as an impossibility. Their presence on campus was the first perceptible evidence that third-level education had changed, and they were determined to bring about more change and make their mark on the system, as Gilmore explains:

> We were the first batch I think of the people who had gone to second-level schooling on the free-education scheme. We were early in the grand scheme, so there was a different kind of batch of students, and therefore there was a mood among the student body that they wanted student elections and that, that they wanted a kind of a new broom and whatever. And there was also this thing that student politics had been controlled by what was known as 'the machine', that it was kind of being passed on from one to another … and there was very much a sense that people wanted a break with it.

And a break was exactly what they got, with the election of a very good team of students union representatives, as Eamon explains:

> The student executive that was elected that year was myself as president, Pat Fitzgerald, vice president, he played football, won a couple of All-Ireland medals subsequently, for Offaly. The secretary was Carol Hannay, to whom I subsequently became married. Joe McDonagh was the sports officer, and Ollie Jennings became the entertainments officer.

Ollie Jennings' appointment as entertainments officer began a career in entertainment management that has seen him take on a host of high-profile roles over the years. But this first appointment came about almost by accident, as Eamon Gilmore recalls:

> I remember meeting him, and I was in a little bit of a pucker because the tradition was that the vice president of the students union would organize

the dances and the concerts and so on, and Offaly were doing very well in the championship, and there was no sign of Pat, Pat was training. So anyway I talked to Ollie, and Ollie said he'd give it a go. And the rest is history, he just took to it and he became very successful.

However radical students might have been in the mid-1970s, there were still a great deal of conservatism in Irish society in general, and Eamon Gilmore recalls one incident that brought home clearly to him the fact that if Irish society were to change it would change very slowly, and that it would take considerable determination to make it happen:

> The only place that contraceptives were available at the time was through the Family Planning Clinic in Dublin. So a group of people got together and they decided they would set up the Galway Family Planning Association, that was 1976. College Week used to raise serious money, so the idea developed that the College Week money should go towards the Family Planning Association. So there was a meeting of the Student Council and the decision was taken: the proceeds from the year's College Week money will go to … setting up the Family Planning Association. And there was provision in the students union constitution that a general meeting could be convened on the signatures of 150 students – never been used before, most of us had forgotten it was even there – and that a general meeting of the students could overturn any decision made by the Student Council. And before you could say 'Bob's your uncle', mainly Opus Dei-inspired from what I could see, the 150 initials were gathered and lodged in the students union office, and the meeting was convened. And it was held on the Concourse, and it was packed. And there were so many we ended up creating lobbies for the voting … and I think we lost it by about 30 votes. Even in retrospect it still surprises me.

Elected as an 18-year-old as student-union president, Eamon Gilmore had a lot to learn, and learnt quickly:

> I suppose one of the things that struck me about it was the formality of it … I learned how meetings were conducted properly, minutes properly taken and all that type of thing. You just learn the tricks of the trade, you know, how, if you're on a body like this, how you put stuff on the agenda. How you watch out for how a decision is made, but also how you build alliances. How you find you're the sole student on this [governing] body, on this committee, and you look around and the first thing you decide is I gotta make some friends here, I gotta make some alliances.

For Brendan Smith, who was students union president and sat on the Governing Body, the experience was similarly instructive, and as he recalls, while he was always prepared to fight his case, he noted that, 'We may not always have agreed, but you respected people for their points of view and so on.'

Far from detracting them from their studies, for some, the experience of taking on the presidency engendered habits that greatly benefited them not only in their future careers, but also in the continuation of their studies, as Eamon Gilmore explains:

> I missed a lot because I was active in student politics, so I was involved in the Debating Society and I was involved in the Drama Society very much in my first year, and so I wasn't the most diligent of students, until actually after my year as president of the students union.[27] Being president of the students union gave me great discipline. It gave me the discipline of work. Because I'd to be in the office at nine in the morning, you know, and you worked a full day, and I just continued that practice ... I mean up to the time I became president of the students union I probably, you know, when is the first lecture, and that's what you got up for. But after that I'd get on my bike and I'd be in the grammar school at nine every morning, no matter whether I had a lecture or not, I just applied myself to it, and you know I got quite a good degree in the end out of it.

CHILDCARE ON CAMPUS

With a changing student profile in the '70s and '80s the need for a crèche for students who had children became an issue for the students union, one they took up with remarkable success. However, as Eamon Gilmore recalls, this process was not without problems:

> We opened the first crèche, and that was actually run by the students union. And it was the biggest nightmare I had during my term as president. Because there were always rows between the parents. I mean it started off as a facility for students ... but what happened in practice was, you know, what's a student? Mainly it became the post-grads, and the PhD students, and then it became lecturers and so on, so it actually grew. So we started that in a house down in Munster Avenue that we got, and the college were very good with all this, I mean they rented stuff for us. Now they wanted a kind of an arm's-length arrangement, so the students union was the vehicle for doing that.

Increasingly, the responsibilities placed on students union officers became arduous and occasionally stressful. The perception of some students was that the students

27 Eamon Gilmore was president of UCG Students Union from July 1974 to June 1975. From 1976 until 1978 he served as president of the Union of Students in Ireland (USI).

union representatives were there not only to represent them, but also to take care of their needs, something for which the young student officers were neither properly trained nor prepared. Brendan Smith, who at one point held the position of welfare officer (prior to becoming students union president), recalls how difficult his role occasionally was:

> I was welfare officer and I helped bring out booklets on contraceptives and advising people to watch out for drugs and all the rest, and helped people out on issues like paying rent and so on. But I was not a trained psychologist or anything like that, and people would come in and say, 'Look, I have this issue, I suffer depression', or whatever, 'and your job is to look after me'. That's a heavy burden. But we did manage to get in a student counsellor to handle that. So there were things that we just couldn't … we were all untrained, we were referring rather than trying to solve.

The role of welfare officer did have its humorous moments however, as Brendan Smith explains:

> Condoms were quite funny because there were people asking me for condoms and explaining, look, they just want to play safe, just because they're going away with somebody doesn't mean anything, but they want to be safe now, and I said, look, I am not interested in your private life, take the damn things and go. It was quite funny because I mean those type of things were very new to people. But most of the time it was just pure innocent fun in the nicest way. But most of us studied hard, as I say, and you know the politics was part of learning about life and trying to make the world a better place.

4

The sporting life

With hundreds of fit young people arriving into college each year, participation in sport was extremely important in students' enjoyment of their time at university. The college was fortunate in having plenty of playing fields at their disposal. It was also fortunate in its location, with the River Corrib running right through the campus, and rowing on the river, either competitively or simply for pleasure, is something most former students recall with great affection. The college traditionally took a proactive approach to the promotion of sport among the student body, and individual professors were allocated responsibility for promoting specific sports, with varying degrees of success. UCG was remarkably successful in its sporting exploits, given its small size and limited resources, relative to the other universities at the time.

GAELIC GAMES

After independence there was some degree of carryover of staff from the previous regime but, increasingly, new lecturers and professors were appointed, and most of these would have been keen enthusiasts of the Gaelic Ireland envisaged by the founding fathers of the state. This extended to an enthusiasm for the Irish language, and of course Gaelic sports. Budge Clissmann recalls that this caused a degree of friction when her love of sport overrode her own keen Republican politics, and inadvertently brought her into conflict with one of the college professors:

> Irene Bodkin was a very good hockey player, and she was very keen.[1] There had been a Hockey Club in the university, but with the Gaelic enthusiasm it had lapsed, there was a Camogie Club, and the Hockey Club just shrank and almost disappeared. But I had played hockey in school, and I was very keen to have a Hockey Club. So we got a Hockey Club up and running in my first year in Galway, the first winter, and we applied for status, to be recognized by the Athletics Board, there was so much money from the Athletics Board. And we applied and there was an awful lot of humming and hawing ... and the one who didn't look on us well was Professor McKenna,[2] he was Siobhán's father. And he wasn't keen on this English sport being revived. We had to fight our corner, we got ourselves

1 A fellow student of Budge's per the College Calendar student list for 1931. 2 Eoghan Mac Cionnaith (McKenna) was appointed professor of mathematical physics in 1934.

recognized, and so we could have our annual dance. But there was one funny episode, it must have been in my third year. The Camogie Club got stuck, for I think it was the Inter-Faculty. I was arts, and the arts team were short, and they said, 'Will you not come and play?' and I said, 'Well, I'll be playing hockey, I'll play as much of the camogie as I can learn quick, so I did play. And we won the Inter-Faculty Cup, and there was a lovely presentation. McKenna was the chairman of the athletics section of the college, so he was there, there was a formal occasion in the Aula, for us to be presented with our cups, and he nearly fell out of his standing when I came up … 'Ooh yeees, you're part of this team?' And I said, 'Oh I'm part of this team, yes.' It was very funny.

Dr Sheila Mulloy was a keen camogie player, and during her time in the college the team took the somewhat unusual step of designing their own uniform:

You see Ó Máille's opened that time in Dominick Street,[3] and they had a dressmaking section … and we got them to make the uniforms. And they were wearing those for ages after we left actually. It was maroon, and you wore a belt, which was maroon and white, a kind of knitted affair, and you wore a white blouse, any white blouse. It was quite free and easy. And then most people tied a ribbon or something around their hair.

One of the great advantages of being associated with sporting activities in the college was the fact that it allowed students to travel around the country to other colleges in order to compete. Eibhlín Uí Chionna recalls her efforts to bring the Camogie Club to Belfast in 1945 to compete in the Ashbourne Cup:

Now the war wasn't quite over at this stage, and we were all dying to get up North, it was like getting out of the country into a new country, because during the war you never left the boundaries of the twenty-six counties. So Dublin got leave to go, and I was on the phone to the secretary of the camogie team in Cork, and she said it was in the balance. And so the two of us hatched a plan and decided each of us would go along to the president … so in I went to [the new UCG president] Monsignor de Brún, in my best Gaeilge you see, and I said that they were all going off to Belfast now for this, because the war is nearly over by now, and of course we'd have the lady superintendent with us and all this kind of stuff, and that Dublin is allowed go and Cork is allowed go, and we have to get permission from you, isn't that alright? And so he said, 'Oh certainly.' Of course the exact same thing had happened in Cork.

3 Ó Máille's was founded in 1938 by the Ó Máille family. The shop specialized in hand-knit Aran sweaters and hand-woven tweeds, and continues to be Ireland's leading retailer of traditional hand-knit Aran sweaters.

Although the wool may well have been pulled over the president's eyes, the lady superintendent, who would be accompanying the students, was still unsure of the wisdom of making the trip:

> The lady superintendent was not all that happy about it, she was a little worried about getting us off to Belfast. I was dying to go up, and a couple of us were, so the chief problem was we had to organize a team, eleven, plus a couple of spares, and you also brought up your coach, that meant two lads, and quite a few of the team would be hard-up for cash. We had enough funds provided everybody could put in something like five shillings. And you had to then go round the people and say, could you manage five shillings? And you had to be careful, you had to not presume, and then you'd say to such a one, 'Maybe your landlady would allow you a little bit off because you'll be away so many days?' So we all managed it, and we had a whale of a time in Belfast of course. And all the nationalist crowd out of Queen's, of course they all turned out to entertain us, you know? You'd have had all these *céilís* at night, they are far more into that kind of stuff there. And we were all walking down the street singing some nationalist song or something, and I didn't realize it was outside Crumlin Road jail. And then of course naturally we were moved off fast by the RUC. Galway did extremely badly, which made us even more popular. I think Belfast beat us.

One student who played camogie with Eibhlín Uí Chionna in her first year in college was the actress Siobhán McKenna, whose father, as we have seen, was professor of maths physics in the college. Eibhlín recalls that Siobhán was a formidable camogie player, something which was clearly greatly appreciated by her father:

> Siobhán McKenna was very good at camogie, a very quick runner. And the story is that her father would be on the sideline when she'd be playing and that he was quoted as having said when she put a good one in, 'Ah, there was porridge behind that one!'

The college enjoyed remarkable success with the Ashbourne Cup in camogie, and Prof. Elizabeth 'Nelly' Lee of the Chemistry Department was a dedicated president of the club from 1965 until 1994, and presided over many of the fifteen Ashbourne titles won by the UCG team over the years.

At Sigerson Cup or Fitzgibbon Cup level, the playing of college football and hurling was intense. But for those who didn't have the necessary skills to compete at such a high level, Gaelic games were still an important sporting and social outlet in the college, as Christy Hannon recalls:

> I used to play a bit of football now, not very well, not nearly as well as I would have liked to. So I played in the faculty leagues, I played for arts

against science once or twice out in Fahy's Field, in Renmore. And often-times we'd go up to St Mary's college, a few of us, and Fr Leo Morahan was teaching there at that time, so he would always let us in and there were changing-room facilities there. But I think Fahy's Field was the official GAA playing grounds, that's where all the faculty GAA games were held.

THE SIGERSON AND FITZGIBBON CUPS

The Sigerson Cup, an inter-varsity competition in Gaelic football, was, and still is, a much-prized trophy, and since its inception in 1911 UCG/NUIG have won it no less than twenty-two times – second only to UCD, with thirty-four wins to their credit.[4] Prof. Dan O'Donovan, later professor of physiology at the college, first came to UCG as part of a Sigerson team from UCD and recalls that his team, and their supporters, didn't exactly make a good impression on the president:

> I remember Monsignor de Brún, president of UCG. When I came down to play the Sigerson in 1954, and the Sigerson then it was a kind of a rowdy affair, students were throwing the scones and everything at each other and I remember the president stood up, he was sitting way up at the top, and I remember he called us a '*scata barbarí* [a crowd of barbarians]'. I knew enough Irish to know that he wasn't praising us.

Sigerson football was clearly not for the faint-hearted, but the intensity of the games also threw up occasional feats of individual sporting excellence that remained long in the memory, as Christy Hannon, recalls:

> I was at a Sigerson final in Pearse Stadium. UCG and Cork. I always remem-ber Cork, they had the skull and the crossbones, the sign of the pirates, the death's-head jersey. That was 1962 now, and UCG won. And they won the year after as well. But I remember there was one particular incident in it. There was a Dave Geaney playing for UCC, I think he's a doctor now, but he was a small lad, he played for Kerry as well, but he got a ball around midfield, and he travelled about thirty, forty yards, and he was hauled down in the square, and he took the penalty himself and scored. I thought it was a great individual feat that, you know? But UCG won the match.[5] Very tough Sigerson football. Very, very tough, and very competitive. Well I think play-ers regarded it as second only in importance to winning an All-Ireland medal.

Even matches with local teams could become somewhat fraught at times, as Peadar O'Dowd recalls:

4 Statistics reflective of wins up to 2018.   5 UCG won the match 1-09 to 1-03.

One of my abiding memories is the college playing Tuam Stars out in the stadium, and Tuam Stars were really the top at the time. I had left college at this stage, but I still followed them, it was about 1966. And one of the chaps that was in my year … the poor oul' college were getting killed, and he said, 'The only thing, we'll have to start a row, a fight.' So he ran out and he hit one of the Tuam fellas. Ah sure he was mad as a hatter this guy, so, we went out to try and help, and there was a free-for-all anyway, and I'll always remember Sean Purcell,[6] Lord have mercy on him, and he had a big arm around this fella and he said, 'Will you ever take this *amadán* in before he's killed.' Even though Purcell was a Tuam Stars man, he protected that idiot.

Members of the college teams – be they Sigerson, Fitzgibbon or Ashbourne – were required to be formally registered students of the college. But Tony Bromell recalls that there were a couple of cases during his time at UCG (1951–5) where doubts hung over whether some members of a particular Fitzgibbon team were bona fide students of the college or not:

> Do bhuaigh Gaillimh, ach bhí ceist ann … an raibh cupla duine as an gCaisléan Gearr ag imirt do Ghaillimh ag an am? Bhí scéal faoi lad as an gCaisléan Gearr, nuair a bhí an Fitzgibbon thíos i gCorcaigh bliain amháin, agus bhí sé ag damhsa le cailín ag an damhsa, agus chuir an cailín ceist air cad a bhí á dhéanamh aige sa choláiste. Agus dúirt sé, 'Sums.'

> Galway won, but there was a question mark – were a few people from Castlegar playing for Galway at the time? There was a story about a lad from Castlegar, when Fitzgibbon was down in Cork one year, and he was dancing with a girl at a dance, and the girl asked him what subject he was doing in college. And he said, 'Sums.'

UCG's first really successful teams began to emerge in the 1930s, coinciding with the arrival of Eoghan Mac Cionnaith (McKenna), who came in 1929 to teach mathematics through Irish. McKenna was, as we have seen, a keen GAA man, and under his guidance, as Keith Duggan recalls: 'In the 1930s Galway fielded a series of college teams who practically ruled the competition.'[7]

The honour of playing for the college was a tremendous incentive for players to work hard to earn and maintain their places on the team. A talented Sigerson and Fitzgibbon player, Bobby Curran, recalls that his devotion to playing and training affected his choice of subjects for his degree.

---

6 Born in Tuam, Co. Galway, Sean Purcell was a Gaelic footballer for Co. Galway, whose career spanned three decades, from the 1940s to the 1960s.   7 Keith Duggan, 'A sporting legacy', *Cois Coiribe* (2007), pp 20–5.

I looked at the schedule for chemistry, you'd have a practical every after-noon nearly in second year, three evenings a week or something like that, and that would have interfered with my hurling and football. So I went for maths and maths physics, and physics, and the reason I went for the physics is because they didn't have practicals on three afternoons per week, they had only two. Well you know young fellas make decisions that, you know … rationally enough from my point of view, I mean I wanted to play football, I played Fitzgibbon from 1955–60, and Sigerson from 1955–60.

Curran went on to be a great supporter of sportsmen in college when he returned to teach there in 1968. However, the lecturer in mathematics was nonetheless mindful that students, no matter what their sporting prowess or commitments, still had to attend lectures and pursue their studies:

I used to have a 9 o'clock of a Saturday morning … I used to have a full house, well, bar one or two. I knew them all you see because of the football and hurling. I used to say, 'Where's X?' … silence. And I'd say, 'Just because he's got on the [county] football team he thinks he can miss his 9 o'clock lecture.' He had a mate in the class, and I'd tell him, 'Be sure to tell him to be here next Saturday.' And he would be.

Curran was a very popular and highly regarded lecturer, but wasn't averse to hav-ing a little fun with his sports-playing students at the same time, as the following story relates:

There was a terrapin building, a big flat terrapin, 'twas a terrible place to be lecturing, you see, with all the people, ninety of them. And the guys at the back could only see one-half of the blackboard. At the back anyhow there was this fella … played for Sigerson one year, and he was at the back, he was a bit of a joker, and everyone would be around listening to his latest joke, you see. So I started writing anyhow, and the jokes were still going on and I stopped. And I said, 'So and so, stand up.' He stood up. I said, 'You're very fit.' He relaxed, he thought he was away in a hack. 'I am', he said, 'quite fit'. I said, 'Would you ever run over to the Archway and get a duster for me?' I never had trouble with him after that.

BASKETBALL

The coming of the American medical students to Galway in the late '40s heralded a whole new phase in UCG sports, as basketball was introduced to the college for the first time. Dr Ben Corballis recalls how the American ex-servicemen pursued their love of the game on the only court available in Galway at that time, in the army barracks at Renmore. In time, they also looked to expand their horizons and play more competitively. An opportunity arose in 1952, and, as Dr Corballis explains, they were determined to bring to the proceedings not only their expertise on the basketball court, but a little American razzamatazz:

> Somewhere along the line we read about the fact that they were going to have an all-university basketball tournament in Dublin. And we said, 'We'll enter.' And we said, 'We've gotta have uniforms.' Well we all had T-shirts, and we could buy tennis shorts. And we got some maroon cloth, and we cut out all kinds of things. Miss Cloherty had a sewing machine, and we sewed up a bunch of uniforms.[8]

A photograph of the team reveals Miss Cloherty's handiwork, as team members have not only their numbers but also the letters 'UCG' clearly emblazoned on the T-shirts in the maroon of Galway. At a time when most of the college teams would have played in a mixture of mismatched sports attire, the uniforms of the Galway team were a sensation. 'We ran on the court and everybody "oohed" at the uniforms, they were really impressed, you know?' But as well as looking good, the Galway team could also play:

> We beat Cork in the semis, and in the final we beat the College of Surgeons for the title. And we brought the cup back to Monsignor Browne, and, well, he was thrilled. 'My Americans!' And we not only took the cup … we actually had the cup three years in a row. And Queen's did not take part in the tournament, but we went up the following year to play them.

TENNIS

The college was fortunate in having some fine tennis courts on campus, and in the '40s and '50s in particular these were very popular with some students, as Budge Clissmann explains:

> You'd only play tennis of course in the summer term, and then in the summer Galway has about half an hour more daylight than they have in Dublin, and so we could play tennis until about a quarter to eleven, twenty to eleven, and the train came in from Dublin at about ten minutes or a quarter of an hour later, and it brought the evening papers. There was no *Herald*, or you know an *Evening Mail* or *Herald*, in Galway until the train came in. And so we'd wander from college down to the station and pick up the newspaper and go home then. And we had to be in the hostel by eleven.

---

8 Miss Cloherty was the landlady of the house in which the American students were staying.

Tennis was not only played by the students, but was also popular among some of the staff. Donal Taheny, who came to college in 1936, recalled himself and a group of his fellow students being invited to play tennis with his history professor, Mrs Mary Donovan O'Sullivan, in the years immediately preceding the Second World War. Mrs Donovan O'Sullivan had a tennis court at her house in Rockbarton, and the tennis parties only ceased when war shortages began to bite, and the afternoon tea that followed the mixed doubles had to be abandoned.

RUGBY

For those playing rugby at UCG, practice took place in Fahy's Field and a number of other locations around Galway, as Dr John O'Donnell, who was a student in the early 1960s, recalls:

> At that time rugby was big in the college. I think the strength of the rugby team had varied a lot and hadn't been very strong then, but when I was there more people came to college who had played rugby at school or more people joined the rugby club who happened to be very good at it. There were some international players, like Mick Molloy and Eamon McGuire. And there were more – you know, the college team won the Connacht Rugby Cup. They went from not having been a strong force to winning the Connacht Senior Cup a number of times. Practices took place in Fahy's Field. And you could actually get into the sports ground and train a bit, some training was done in the sports ground. The college bought the Grammar School at that time,[9] and that had a very good pitch. It wasn't a full size pitch, but the quality of the ground was very good. And matches, you could get a turn in the sports ground, the Connacht branch had the use of the sports ground, and different clubs would take it for different Saturday or Sunday afternoons for the season. There was a kind of auction where they'd say I'll take that one and I'll take that one, I'll take that one. And the rest of the time matches were played in Fahy's Field, or away in other clubs you had to play. But there was no hot water in the shower itself, cold showers! You can imagine in the winter, covered in mud and having to get into a cold shower, the only way to get clean enough to put your clothes on again. So it was kind of primitive. Things have changed for them now, the facilities are better.

Subsequent college rugby teams continued the great tradition, and one of the major stars to emerge in the 1970s was Ciaran Fitzgerald, who graduated with a B.Comm. in 1973, played for the college rugby team, and went on to play for the Irish rugby team in the Triple Crown years of 1982 and 1985.

9 The Grammar School was a Protestant institution established under the Erasmus Smith Trust, and located at College Road since 1815. In 1950 a wing of the school was gutted by fire, and the school finally closed in 1958. The building was subsequently purchased by UCG.

THE MEN'S CLUB

The Men's Club was something of an institution on campus, and for some students it became a home from home for them – sometimes to the detriment of their studies – but it was undoubtedly a place for socializing, fun, or, as Peadar O'Dowd puts it, 'devilment':

> Everything was money of course, you played everything for money. You played cards for money, bridge was even played for money, and snooker and billiards and all this sort of thing, was played for money.

Prof. Seán Lavelle recalls that in some cases the money earned in the Men's Club was destined for purposes other than mere socializing: 'There was a poker school that used to go on all night, in the Men's Club there. Some of the fellas were reputed to pay their fees by the assets they gained.'

Chess was also played in the Men's Club, and Chess Club member Peadar O'Dowd recalls:

> When I was in the Men's Club I played chess, but I played it for money as well. And one of the greatest treasures I have is a letter showing that I'd been thrown out of the Chess Club here in the college, for bringing the game into disrepute. For playing for money.

At the Chess Club on the main campus, facilities were somewhat limited, particularly when it came to travelling to away matches, as John O'Donnell recalls:

> I joined the Chess Club, and matches took place in empty classrooms in the evenings. We got the keys and we used them. They were a bit cold as far as I remember. We had a very strong chess player, a fella called Diarmuid McDaid, who was nationally a very strong chess player. I was about three or four on the team, and about six players would go off then to represent the college. We went to Trinity one year, and we went to Cork another year. Of course the Chess Club had no money, so you had to pay some of your own way, with minimal help. We could barely afford chessboards, and chessmen and clocks. You have to have clocks for competitive chess.

Considering the college's success in basketball during those years it is somewhat surprising that basketball did not really become a part of the college's sporting life for some time. It appears that once the American students left, there was no longer a core group of players available from the general student population to form a team that could compete in inter-varsity and national basketball leagues. Certainly by the 1960s basketball appears to have faded on campus, but it seems that the caretaker of the Men's Club, the well-liked Peter Curran, was determined to change that, and ensure that the young men in his charge would get some much-needed exercise outdoors in the process, as Peadar O'Dowd, recalls:

> I remember we were playing snooker one time … and Peter came in, the caretaker, and he had his hand behind his back, and all of a sudden he produced a huge big ball down on the snooker table, and scattered the balls. 'Why don't you go out into God's fresh air and play a really good game? Now!' he says. 'What's that?' He said, 'Play basketball.' And we said, 'What's basketball?' We never heard of it, we didn't know what it was. 'Well if you look there', he says, 'you'll see they're after putting up two baskets, and what you do is you put the ball into the basket and there's two teams, you see'. So we decided to take him at his word, and this is I think one of the funniest things ever I remember in my time in college. We got everybody out, there were twenty-one of us. So being very good at mathematics we put ten on each side, and one tiny little fella, we tossed for him you know. I think there was a shilling a man, or two shillings a man, or whatever. So after about three hours anyway, and after about three guys going up to hospital, you know, we found that it was a non-contact sport, and we said, ah forget that so … Oh yes, fisticuffs and everything used, we'd no idea of the rules at all, it was a total free for all. Oh there were rugby tackles, there was every sort of tackle. Fisticuffs breaking out every so often. 'Twas fun.

JUDO

Judo was a sport introduced to the college in the 1960s, and as one of the earliest members of the college Judo Club, Adrian Ryder recalls that it was very much a case of 'learn as you go'.

> There was a Judo Club just started, Professor Lavelle was involved in that.[10] And I remember the highest belt we had when I started in the club was a yellow belt. This was the big deal, a yellow belt. A month after I joined I got a yellow, and the yellow belt got orange, so they were up to orange, big improvement. So I was in it at the very, very early part of it, it came on then. But we'd have been sitting there, we'd have books, and we'd say, looking at the picture, 'I'd say this is done this way,' 'No, I think it's done that way.' We'd try it out, come to a consensus, 'Yep that's the way we'll do it.' And I think we did better because we knew we knew nothing, so we weren't afraid of somebody else suggesting … compared to now. You can't have an instructor who's less than a black belt.

10 Prof. Séan Lavelle of the Department of Experimental Medicine was the patron of the Judo Club.

The Judo Club, however, became firmly planted in the university and continues to thrive.

TABLE TENNIS

Although facilities were improving throughout the college in the 1970s, UCG still lagged behind its fellow colleges, a fact that was brought home very strongly to Grace Timlin when she travelled to Queen's University for an inter-varsity table-tennis competition:

> Of course we nearly died of shock when we got there, because at the time Queen's University had this massive sports centre, this was around 1972/3. They had an artificial ski slope indoors, imagine! And we were shocked. They must have had twenty table-tennis tables set up for this tournament, it was so well done. And they had a fantastic cafeteria where we ate, and of course we had seen nothing like that before. You know, the amount of facilities they had, we had nothing here. Well we had to go to the Commercial Boat Club or somewhere to play and there was another building up in College Road, the Grammar School, we used to go up there as well to play our table tennis, because they had no facilities, none. And it was the time of the Troubles and I can remember somebody threw a brick in, we were staying in this hotel on the Malone Road, somebody threw a brick in the hotel window when we were in there.

Thankfully the Table Tennis Club returned to UCG unscathed – if a little envious of the facilities available to their Queen's counterparts.

THE SCUBA DIVING CLUB

Diving was another sport that became increasingly popular in the university, particularly among students who were studying marine science in the 1970s. Prof. Maria Byrne recalls that it wasn't the easiest sport for students to participate in, given the difficulty of having to pay for tanks to be filled, and organizing transport to suitable dive sites, but where there was a will there was a way, as she explains:

> It was part of the course, and that's how you really learn. But in those days, sure we didn't even need buses, we just all went off in the back of the van, and off to Carna. But being out there in the real world, seeing animals where they live, that's where you learn. You don't learn from pickle jars and things in the lab as much as you learn from seeing things swimming, you know going snorkelling, so I joined the diving club quite early on in my first year here. But there was a fella up in Shantalla, who was a commercial

diver, and we used to go up there to fill our tanks. We went diving in our spare time really, and that was like doing our own extra-curricular activity. And very often if we didn't all have cars we'd have one car … Dave Niland was involved, Dave was very involved in the diving. But Dave was the only one with a car, so what we used to do was we'd put all the diving tanks in his car, he was very generous, put all the diving tanks in his car, and we'd cycle. We'd get on our bicycles, and we'd put all the other gear on our backs and we'd cycle to Furbo, or Blackrock … I think the furthest we cycled was Furbo. We hitch-hiked as far as Belmullet.

ATHLETICS

The Athletics Club was founded in the college in 1960 by Pádraig Griffin, who later went on to become president of Athletics Ireland. The following story, recounted by Prof. Iognáid Ó Muircheartaigh, reveals how students managed to be serious athletes and yet enjoy themselves. In his own case an inter-varsity athletics meet in UCG sowed the seeds of what was to be a long and distinguished association with the college:

> My first visit here to Galway was in 1964 for the inter-varsity track and field championships, as captain of UCD. It was just a one-day meet, on the Saturday, and on that weekend I came here I ran the 100, 320, 440, won all three of them. We also won the 4 x 100m relay, so I won four gold medals on the weekend, which was very nice. But there was a dinner in the Great Southern that night, a celebration for presenting the cup and there was a party after it … in Roscahill. So after the dance in the Great Southern, at about 2 o'clock, we all headed out to Roscahill to this party. I had my first real introduction to Galway, and it was a long night. And then we came back in eventually, I can't even remember where we stayed, but I know we went for a run then on the Sunday. I mean we'd won, we had our sports on the Saturday, and we were very serious athletes, so we went running on the Sunday, and I remember we togged out down in what was then the Men's Club. And we ran up Taylor's Hill, turned left at Knocknacarra, back down by Grattan Road … I thought, this is a great place. But it never even crossed my mind for a moment that I would come here.

Prof. Ó Muircheartaigh recalls being impressed with the talents of one of the UCG students he encountered:

> In addition to the athletics I was very involved in the Irish-language activities, and there were regular inter-varsity events that were called *comh-caidreamh*. And I came to a *comhcaidreamh* weekend in Galway, and funny enough one of the things I do remember very clearly was one of my vice

presidents [when] I became president of the university, a student here at the time, and I remember being extremely impressed, both with his debating and with his Irish dancing, and that was Gearóid Ó Tuathaigh. He was an amazing dancer, and I think that in a different era he would have been a star of Riverdance, rather than a very distinguished professor of history.

Another student who was initially very involved in the Athletics Club was Brendan Smith. As he recalls, even after his involvement with athletics ended, his reputation as a runner resulted in him acquiring a nickname he has kept to his day:

Even to this day everybody still calls me 'Speedie', the college nickname. Because in those days you had nicknames, and some kind of went and some lived with you afterwards. When I first came to college I was involved in athletics, but I got out of that very quickly because I got involved in the social side of it. And I was running around, doing everything, and the name kind of stuck at that level.

THE P.J. TOBIN CUP

The Engineering Faculty had its own inter-faculty cup for soccer between the First, Second, Third and Fourth Eng. students. Named after the man who endowed it, a very popular former lecturer on the engineering course, the P.J. Tobin Cup was traditionally 'christened' in the appropriate manner in one of the college students' favourite socializing venues, as Dr James Browne recalls:

One of the great things about Paddy Tobin was that he'd always fill the cup with a couple of bottles of whiskey – it was a big cup. And whoever won it then he'd bring it down to the Skeff, and pour in two bottles of whiskey into it. Different times then.

Sports officer Tony Regan recalls that this was a particularly good competition,[11] fostering inclusivity in sport, as it allowed players who, as he says, 'mightn't have got a look in' in other sports to be part of a team and play for their faculty. Tony also recalls that on one memorable occasion two sisters who were engineering students at the time, and members of the well-known MacDonnchadha family from Devon Park in Galway, played in the P.J. Tobin Cup Final, and acquitted themselves well by all accounts.[12]

As we have seen, not all college sporting activities were taken as seriously as the Sigerson, Fitzgibbon or Ashbourne cup competitions. Seán Mac Iomhair recalls an annual sporting event in the 1970s, involving the engineering students, which

---

11 Tony Regan retired as head of sport at NUIG in 2009. The P.J. Tobin Cup final in question took place in 1972. **12** *Cois Coiribe.*

brought a great deal of fun to the college: 'Bhí sé de nós ar feadh roinnt blianta leis na h-innealtóirí cluiche a bheith acu leis an bhfoireann hockey, agus gléasfheadh na h-innealtóirí iad fhéin mar cailíní.' ('It was the tradition with the engineers for a number of years that they would play a match with the hockey team, and that the engineers would dress themselves up as girls.')

Prof. Jim Flavin, however, recalls one occasion when things got a little out of hand following the mixed hockey event, with ramifications for the continuation of the event itself:

> Oh do bhíodh high jinks ann, bhíodh said ollta agus mar sin de, agus chuadar isteach sa coffee shop agus d'ardaigh siad Ma Creaven suas san aer. Agus bhí ana-raic ann ina dhiaidh, an Discipline Committee agus mar sin de. Agus de réir dealramh cuireadh deireadh leis an mixed hockey ansin.

> Oh there was high jinks happening, they were a bit worse for the drink and that, and they went into the coffee shop and they lifted Ma Creaven up in the air. And there was awful trouble afterwards, with the Discipline Committee and all that. And after that then, apparently, that put an end to the mixed hockey.

THE RIVER

Given its location right beside the River Corrib, the college rowing boats were a major source of enjoyment, as well as exercise, for students. Budge Clissmann recalled taking to the river in order to study in the run-up to exams:

> You only had to pay a small fee to join the Boat Club, and then you could take a boat out any time you liked. In the fine weather I would take a boat, and my books, and row up the river, pull into some reeds, and lie back and read away to my heart's content. It was absolutely wonderful, a wonderful facility.

Prof. Seán Tobin also loved the river, but felt he and his fellow non-Galwegians were at a distinct disadvantage when it came to using the rowing boats, as he explains:

> The college had some lovely boats, rowing boats, really nice, light, elegant boats, these weren't put out until the 1st May … and we were all gone in June. And I remember complaining about the fact that the students who lived in Galway had the use of these boats all summer long, and poor idiots like myself who lived in south Tipperary couldn't benefit from them at all, well we could for a while.

The oarsmen and women who took to the water in the university's Rowing Club were less interested in the pleasures of leisurely trips on the river, and more interested in the intense competition that has seen the club earn an international reputation for itself over the decades. Generations of college students have rowed competitively with the club – many, as Keith Duggan recalls, 'learning to row in the shadow of the university'.[13]

The sporting life of the college has been at the heart of what makes UCG such a special university. Whether in terms of the significant achievements of its sportsmen and women, in both national and international arenas, or the collegial pleasures derived from a soccer kickabout on the lawn in front of the Aula, with jumpers as goalposts, UCG has always been willing to include everyone in the fun and camaraderie that can be derived from sport. But as Keith Duggan recorded some years ago in his review of the sporting history of the college, it was never just about excellence:

> In December 1933, some 3,000 people – including, most likely, the entire student body of 600 – turned out on the streets of Galway to welcome the Queen's University team, visiting for the Sigerson Cup. A torchlight procession guided their way to the Aula Maxima. The Belfast college was the first Ulster team to play a competitive GAA fixture in Connacht since partition. The sporting welcome was one of the most memorable in Irish college history. It set a tone that would – and will – continue.[14]

As indeed it has.

13 Keith Duggan, 'A sporting legacy', *Cois Coiribe* (2007), p. 22.   14 Ibid., p. 25.

5

The view from the front: experiences of academic life

The college changed dramatically in the fifty years from 1930 to 1980 in many respects. As we have seen, student numbers increased significantly, and as a result more academic and administrative staff were required. New academic disciplines and courses came on stream. The physical expansion of the college continued apace, and new teaching methods, and a more focused approach to research, heralded a new era as the college approached the end of the twentieth century. But one fact remained constant: the turnover of academic staff was minimal. The academics who came to teach at UCG tended to stay there, even when there were perhaps greater professional opportunities to be had elsewhere, and greater obstacles to be overcome in teaching and researching in their chosen discipline in Galway. The college was particularly fortunate in attracting some extraordinary scholars, gifted teachers, and groundbreaking researchers, all of which combined to create something of a renaissance in the university's fortunes during a critical fifty years in its history. Why they came, what they accomplished, and why they stayed will be examined in the course of this chapter.

NEW BEGINNINGS – THE ADVENT OF LECTURESHIPS IN IRISH

The fortunes of the college improved considerably in 1927 with the introduction of three new lecturships for the teaching of economics, history and mathematics through Irish. So successful were these appointments that the government of the day agreed, some years later, to the establishment of three more lectureships – for the teaching through Irish of Latin, Greek and the theory of education. The college was fortunate that the professors appointed to these new positions were not only committed to the revival of the Irish language, but also happened to be exceptional scholars and teachers.

In a contribution to a 1934 Dáil debate on the financing of universities and colleges, Helena Concannon TD, herself an historian of some repute, urged the Committee on Finance to increase the salaries paid to the earlier appointees at UCG, and declared, 'I do not know of any expenditure of public moneys which has given a richer return than these lectureships through the medium of Irish in University College, Galway.'[1] She went on to commend the lecturers concerned, and the university, for 'the part Galway College is playing in the revival of the use of Irish as a full-grown literary language':

1 Dáil Éireann Debates, 21 June 1934.

The lecturer in Greek, through the medium of Irish, has edited in Irish a number of Greek plays and has done his work with such scholarship as to earn the praise of distinguished critics. The lecturer in mathematics has, with An Gúm,[2] ready for publication some important mathematical works. The lecturer in education is busy with an authoritative work on the theory and practice of education. The lecturer in history – a brilliant woman – is engaged on a history of Ireland in Irish, which will fill a clamant need. The lecturer in economics, who has done remarkable work in his faculty, is, I am glad to say, about to extend beyond the circle of his fortunate students the benefits of his work by the publication of a book in Irish on national economics. The lecturer in Latin – another brilliant woman – has in hand a Latin grammar in Irish. It will thus be seen that in the production of textbooks on subjects of vital national and educational importance the Irish lecturers in Galway College have deserved well of their country.

Deputy Concannon's praise for the women lecturers of UCG (Síle Ní Chinnéide and Máiréad Ní Éimhigh, respectively) is striking, and relative to the number of its staff, UCG had a comparatively high number of women professors at that time. There were two professorships held by women in 1930: Prof. Margaret Shea (in German) and Prof. Mary Donovan O'Sullivan (in history). By 1940 these women had been joined by yet another female professor, Cáit Ní Maolchróin (in Old and Middle Irish), and these were joined later by Máiréad Ní Éimhigh (in classics). By 1970 there were five women professors, some of the older women having retired, and some new appointments of female professors having been made, including Lorna Reynolds in English, Máirín de Valera in botany, Síle Ní Chinnéide in history and Mary O'Reilly in Spanish. Brilliant women they undoubtedly were, but in the academic climate that existed in the 1930s, '40s and '50s, intellectual brilliance alone was generally insufficient to allow women to ascend to the highest levels of academia. The question remains: why was UCG exceptional in this regard? Why were there so many women in senior lecturer and professorial positions in Galway? The answer perhaps lies in an anecdote related by Budge Clissmann, a student who graduated in 1934:

> The English professor, he was very old, he was a really nice man, he lived out in the Eglinton Hotel in Salthill, and if you went to visit him he was delighted and he played the piano for you, and he would tell more or less the same story about how somebody had suggested to him that he should do a new doctorate of literature in Galway or something, and that he had said to them, 'And put that on top of my Cambridge MA? I will not!'[3]

2 An Gúm was an Irish state company, founded in 1925, which was part of the Department of Education, and tasked with the publication of Irish literature, especially educational materials. The agency now forms part of Foras na Gaeilge.

In her obituary for the late English professor, Catherine Donnellan, in remembering a man having 'talents amounting to genius', somewhat tellingly commented: 'Studious, intelligent, sensitive and gifted with the gift of poetry, life seemed to hold more in store for him than a professorship in a provincial town.'[4]

There is a sense then that, at least in the early days, until the introduction of Irish language scholarships began to attract the better students in the late 1930s and 1940s, and thereby began to produce top-class graduates, UCG was regarded in wider academic circles as something of an academic backwater. In short, male academics simply didn't consider academic appointments to Galway as sufficiently prestigious to even apply for, and so eminently qualified women were given their chance to shine and begin scaling the academic ladder by taking up these appointments. That this was the case is somewhat confirmed by the fact that by 1980, the number of women professors had declined to just one – Prof. Elizabeth Lee in chemistry. The female lecturers and professors who retired, many of them in the late '70s, were in every case replaced by male candidates, and it was some time before more women were appointed to senior academic positions again.

COMING TO UCG

With relatively small student numbers and somewhat limited facilities it is remarkable that academics of immense ability chose to come to Galway to take up lecturing or professorial appointments. But come they did, and for many and varied reasons.

In 1960 Prof. Seán Lavelle, a medical graduate from UCG, chose to return from a prestigious position in Pittsburg to take up a newly established chair of experimental medicine and practical pharmacology. The establishment of this new department had come about in an interesting way, as Prof. Lavelle explains:

> Well, pharmacology wasn't being taught here as they thought it should be, and the GMC issued an ultimatum to the college,[5] at least that's my story, that I heard, to get a pharmacologist, and they knew that nobody would come in pharmacology. And it had been a tradition in Galway to keep an eye out for the people that were able and offer them a place on the staff if they could. And most of the people who were there at the time had come up that route. And they said there's a chap here who's done a lot of experimental

---

3 The person in question was William A. Byrne (1872–1933), who was professor of English from 1917 until his death from a heart attack in 1933. According to Kathleen Benson ('The forgotten poet of Co. Kildare', *Journal of the Co. Kildare Archaeological Society*, 1:14 (1964–5), p. 54), Byrne went to Cambridge in 1915 and took his degree 'with such brilliance' that he was selected for the chair of English at Freiburg University. However, somewhat ironically, in view of the above, it emerged that Byrne's degree was, according to Prof. Tadhg Foley, 'an external one from London University, not a degree from Cambridge'. 4 'Kay Don', 'The late Professor W.A. Byrne', *UCG Annual*, 9:8 (1933–4), p. 15. 'Kay Don' was presumably Catherine Donnellan. 5 The General Medical Council was the regulatory body for doctors in Ireland.

work, and they changed the name of the thing to experimental medicine and practical pharmacology, and I applied for it and I got it.

Interestingly, Prof. Lavelle recalls that:

> At the interview the most searching questions were asked by people who weren't in the medical faculty, I think because they were concerned with tuition, with education, and the other people would be more concerned with technicalities.

Prof. Lavelle's recollection of his interview for the position reveals something of the changes that were to await him in Galway:

> I was asked how many medical students were at Pittsburg, where I was at the time. And I said 100 per year, that's 400. And they said how many staff? And I said well the last faculty meeting I was at there was 1,200. And there was silence, total silence.

There were also financial differences. Prof. Lavelle recalls that, like many of his contemporaries: 'I came home then to a drop in salary ... I was tax-free in the States. I think it was about a third less.'

Prof. Turlough Fitzgerald's decision to take up a position as chair of anatomy in 1968, having, like Prof. Lavelle, previously taught in the States, came about in a somewhat similar manner:

> In 1966 I went to the University of Washington in Seattle and it was one of the top four medical schools in the US. And I thoroughly enjoyed Seattle. And then this chair came up, and although we were negotiating buying a house in Seattle, because I was granted tenure, there was this drag, because there were thirteen teachers of anatomy in the University of Washington, and in Galway there were two, of which one (the chair) had just resigned. Leaving a total of one. And a total of two years, eighty students a year. So I decided I might turn out to be a big fish in a small pond, and decided to apply.

Prof. Eamon O'Dwyer, who arrived at UCG in 1958, was similarly motivated by the opportunities afforded to an enthusiastic young man to make his mark in his chosen field:

> I was in the National Maternity Hospital, and there were ten of us consultants. I was the youngest one in it, my ambition would be to be the master of the hospital. But you were looking also at so-and-so, and so-and-so, and so on, and I said ah I'd be 55 if I'm ever going to be master

here, and that'd be too late. So I worked with two people, we worked as teams in the National Maternity, the late John Cunningham, who was the professor emeritus of University College Dublin, and the other person we worked with was the late Éamon de Valera, who then became professor subsequently. And one day John Cunningham said to me, 'Eamon', he said, 'the chair in Galway is vacant, would you think of that?' 'Oh', I said, 'I hadn't thought about it'. 'Well it is vacant, you know, and you might just think about it and you know, you could do worse.' I said, well, if I go to Galway I'll be 34, I'll be the boss, I'll have my feet under my own desk, and that'll be it. But I'd be single-handed. There'd be no other consultant in the hospital, only me. I came down, after a lot of soul-searching. I went off to Sweden, with Éamon de Valera, we went on a sort of a learning visit as it were, and I met John Kennedy there.[6] And he said, 'Oh you're coming to Galway, aren't you?' And I said, 'I don't know.' And the minister's wife in Sweden said to me, 'Oh Eamon, don't be mad going to Galway, you're a consultant in Holles Street and you're a consultant in St Luke's in Rathgar, why would you go down to Galway? You'll make a fortune in Dublin if you stay there.' 'Oh leave him alone', says Kennedy, 'he's coming down, because we need him'.

Times were changing and in the range of new appointments, particularly in the 1960s and '70s, it is clear that some of the 'old guard' recognized that new, energetic, ambitious academics would be needed to bring the college on to the next phase of its development. Prof. Richard Butler's account of his interview for a one-year position as a lecturer in the Chemistry Department is indicative of the kind of challenges facing the college, and the kind of 'can-do' attitude that would be needed to bring about change:

> I always remember one of the interviews I was in, there was Máirín de Valera, and a lady from classics, Margaret Heavey. And they were there on the interview board, and there was about five or six, maybe ten people, big boards then. I'd been explaining to them [about] the chemistry I'd been doing in the University of Leicester where I had been working, we were doing wonderful chemistry there, and they said to me, 'Is there any reason why this chemistry couldn't be done in Galway?' And I quite innocently said, 'No, no reason at all, all you need is money.' And they all burst out laughing.

Prof. Butler was one of those who chose a career at UCG over a more lucrative position as head of the newly established Sligo RTC, a position to which he had

---

6 John Kennedy came to UCG in 1948 as professor of pathology, and pathologist to the Central Hospital.

been appointed at the age of just 27 in 1970, following his return to Ireland from the University of Leicester. Resigning his position to take up a one-year lectureship in the UCG Chemistry Department in 1971 was something of a risk for Prof. Butler, but one he was prepared to take, as he explains:

> I realized eventually that I wasn't a political administrator and that the job didn't particularly suit me. I wanted to get back to research in chemistry, and I came here. But I had to explain why. I had a private session with the president of the college, who was Martin Newell, and I had to explain to him why I was going to come down here as a junior lecturer in chemistry from being head of the college in Sligo, and half the salary. It was very significant, because the salary up there was £2,800 a year and it was £1,400 a year [at UCG]. I remember telling him that I was a very good chemist, that I was going to get a D.Sc. degree in a few years because I knew, I had the research done, a lot of it, I knew what I was going to do, and he looked at me and he said, 'If you get a D.Sc. degree we'll make you a professor.' So that was then '71. In '74 he conferred me with the D.Sc. degree and I went up to him the following day and I said, 'You told me you'd … ' It took him two years to make me associate professor, and he retired in the interim, but it was that kind of world, you know?

Before the process for appointment to the academic staff of the university was revised in the mid-1960s, it was necessary for applicants to supply copies of their applications for every member of staff who had a vote on the Academic Council. In the case of Prof. Jim Flavin, when he applied for the position of lecturer in the Department of Mathematical Physics in 1962, this was a singularly daunting task, as he explains:

> Bhíodh ort 135 cóip den iarrtas a cur ar fáil, ar do chostas fhéin. Cén fáth an oiread sin? Mar bhí ceann ag teastáil le haghaidh chuile dhuine a raibh vóta aige. Nuair a lúaigh mé leis an Ollamh a bhí agam i Newcastle-on-Tyne go raibh orm é sin a dhéanamh dúirt sé, 'But this is ridiculous!'

> You had to make 135 copies of your application available, at your own cost. Why that many? Because every person who had a vote had to have a copy. When I said this to the professor I had in Newcastle-on-Tyne, that I had to do this, he said, 'But this is ridiculous!'

Although not required to make quite so many copies of his own application, Prof. Etienne Rynne vividly recalls the interview process for his position as the first statutory lecturer in archaeology in Ireland in 1967. By all accounts it was a gruelling process, as he explains:

> You couldn't get a job, a statutory job, without interviewing. I had to be interviewed by forty something people, bishops and everybody else, I have a list of them here. But I had a list and I ticked off all the ones that I had met. I had to call on Bishop Browne … We had to visit everybody, personally visit them all.

In the course of his interview for the position with Prof. Michael Duignan, the young Prof. Rynne was asked to wait in the staff room, where he first became aware of the wonderful art collection which the college had acquired over the decades. But his appraisal of one particular painting almost caused him to fall at the first hurdle and jeopardized his future career with the college, as he explains:

> Behind the sofa in the staff room there was a nice painting. And just for want of something to say, I didn't know what to say, but I knew Duignan thought he knew something about art and all the rest because he had bought paintings for the college etc. And so I said to him, 'By the way professor, do you mind me asking, who did that painting up there?' 'It's of the Holy Family.' 'Who did that do you mind me asking?' It was cubist kind of stuff. 'Oh', says he, 'I'm surprised at you Etienne, I thought you knew your art, I thought you'd know a Mainie Jellett when you saw one'. And I said, 'That's not a Maine Jellett is it?' And he said, 'It is indeed, sure I bought it myself for the college.' And I said, 'Well professor, I don't think it's a Mainie Jellett. If you don't mind me saying so', I said, 'it looks much more like Jack Hanlon', says I. 'No, I got a Jellett,' says he. And I said, 'Well, I was a student of Mainie Jellett's,' because I was a student, when I was six or seven years old. But later on when I got the job and when I had the chance I went up and I tried to look and see was there a name on it. Couldn't find any name on it at all. So I waited until I got the room completely empty one day, and I took it down from the wall and looked at the back … Jack Hanlon.

Perhaps wisely, the young archaeology lecturer did not raise the matter with his new boss again.

Prof. Iognáid Ó Muircheartaigh's arrival at UCG came about as much as a result of chance as anything else – but he was fortunate in having just the skills that were needed in UCG in the early '70s:

> I was a PhD student at Glasgow University at that time, and my professor there, David Silvey, received a phone call from Seán Tobin, professor of maths at UCG, asking him, 'Do you have any statisticians over there, we're looking for a statistician.' Silvey asked Tobin, 'What kind of statistician are you looking for?' and Tobin replied, 'Just a straight-forward statistician', to which Silvey responded, 'Well we have a somewhat bent one over here.' He had a good sense of humour.

In what might have been seen as a long-shot, Prof. Tobin added another stipulation to his search for a 'straight-forward statistician': 'ideally one with Irish'. In Iognáid Ó Muircheartaigh they had found not only their man, but a future college president.

Prof. Jim Flavin was another academic whose arrival at UCG in 1962 happened at just the right time. A graduate of UCC, and a fluent Irish speaker, Prof. Flavin arrived to take up a position as lecturer in maths physics, but as events unfolded, his promotion to professor of the Department of Maths Physics was remarkably rapid, as he explains:

> Tháinig mé go UCG i 1962 mar Léachtóir. Fuair mé an Ollamhnacht an bhliain dár gcionn. Anseo mar a tharla. Nuair a tháining mé anseo bhí Eoghan Mac Cionnaith ina Ollamh, ach bhí sé ar phinsean an t-am sin. Ní fuaireadar iarrthóir sásiúl le Gaeilge. Forgraíodh an Ollamhnacht an bhliain sin, an bhliain a thainig mé, ach ní bhfuaireadar iarrthoir sásúil ar bith. Chuala mé ina dhiaidh sin gurbh é an rud a dúradh ná gurbh céim ar gcúl é duine gan Gaeilge a cheapadh. Seacht bliain ina dhiaidh sin, sin '69 is dócha, an céad uair a fostaíodh Ollamh gan Gaeilge. Fograiodh an post arís i 1963, so bhí an t-áth liom.

> I came to UCG in 1962 as a lecturer. I got the professorship the following year. This is how it happened. When I came here Eoghan Mac Cionnaith was professor, but he was on pension at that stage. They didn't get a suitable applicant with Irish. The professorship was advertised the year I arrived, and they didn't get anyone suitable. I heard afterwards that what had happened was that it was considered a backward step to appoint anyone who didn't have Irish. Seven years after that, that was in 1969 I think, was the first time a professor without Irish was appointed. The post was advertised again in 1963, so I was lucky.

BEING APPOINTED

The system of appointing staff to positions was somewhat haphazard at least until the early 1960s, and it was often the case that staff had to take up a position (having already resigned from another position on occasion) without having been formally appointed. Prof. Pádraig Ó Céidigh's appointment to an assistantship in zoology was a case in point:

> Prof. [Thomas J.] Dinan introduced me to the registrar, Mitchell, who explained to me that I wasn't legally appointed at all until the end of October, but that it was 'highly unlikely' that they wouldn't appoint me. Well I took the chance on it anyway. But anyway I met Coll,[7] who'd just been appointed to

7 Proinnsias S. Ó Colla was professor of chemistry at UCG 1954–81.

Dillon's job, Dillon had just retired that year, but he told me, 'We appointed you today,' he said – there was a [meeting of the] Governing Body at the end of October, so I'd been teaching for about three weeks before that.

Academics and medics were attracted to UCG for a number of reasons, but for some, specific incentives were offered to encourage them to take up positions in the university, as Prof. Eamon O'Dwyer recalls:

> I was a graduate of UCD and I came here in 1958 as a consultant from the National Maternity Hospital. When I came first, Monsignor Padraig de Brún was the president, and he said to me, 'If you come and join us I'll give you that garden all for yourself, because you're a good gardener I believe?' And the garden I was to get was the late Máirín de Valera's botany garden at the college.

It is rather doubtful that this offer was made with the prior knowledge of the eminent professor of botany.

Having opted to resign his position in Dublin, Prof. O'Dwyer found himself taking something of a chance in taking up the chair of obstetrics and gynaecology in UCG:

> It was a funny sort of way in which the appointments were made then. You were appointed to the hospital first. And I was an acting professor for some months. Then I had to go through all the rigmarole of applying to the senate of the NUI to be appointed to the permanent post. The medical school here was under a cloud at the time. Now, it had been the best – there was a survey carried out by the Americans, and our school here came out on top.[8] But the government had decided at the time that I think they were going to rationalize, and that three medical schools – Dublin, Cork and Galway – were too many, they'd get rid of one. And the one they were going to get rid of was this one. When I came the monsignor said, 'Now you know there's a threat to close the school.' 'I do', I said, 'and you'll come nonetheless?' 'Oh I will', I said, 'I'll take my chance'. 'Well', he said, 'look, if it's closed, you'll always get your pension'. I was just 34.

Prof. O'Dwyer's found that his first few years were taken up with the stresses of working largely on his own, and at the same time trying to save the medical school,

8 The visit referred to was conducted by inspectors from the American Medical Association in August 1955. Although the report did criticize the poor ancillary facilities and the paucity of junior staff and researchers, the overall report was very favourable, praising in particular the close association between the university and the teaching hospital, and especially the clinical professors being also on the staff of the hospital. See 'The American visitors' report', *Journal of the Irish Medical Association*, 33 (1953), pp 183–5.

which was not only employing him but, as he soon realized, was providing an essential service to the west of Ireland. A spirited defence of the medical school in Galway saved the day, as Prof. Éamon O'Dwyer recalls:

> I came in 1958, and a year or so later we had an inspection by the General Medical Council in London of our school, and of course instead of them inspecting us, we were sort of inspecting them. We took them to lunch, the late John Kennedy and I, and we told them that the school was under threat here. And that this would be a disaster for the hinterland, the whole West of Ireland was depending on this medical school. And they wrote their report. And in their report, they put an addendum for the government on top: 'DO NOT CLOSE THAT SCHOOL, because it is essential for the well-being of the people of the west of Ireland.'

Even when the medical school began to thrive, and was producing excellent doctors, staff resources were still very limited, and Prof. O'Dwyer recalls that the luxury of secretarial assistance to cover his college and hospital work was something he could only dream of:

> I had no secretary in the college. The grant I would get from the college, it might be £20-a-year type of thing, it wouldn't buy a book of stamps. I had a part-time secretary in the hospital, and I had her for years and years. And then I finally got a full-time one. Eventually I got the deanery for six years, and I acquired a full-time secretary with the deanship. But there was no office – I gave *them* the office, I gave them the office in the Maternity Department.

BECOMING ESTABLISHED

Prof. Dan O'Donovan, a UCD graduate who had studied for his PhD in physiology at the University of Rochester, found the change in scale of the college in Galway somewhat startling when he came to take up a position in the Physiology Department in 1965.

> It was quite small, even relative to UCD, it would have been small. It was the Quad really. There was nothing outside of that, everything went on in that, and when I came that was it. I remember there used to be a joke because I used to say, well I was coming back from America where everything was big and all the rest, and when people would say something about, 'What was going on now?' and I would say, 'Well it's in a state of flux.' In other words, it was changing, but it still hadn't changed yet.

For many the sheer size of their departments put them at a distinct disadvantage in terms of the work they were able to undertake. As Prof. O'Donovan recalls:

I used to go back on sabbaticals to the States, and I'd go to international conferences, and they'd ask me, I mean, I was in penal physiology, and I would tell people that I was lecturing in the alimentary tract, and muscles and nerves and all these things. And they would say, 'Ah that's academic suicide, you shouldn't do that.' And I'd say, 'Well what can I do, there's only two of us in the department, two or three.' I mean before I came there Prof. Donegan literally taught on his own, he was professor of the subject. And in fact, if you go back to those times physiology and anatomy were sometimes one department, of course anatomy is the structure, physiology is the function and one person taught it all. I suppose physiology grew out of anatomy, and biochemistry would be part of physiology, and when Professor [Colm] O'hEocha was appointed lecturer, professor of biochemistry you know, he was taking I suppose a slot out of physiology, because we'd be doing experiments in physiology which they'd be duplicating in biochemistry. So that's how departments grew. But I mean, you had a professor and an assistant and the assistant cleaned the blackboard for him and all the rest.

With the expansion of the college, particularly in the '60s and '70s, came demands for office space for new staff, and with budgets tight and resources stretched to the maximum, a spirit of DIY appears to have prevailed. This was particularly so in the case of appointments to new positions, and the establishment of new departments, as the following account from Prof. Seán Lavelle vividly recalls:

When I found the reality here it was very hard to take. They asked me how much I would want, and I said I'll have to think about that. And while I was thinking of it I ordered my first piece of apparatus, or I didn't order it, I got the data on it. It was more than the amount of money I was actually given ... wiped out my budget. And I was given £138 a year to run the department. Now I've forgotten how much, but it was so many millions to run the department in the States. I had no place to unpack my bag, and Johnny Kennedy, who had been my boss before I left pathology, he gave me a storeroom that he had, a side room, which was about 8 x 6ft, to park my bag in. Then somebody decided that I could have the old Pharmacology Lab, and it consisted of two benches, and an island bench in the middle, and there was about 4ft between the benches. There were three sinks in each bench. There were two electric outlets. And there was the old gas heater, the old gas system was still connected there. So you turned on the gas heater to get hot water. And after a wait of half an hour or so it came on.

I had thirty-two pieces of apparatus. I got the Medical Research Council to give me the big piece, and I spent the rest of the budget on modern equipment that would be necessary in any lab. I had thirty-two pieces of equipment to be plugged in, to these two outlets.

Prof. Lavelle was undaunted and anxious to begin work:

> So I rigged up a network of cables. I had no assistance, I had to do it all myself. I rigged up a network of cables from the light. I got one of these double adaptors on the light and put a light bulb in one and ran the other thing from it. And thanks be to God we didn't have a fire.

Prof. Lavelle's research involved the use of rabbits, and, as Prof. Tom O'Connor recalls, occasionally the professor's research subjects brought some light relief to the solemn atmosphere of learning in the Quadrangle:

> Seán Lavelle was in the north side of the Quadrangle, where the Finance Office is now. He had some of his labs there, and his white rabbits, his cages, were there. They used occasionally get out and be hopping around the Quadrangle.

In a university where, for most of the period covered by this book, blackboards and chalk were the main teaching aids, it is extraordinary to note how even those basic 'tools of the trade' were subject to restrictions, as Bobby Curran recalls: 'Back in the '70s the dusters were held in the Archway. That's a fact. There was a box of them there and you'd pick up a duster and clean the blackboard and bring it back again.'

FINDING AN OFFICE

Like many new staff who arrived in the college in the 1960s and '70s, Prof. Dan O'Donovan found himself without an office:

> I had a lab but I had no place to put my books or anything. And there was a lab, and I got up and I sealed off this little corner, a little wooden thing. And it had a sliding door, with a filing cabinet here, so to open the filing cabinet I had to close the door. And the books were all up on the shelf. And then I went to the buildings officer, Gerry Lee, and I told him I needed more space, I was really cramped. And they asked him, 'What kind of office does he have?' 'Well', he said, 'Put it like this, I went to visit him and when I went in to visit him, I wasn't able to turn around, I had to back out of the office. 'Twas too small to turn around!' That will tell you the size of it, 'twas very, very small. And I was just trying to save them money ... I just made a little temporary wooden hut.

Prof. O'Donovan's cramped office space eventually expanded, as he explains:

> I blocked off the stairs, made a floor out of it, and I broke a door, which was a kind of an Archway from the lab, and from the main big lab

outside, and I had two doors out of it. And I made a cupboard out of a little alcove that they had for a press as well, but I had an office now, which was about four or five times the size of what I had before. And I remember our technician came in one day and he said, 'Where did you get all the books?' I said, 'I always had those.' 'No, no', he said, 'this place is full, you were in a little corner'. 'Well', I said, 'I've just spread them out more, they were all in there but I had them tightly organized and they fitted well'.

Prof. Jim Flavin arrived in the college in 1962 as a lecturer in the Department of Maths Physics. He found himself operating without an office, and pretty much running the department on his own, the position of professor of maths physics having just become vacant on the retirement of Prof. Eoghan McKenna. During his first year, Prof. Flavin lived in a hotel behind Scoil Fhursa on Taylor's Hill, and carried his work in and out with him during the academic year. However, anxious to avoid the cost of staying in a hotel for the summer months, and with nowhere to deposit his teaching and research material in the college, there was but one alternative open to the Corkman, as he explains: 'Deirfheadh General de Gaulle, "I am France", you see, agus is mise "an Roinn" agus do theadh "an Roinn" go Corcaigh i rith an tSamhraidh.' ('General de Gaulle used to say, "I am France", you see, and I was "the department", and "the department" would move to Cork for the duration of the summer.')

For Iognáid Ó Muircheartaigh, being the owner of a large car was to prove useful when he arrived to take up the position of statutory lecturer in statistics at the college:

> I had bought a car in Glasgow a year earlier, and it was a beautiful car, it was a Daimler Benz, huge thing, a tank, lots of leg room, leather seats. I bought it for £85. And it lasted a year, and it was a bit dodgy, but I brought it anyway. And I arrived in to UCG in it, all my belongings in this car. I made a big impression I have to say. But it turned out then I had no office, there was no office, so this car was my office for a year I'd say.

For many, however, the 'greenfield' element of UCG was one of its biggest attractions. Prof. Richard Butler, having weighed up his options, the attractions of working at the Chemistry Department of UCG and being allowed to undertake research as well as teach were enough to outweigh the financial rewards of his position, and convince him to overlook the disadvantages of the position on offer and look to the future:

> The reason I was here was because there was a big hole, they were building a new Science Block, and I knew that there was going to be good facilities in the place, and that was why I was very interested in getting in here, because

they were building this whole building.[9] I was going to be in on the ground floor effectively. I mean this building opened in 1973, I came here in '71, so I knew what was happening.

SOURCING FUNDING AND LEARNING TO INNOVATE

UCG was fortunate in that its academics rose to the challenging of expanding their departments, even though this involved a great commitment of their time in making grant applications, sourcing sponsors and finding new and imaginative ways of making a little go a long way. Prof. Butler was typical of many such academics:

> When the new building was opened, the department got a grant of money for equipment for it on the basis of square footage. And Frank Coll had £50,000. And of course I wanted to buy a new nuclear magnetic resonance laboratory, set up this in the country, because I was an expert in this, and it wasn't in the country. And it was £15,000 ... and the idea of spending £15,000 on it! So in those days what you did with £50,000 is you bought hundreds and thousands of beakers and glassware. So we persuaded him ... we got a deal with a Japanese company that made these machines, JEOL, and we got a deal that we could pay over three years, if we got 5,000 down. So myself and Pat McArdle[10] persuaded Frank Coll to put 5,000 down, which meant that he was now on the hook, because he had to pay the balance the coming years, so we got the NMR machine put into the place. That was the first step I think, the first major step in my opinion anyway, in bringing the Chemistry Department into the modern era. In that period from 1971 to '75, we got a whole lot of first-class equipment came in. I think the practical classes improved, everything improving enormously, it was an exciting time.

Tenacity and innovativeness certainly paid dividends, but luck occasionally played a part also, as was the case when Prof. Butler applied for funding for yet another important – and expensive – piece of equipment:

> We went to the Higher Education Authority directly, which I don't think you could do that now. We just wrote out an application, myself and Pat McArdle, and we got into the car and drove to the Higher Education Authority. And we went in, and I always remember before we went in to the HEA there was an article in the paper, and there was one of our competitors, attacking the HEA. And I said, great, they couldn't have done it on a better day. This was in the *Irish Times*. And following that the HEA realized there was a need for what they called a 'Big Item Fund', and they

---

9 The reference is to the arts/science building, now more commonly known as the main concourse.   10 Prof. Patrick McArdle was first appointed to the Chemistry Department in 1972.

set up a scheme for the whole country. So there was one big item every year, and people could apply for it. It all became very formal, but the very first one, there was a carbon-13 NMR, or a Highfield NMR machine, and that's how we got it. So we had the first Highfield NMR in the country, and in a short while we were providing a service to all the other universities. But then UCD got one, as soon as we got one, UCD had to get one. Well we were doing that all the time in those times. Then we got an extra crystallography facility, and you know the whole place changed dramatically.

Developments in the field of mathematics, and applying mathematics to the needs of modern society, was another field in which UCG took the lead – but not without some resistance, as Bobby Curran explains:

They have degrees in applied mathematics, and financial mathematics and what have you now, but we opened it up. That wasn't easy by the way, I'll tell you what happened. I was lucky, I suppose, to be head of department that year. I also had a couple of good friends in UCD, Prof. Power's daughter, Sheila Tinney, she was associate professor of mathematics in UCD. The mathematics departments and the maths physics departments in all of the other universities and the maths physics people in UCG went cracked. They saw it as the end of the line etc. etc. they wanted to keep it very pure, mathematical science, if there were only two or three coming out, that was good enough and so on. I had to fight that one, and I won it. Then I had to go and fight these guys. I went up to Dublin anyhow. Iggy was with me.[11] There were two of us, because there was stats in it you see as well. And we went up anyhow, and they were dead against me. But she came in and said that 'I think in fact Galway should be allowed to do what they want to do,' and that clinched it, and so we got it going. I also got, at the M.Sc. level, numerical analysis recognized as a subject.

The latter proved to be an inspired move, and added considerably to the college's reputation in the rapidly progressing fields of numerical analysis, statistics and computing, as the following account, from Bobby Curran, attests to:

John Shiel was the first guy that did his M.Sc. with me,[12] and the external examiner was a man called Leslie Fox, who is famous, he was head of the new numerical-analysis laboratory and professor of numerical analysis in Oxford.[13] There's a Leslie Fox Prize, he was famous. And he said about John

11 Prof. Iognáid Ó Muircheartaigh, known to students and staff alike as Iggy, was a lecturer in statistics at that time. 12 Prof. John Shiel was appointed a personal professor in the Department of Industrial Engineering at UCG in 2002. 13 Prof. Leslie Fox was director of the Oxford University Computing Laboratory 1957–82 and professor of numerical analysis 1963–83.

Shiel's answering at the M.Sc. that it was the best answering he had seen from any student anywhere in the world.

THE DAWN OF THE COMPUTER AGE

UCG was quick off the mark in providing postgraduate M.Sc. courses, and in this regard achieved a first in the Ireland, as Bobby explains:

> The first computer science postgraduate in Ireland was a guy called Tony Johnson, who did an M.Sc. with me, and he and I wrote the first computer-ized admissions system for UCG, and UCG used it from about '71 to '74. And would you believe it, they're still using the programme that we wrote to print labels? It was so good. We wrote it in Fortran and it's still being used. So myself and Tony Johnson ran that system, and all the students that came into UCG that year, 1972, were computerized for the first time. He got an M.Sc. out of it, that was part of it anyway, he'd to do exams as well. So he was the first M.Sc. in computing in the National University of Ireland in 1972.

FUNDING FOR RESEARCH

Finding the necessary resources to conduct research, or indeed to fit it into a busy teaching schedule, was a constant difficulty for academic staff at UCG. This situation was further exacerbated during the Second World War, as explained in the obituary for Prof. Máirín de Valera, who died in 1984, which was published in the *European Journal of Phycology* in 1985.

> Subsequent to her appointment at Galway in 1939, there was only one publication during the next decade, the rather significant (but frequently overlooked) paper dealing with the first record for the occurrence of the red alga *Asparagopsis armata* in the British Isles. This dearth is under-standable, bearing in mind that Máirín was an isolated phycologist in a department then with minimal facilities where she carried a horrendous teaching load, and in a country which, although neutral, was enveloped for many years by the Second World War, so that resources of all kinds were at a premium. Whatever spare time there might have been was largely spent assessing and evaluating the potential resources of Gelidiaceous algae throughout the west coast of Ireland as sources of agar. Due to wartime restrictions, this work was largely undertaken with a bicycle as the only means of transport.[14]

14 M.D. Guiry and P.S. Dixon, 'Máirín de Valera (1912–1984)', *European Journal of Phycology*, 20:1 (1985), p. 82.

Prof. de Valera's dedication to her research during the difficult war years was to pay major dividends, not just in terms of papers published, but in terms of the extensive knowledge she gained from her field studies, which she was determined to pass on to her students. The obituary referred to above went on to say that:

> Subsequently, her research was largely concentrated on field studies, particularly on the distribution, ecology, life histories, and phenology (both in terms of occurrence and reproduction) of marine algae so that there was a constant production of papers based essentially on the work of earlier years but reinforced by further field investigations. In general, regardless of the particular requirements of the many marine phycologists who visited Galway, the location of rare or interesting material was described in detail so that all came away with a deep respect for her abilities. If one were to ask where to find a particular species, the reply would be immediate, 'over the bridge, turn left, and there is a large pool by a big boulder' and, sure enough, there it would be.[15]

Research is at the heart of what today's universities need to do in order to establish and maintain reputations for academic excellence and innovation. But it was not always so. When Prof. Seán Lavelle returned to the university to take up the chair of experimental medicine in 1960, he found that his interest in research was not greeted warmly by some of his colleagues, as he explains:

> Nobody worried very much about it at that time. You went on automatically to 70, and you came in and you gave your lectures and that was it, there was no money for research. And that was the biggest battle I had when I came back here, was to get funds for research. I remember getting up at the Academic Council and saying that the primary duty of a professor was to carry out research in his discipline. And in the next few days four of the Academic Council came to me and chided me gently, and reminded me that UCG was a teaching institution.

As one of the smaller colleges, Galway was particularly at a disadvantage in securing funding for research. Yet with a good deal of resourcefulness and tenacity funding *was* found for some important projects. Prof. Richard Butler recalls how he and his colleagues at UCG became very adept at fighting to get funding:

> There was no money for research, there was none of this kind of thing that's going on now, Science Foundation Ireland – that was eons before that ... but we managed to get it. There were capital grants that you could get. The college used to get a capital grant, and you got a small capital grant

15 Ibid., p. 82.

each year. And we used to do deals with the people in the accounts office, they were always extremely helpful. We would accumulate … I'd say I want to accumulate our capital grant for the next few years because I want to buy a machine that's going to cost £60,000, and get me twenty a year, and they would do that. Because it was almost survival actually, and we were great survivors. I always felt we were great survivors when there were only crumbs around. It's actually harder to survive when there's loads of food around.

TEACHING AND RESEARCH: FINDING THE BALANCE

Balancing the demands of teaching and research is a constant struggle for most academics, and UCG was no exception. But academics came up with innovative ways of pursuing their own research, and meeting their teaching commitments, by the careful management of their time, and an enormous personal commitment. Prof. Dan Donovan recalls his own efforts in this regard:

> I had a little thing, which I got in America, on my noticeboard in the office which said, 'Research is to teaching as sin is to confession, if you don't commit the one, you've nothing to tell in the other.' So in other words, if you go in to teach people and you are saying, well, I read this in a book yesterday, this is what it says, instead of saying well we did this experiment last week, and this is the result we got, telling people the practical things that you had actually found out, rather than rehearsing something from somebody else, you know? And it keeps you more alive as well, of course.

Prof. O'Donovan echoed the sentiments of many of his colleagues when he said, 'You wouldn't survive academically, if you didn't go away' on sabbaticals.

But with a shortage of staff and increasing student numbers the demands of teaching and administration made designated research time difficult to come by. For many the answer was to block their teaching together as best they could and use the summer months judiciously, as Prof. Dan O'Donovan endeavoured to do:

> In 1970 I went to Cornell Medical Centre in New York. I sequestered all my teaching into maybe two-thirds of the year, so whatever lecturing I was doing in April and May, I gave those earlier and then somebody else filled in for that time. So instead of going just for three months in the summer, I went for six months, so I was able to go from April until October. And what I did in that particular case, and which I did afterwards as well, was that I went over during the Easter holidays, which might be early April and I wasn't losing any time here, and the last term would be very short anyway, it was May, maybe three weeks or something, and I had already given those lectures earlier. I would go and fix up housing and all the rest for the family,

and the family would go out during the summer. So I'd come back then in June for a two- or three-week slot where I could do the exams, correct all the exams, and do the orals, and the practicals and all the rest. So in other words, I gave all my teaching, I did all the examining here, and still got officially six months away. And so when I published then, even though I continued some of the same work here, it was mainly due to what I did over there, from the communication with international people. So, that was the way that I kept alive academically, and how UCG got the name of producing a lot, whereas in actual fact it should be credited elsewhere. And then three years later I went to Munich and did the same thing, I spent six months there.

Others, like Prof. Tom O'Connor, were forced to take even more drastic measures in order to take time out to do some designated research:

> I went to America in 1963/4 on a Fulbright. But at the time I had been appointed a statutory lecturer, I'd been assistant up to '62, and then I was fifteen months as a statutory lecturer. But I had to resign my statutory lectureship so that I could get away, because the situation was that we were looking for more staff, and the question was how could you let somebody off on a sabbatical when you're looking for more staff? So the idea came to Professor Ó Brolcháin that I would resign, and go, and reapply. I was taking a bit of a chance on it. So as it turned out I did have to come back from America and do an interview again to regain my position here.

Prof. Iognáid Ó Muircheartaigh found that undertaking research in the United States was extremely important to him in his subsequent career:

> I got a sabbatical in '75, so I was here five years by then. I taught and learned, my teaching was getting going by then, but I'd done very little research. And you know you're going nowhere without research in academic life. And I was very fortunate, I got a Fulbright fellowship to Stanford University. So in 1975 I was 32 years of age, and I was able to walk into one of the best universities in the world and be treated like a very distinguished visitor. And they were so nice, I mean these people were the equivalent of Nobel Prize winners of statistics, and I was sitting between these different offices, knowing them on first-name terms, so it was a huge, unbelievable break. I got started on research. When you meet someone like that, or you find a project that suddenly grows into something bigger, you know you just have to be lucky. I was extremely lucky.

The fact that UCG was a relatively small institution in some ways paid dividends in facilitating the coordination of research and exchange of knowledge between departments, as Prof. O'Donovan explains:

Seán Lavelle used to organize research meetings between us. And I would go in and tell people, maybe people even in physics and experimental medicine and biochemistry what I was doing. And they would come in the next day, and tell what they were doing. And we sort of knew what each person was doing. Because it was possible, in a small university. I remember a story that this guy, an American, was giving a talk in Tokyo, and someone in the audience raised his hand and said, 'I'm very interested in your talk, I must have a chat with you sometime about it.' And the speaker said, 'Well, any time you want to, come up the stairs, in America you're only one floor down from me.' In other words, they were in the same building, and they wouldn't actually talk ... they'd be all doing their own research, and not communicating, and this can happen.

Maureen Langan-Egan, a UCG graduate and subsequently a lecturer in the Education Department, recalls how in her field, teaching was also an essential part of the research process:

It is very important that people go out and see people teaching in the classroom, because you can become very cut-off from reality if you don't. And you learn a huge amount by going into the schools, by seeing. You can be inspired by fantastic ideas that these young teachers come up with. It re-energises you, because there is always the danger of becoming an academic ivory tower, particularly with a practical programme. This is heresy now but I'm going to say it anyway ... there's a huge emphasis on research at the moment ... but in education I say where are you going to get the people who are going to do the research in a number of years if you don't turn out good practitioners first?

ATTENDING CONFERENCES

Attending international conferences and meetings of professional associations also proved rather difficult for UCG academics, as budget restrictions meant that in many cases they had to fund at least part of these trips from their own pockets, as Prof. O'Donovan explains:

I would go to meetings of the Physiological Society, and they were always held in London or Oxford or someplace, and you had to fly over, you had to stay, you had to feed yourself, and all the rest, and ... you'd apply to the Finance Committee for money to go. And if you applied for £100 you got £50, and if you applied for £200 you got a £100, which they never gave me, and I remember the big thing was that they give you the flight. I remember saying to one of the staff members one day, 'How do they expect me to stay at the meetings, spend three days there, book into a hotel and all the rest?'

'Well', he said, 'what you're supposed to do is to fly over to London or Oxford and sit on the steps and put up a notice saying, 'I'm from UCG, I've no money to stay in a hotel, please help me out.' It was hard going.

Things did improve over time, however:

> Well, after some years then … we got what is called the Triennial Grant. Now that was tremendous … it wasn't that it was very high, but at least you could plan. So in other words in 1976 say, you see that until 1979 I have this much amount of money, maybe £300 or so. And I can use that to go to an international meeting in the States, or in Japan or wherever it would be. It wouldn't pay fully, but you could keep it all for that, or you could spend it on going to smaller meetings elsewhere, and so on, so 'twas yours. The college didn't worry too much so long as they knew you were going and giving your paper. The other thing is there was no question of going to a meeting without giving a paper … I mean your paper would be published and to survive you had to, it was pointless going to meetings without giving a [paper].

Attendance at international conferences not only benefited the academics who attended, keeping them in touch with the latest research and promoting their own research, it also was important in promoting the reputation of the university abroad. Prof. Eamon O'Dwyer was one professor who very much appreciated this fact:

> I belong to a group called the Gynaecological Visiting Society of Great Britain and Ireland … and they used to call me, jokingly, the Aer Lingus Travelling Professor of Obstetrics. I was always either coming or going from some meeting. I went to Norway, for example, on behalf of WHO to advise the Norwegian government on primary health-care education in the Arctic Circle. I went to Warsaw with the secretary of the Department of Health in Dublin as a member of a team to advise the Polish government on what was called C&C, collaboration and cooperation, how could they get better service, and we were there for the Solidarity uprising. It was very important, and I'll tell you why. When I first went to the UK, to one of these gynaecological meetings, a fellow said to me, one of the members, 'I know where Galloway is, that's in Scotland', he said, 'but I don't know where Galway is.' 'It's in Ireland,' I said. 'Ah yes, I know it's in Ireland, but where in Ireland?' 'Well you know where Shannon Airport is?' 'I do'. 'Well if you get out at Shannon Airport and go directly north for 50 miles you'll hit Galway.' So, they all knew where Galway was after that.

SHORTAGE OF TELEPHONES

Telephones were in short supply in the university for many years, and the telephone in the porter's lodge in the Archway was among the busiest of those that were available. Prof. Jim Flavin recalls that for the resident porter, Pádraig Ó Fatharta, keeping the lines of communication open in the college was no easy task: 'Do bhíodh ar Phádraig rith timpeall an coláiste, ag feachaint an bhfeadeadh sé teacht ar an duine a bhí á lorg, agus, mar a deirfeá, na coat-tails flying in the breeze.' ('Pádraig had to run around the college, to see if he could find the person that was required, with, as they say, the coat-tails flying in the breeze.')

Although for many years the telephone system in the college was somewhat primitive, as Prof. Tom O'Connor recalls, having a live-in porter, complete with a wife and family, as was the case with Pádraig Ó Fatharta, somehow made the limited system available work:

> The telephone system in the college at the time was they had an exchange there, with about five or six lines, I think one to the President's Office, one to the Bursar's Office, the Registrar's Office, the supervisor of exams, the library, this was in the Quad, and the Engineering School, and the Anatomy School. And it was one of these ones where the little eyeball drops down when you pick it up and you have to ring up and then you have to connect the wires and plug them in to connect various people, one to the other. So you'd have people doing that. But that was the only public telephone in the university, so the calls would come in, and Pádraig's wife, or whoever it was, would direct people, would put them through to the different departments. But inevitably if there was a phone call for me he'd send over one of the children, and you'd have this little one would come in and say, 'You're wanted on the telephone.' And you'd have to trot across to the Archway to take the phone call there.

Pádraig Ó Fatharta and his family weren't the only ones having to tear around the college trying to find people who were wanted on one of five telephones available on campus in the 1960s. Prof. Dan O'Donovan remembers one such occasion well:

> One night, I was going through the Archway, I was picking up my mail and the telephone rang. And Pádraig said to me, 'Oh, this is a phone call from America, it's for Professor de Valera.' And I said, 'I'll go down and get her,' there were no extensions in the place. And I ran down to Áras de Brún, and she had gone, and then came back, breathless, to tell this man from Columbia University that Professor de Valera was gone home. He was wondering why I took so long to answer him.

STAFF TAKING ON MANY RESPONSIBILITIES

With limited numbers of staff available, and both student numbers and departments expanding considerably, it was often the case that academic staff were forced to take on many and various roles in the college, in addition to their teaching commitments. Bobby Curran recalls being told a funny story in this regard by the professor of classics, Mairéad Ní Éimhigh:

> I was very friendly with her when she was dean of arts. The conversation went around to somebody who was a professor in the 1890s or what have you, and he had come from Oxford, or one of these places, and he was asked to assume the professorship of X, I don't remember the details, and then the professorship of Y came up and they said, 'Sure, the professor of X, he'll handle the Y.' So he became professor of Y. And I think there was something else came up after that and he was made lecturer in Z. And talking about him, Máiréad Ní Éimhigh, said it wasn't so much a chair he had as a couch![16]

Most professors and other academics appear to have lived quite close to the college – indeed for a time this was a condition of their employment – and most walked into work each day. In common with many of his colleagues, Joe McGrath recalls that one of his professors, Prof. Mitchell, would have been a very fit man, given the amount of walking he had to do in a day: 'Every day he walked up to the college in the morning, he walked back for his lunch, he walked back to the college again and in the evening he walked home. He had no car.'

The fact that most of the college's academic staff lived relatively close to the university, and in the case of Prof. Stephen Shea, who was professor of medicine, and his wife Prof. Margaret Shea of the German Department, lived right on the river at Newcastle, proved a great boon during the war years when petrol was in short supply, as Dr Sheila Mulloy recalls:

> They lived up Newcastle direction, and they came down by boat to college during the war. You see they lived right up in Newcastle, and college was down here, and you went back for your lunch you see, so they used to come down in a boat, during the war.

Prof. Seán Lavelle recalls that Prof. Cilian Ó Brolcháin was one of the few professors at the time who did have a car, but, as he recalls, he was the least likely to have needed one:

16 Prof. Ní Éimhigh might well have been talking about herself, as she was appointed as lecturer, and later professor of Latin in 1931, the same year George Derwent Thomson was appointed as lecturer, and later professor of Greek. When Thomson returned to Cambridge to teach in 1934, Ní Éimhigh took on both roles, thereby becoming professor of classics.

He lived directly opposite the college gate. And he used to come out of his house in the morning, get into the car, do a U-turn on the road, and drive into the college and park just outside the Archway, on the left hand side. And then at 2 o'clock, he was lecturing all day, he had a lot of lectures, and he would come out, get into the car, do a U-turn in the college, and go out and park in front of the house.

One other lecturer who had a rather distinctive car was Ralph Ryan of the Engineering Department, as George Deacy remembers:

We had Ralph Ryan coming in ... and he was driving the big yellow Dodge, and everyone in the town knew him, knew who owned the big yellow Dodge, because you know they had all the small Fords at the time, and he had this big yellow Dodge. I think he must have brought it in from the States or something. Big leather seats in it. But huge, huge, 'twas like a big Cadillac, he'd be smilin' away and him sat in it.

Early on, professors lived close to college because it was convenient for them, and there was no shortage of suitable houses to be had within the city boundary. However, with the continued growth of Galway city, one of the biggest difficulties facing new lecturers coming to work in UCG in the 1960s was the requirement that academic staff must live within the city boundary, as Prof. Etienne Rynne explains:

Prof Hayes-McCoy changed the whole attitude to newcomers coming to Galway.[17] He lived in Dublin but he used to come down on Tuesdays and go back on Thursdays or Fridays, and he stayed in the Great Southern Hotel. And Professor Duignan felt that Hayes-McCoy had gone up and down and he felt that wasn't good enough. He was the one that brought in the new rule, that all newcomers who were appointed by the college had to live within the city boundary. We started off at the top of Taylor's Hill in a rented house, there were no houses in Galway, the place had got so big. I was eleven months in Galway and I looked for permission to live in Athenry, because I couldn't afford a house in Galway, Galway was the dearest for houses in Ireland at the time. I applied for permission to live in Athenry, and Duignan told me he voted against me because he felt he had to because he had brought in the rule and all the rest. So I got turned down. I remember going to meet President Newell, in the President's House. I went in and talked to him and told him why ... so he gave me permission, he said he would, for a year, and 'perhaps a bit more if necessary while you're moving.

17 Gerard A. Hayes-McCoy was appointed professor of history in 1958, a position he held until his death in 1975.

But you'll keep looking for houses within the time.' So I said, 'Yeah.' So I stayed out here, and I've been here ever since.[18]

Interestingly, the somewhat unorthodox working arrangements of Prof. Hayes-McCoy proved to be surprisingly productive in terms of his research, Prof. Rynne explains:

> Hayes-McCoy managed quite well in fact. The thing is that he managed to write an awful lot. He wrote longhand, he didn't type. He had beautiful handwriting and he used to write on the train, coming down and going back. He did an article for me, and a big important article, I don't know how he did it at all. He was very good. So there was an advantage in the commuting.

Another professor who commuted from Athenry, and who became a great friend of Prof. Rynne's, was Prof. Margaret Heavey,[19] who was recalled with great fondness by everyone interviewed for this project who had known her. Prof. Rynne's recollections of her are typical:

> Margaret A. Heavey, she was Ma Heavey, and she was such an intelligent and lovable person, that when the dean of the faculty came up at some stage she was elected dean, in her old age, probably the first woman dean ever, dean of arts. She was a lovely person, and she was an excellent dean – terribly human ... a gentlewoman if you can say that. And she was also excellent at languages ... I noticed something I found the other day, some little holy brochure or something, in German, she had translated it from the German into English, so she was fluent in languages and suchlike obviously. So she was a marvellous woman. I think she was one of the most loved women I knew in the place.

THE ROLE OF THE PRESIDENT

Prior to his appointment as president, Monsignor Hynes had already served the college in a number of capacities, starting in 1911, when he was appointed dean of residence at UCG, the first Catholic priest to occupy that position since the Synod of Thurles.[20] He was appointed secretary in 1914 and registrar in 1916. In 1924, he became professor of archaeology, a position he retained when he assumed the role of president.

---

18 Prof. Rynne's interview was conducted in his home in Athenry.   19 Professors and lecturers at UCG often used both the English and Irish forms of their names. Prof. Margaret Heavey was also known as Prof. Mairéad Ní Éimhigh.   20 The Synod of Thurles, which took place in St Patrick's College, Thurles, Co. Tipperary, in 1850, was the first formal synod of Catholic episcopacy and clergy since 1642. It marked the beginning of a movement to standardize the administration, religious practices, teaching and discipline of the Catholic church in Ireland.

By all accounts an extremely affable man, with a keen interest in the welfare of students, Monsignor Hynes proved to be a well-liked figure in the college – so much so that he was given something of a hero's welcome when he returned to the college as the new president in 1934, the *Irish Press* reporting that:

> Some 300 students assembled at the railway station to welcome in the new president on his return from Dublin.[21] Fog signals burst as the train arrived. Fr Hynes was chaired to an open car and escorted through the streets by a cheering crowd.[22]

The students accompanied Fr Hynes through the streets as far as the college.

Popular with students as he was, Monsignor Hynes also proved to be an astute administrator, with an eye to an opportunity. As we have seen, in 1910, at a time of acute financial crisis in the college, he had lobbied the county councils of Connacht until they agreed to strike a rate to support the college. His efforts had resulted in an annual increase of funding of £3,000, guaranteeing the college's survival. As president, Monsignor Hynes was also instrumental in identifying another important opportunity for the college. He saw the advantage UCG had in terms of the high levels of Irish available among its teaching staff, and envisaged a new scholarship programme that would not only provide a significant boost to the numbers of students attending UCG but also attract the very best students to the university. His successor, Monsignor de Brún, took up Monsignor Hynes' plan in earnest, and the result was the Aiken Scholarships, initiated in 1947, which transformed the fortunes of UCG.

MONSIGNOR DE BRÚN

In 1945, Monsignor Hynes was succeeded as president by another monsignor and eminent scholar, Pádraig de Brún. The words 'an extraordinary man' were applied to Monsignor de Brún by practically all those interviewed who had had the benefit of knowing him.[23]

Perhaps even more than his predecessor, Monsignor de Brún was a committed proponent of the Irish language, and it was he who would oversee the renaissance in the college's fortunes that began with the introduction of the Aiken Scholarships.

However, despite Monsignor de Brún's undoubted abilities, the administrative skills needed to run a university did not come easily to him. Furthermore, the

21 The local press noted that during Monsignor Hyne's tenure at the college enrolment had increased from 197 in the academic year 1913/14 to 610 in the academic year 1934/5. *Connacht Tribune*, 27 Oct. 1934. 22 *Irish Press*, 27 Oct. 1934. 23 Monsignor Pádraig de Brún (1889–1960) was a mathematician, poet and classical scholar who served as president of UCG 1945–59. He had been taught mathematics in both Rockwell College and Holy Cross College, Clonliffe by Éamon de Valera, who remained a lifelong friend. He was also a close friend of the executed 1916 leader Seán Mac Diarmada.

administration of the college during his presidency was severely hampered by a lack of secretarial support, as Prof. Tom O'Connor explains:

> He had no secretary, nothing of that sort. That was one of the problems that used to keep arising, because he used to sometimes answer students, send back an answer, and there was no record of what he'd said at all. Or he'd write on the back of a letter he'd got and send it back. So Professor Mitchell, who was the registrar, was always trying to chase around, to pick up the bits and see what [had been agreed].

His administrative shortcomings notwithstanding, Monsignor de Brún was a noted scholar, with a special interest in mathematical physics, and during his presidency many well-known academics, scholars, writers and artists visited the college and delivered lectures to which staff were invited. Prof. Tom O'Connor, then a young lecturer in the Physics Department, was often called upon to help out at these lectures, as he explains:

> He used to have all sorts of distinguished visitors, and they would give public lectures in the university. And he used to come in from his office into the Physics Department, and he would say 'Look, we have somebody coming along this afternoon, so would you come and work the slide projector,' or whatever had to be done, 'and come in afterwards for a *deoram* [a small alcoholic beverege]', though I was a teetotaller at the time. Anyway, he used to entertain quite lavishly. I remember Bondi came,[24] and, 'Why is it dark at night?' was one of his talks. Why is it dark at night, it shouldn't be with all the stars that are out there. And there was one very memorable talk he had one night, from Sir Shane Leslie.[25] Sir Shane Leslie was a very gaunt, striking figure with a kilt, but he was giving a talk in the Greek Hall. And at that stage the heating was provided by a turf fire in the room. So he insisted on putting the lights out, because he wanted to talk about you being fey,[26] and the various sort of stories he had from Glaslough and the place he had there. So we had this gaunt figure with the flickering fire, turned off the lights, and you'd these ghost stories. Which I must say was a very memorable night as well.

RELATIONSHIP BETWEEN ACADEMICS AND STUDENTS

The paternalistic/maternalistic aspect of the relationship between lecturers, professors and students extended to both ensuring that the students worked hard and

24 Sir Hermann Bondi was a noted physicist and astronomer.   25 Sir John Randolph Leslie, 3rd Baronet, generally known as Shane Leslie (1885–1971) of Glaslough, Co. Monaghan.   26 The term 'fey' is used to convey an impression of vague unworldliness or mystery. The word comes from the Old English word *fǣge*, literally 'fated to die soon', which refers to the spiritual state a person is in just before they die.

did well, but also, on a more practical level, that they retained their much-valued scholarships. The small numbers in the college, certainly in the early years, ensured that students were well known to their professors, and, within reason, enjoyed a very good and somewhat more informal relationship with them than would have been the norm in larger institutions. This is perhaps best reflected in the appellations 'Ma' and 'Pa' given to various professors and lecturers – and, indeed, presidents – in the college over the decades. Dr Séamus Mac Mathúna reflects on this:

> Bhuel, ar bhealach tá sé spéisiúil, an méid den bhfoireann ban go raibh an t-ainm 'Ma' ag gabháil leo – Ma Heavey, Ma Creaven san siopa caifé, Ma Shea, an tOllamh le Gearmáinis, Ma O'Driscoll, an Feitheoir Ban, agus a leithéid. Agus fiú, cé go raibh sé i bhfad imithe sular tháing mise anseo, tugadh Pa Hynes ar an Monsignor Seán Ó hEidhin, a chríochnaigh suas mar Uachtarán, agus mar an gcéanna tugadh, is dóigh liom, Pa Browne ar an Monsignor Pádraig de Brún, a tháinig ina áit. Mar sin, bhí cineál blas *'in loco parentis'* ag baint leis an áit.

> Well, in a way it is interesting the number of women staff who had the appellation 'Ma' attached to them – Ma Heavey, Ma Creaven in the coffee shop, Ma Shea, the professor of German, Ma O'Driscoll, the lady superintendent, and suchlike. And even Monsignor Hynes, who ended up as president and who had gone long before I came here, was called Pa Hynes, and Monsignor Pádraig de Brún, who succeeded him, was, I understand, likewise called Pa Browne. So there was a kind of *'in loco parentis'* flavour to the place.

Among the most striking elements of this relationship was the fact that it was a common practice to call on professors in their homes in order to establish whether one had passed one's exams, thereby circumventing the long, usually tense wait for the official exam results to be announced, as Eibhlín Uí Chionna recalls:

> When the exams were done and you felt the results were ready, it must have been some grapevine told you that the professors were finished, you got up on your bicycle and you cycled around and went to the professors' houses. I went out to Professor Dillon to say, 'How did I do?' Now I suppose if you knew that you'd failed you mightn't do it, though some did. And then you went off to your physics man, and I remember well going out to Salthill to Martin Newell, a lovely man, he was living out in Salthill at the time, and getting my results. There was a story about Dillon – he was always famous for his smile, he always smiled. And somebody went out to Dillon to see how they did in chemistry, and he replied, 'I'm afraid you've failed,' and the

smile was bigger than ever. He had a lovely smile, and so they always said, 'A man may smile and smile and be a Dillon.'[27]

Prof. Seán Tobin fondly remembers a visit to one of his professors, Prof. Martin Newell, and recalls the warmth and kindness of the professor's wife, Noreen Newell, and her great good humour:

> I suppose it was our first year now, and having seen Tommy Dillon, Professor Dillon, [my friend and I], greatly emboldened, went out to see Professor Newell, who lived at the time reasonably close to the Sacre Coeur Hotel. And Mrs Newell was painting the gate, the wooden gate and gate-post, and we said was it alright if we asked Dr Newell about our results. 'Oh certainly boys, go on in there', she said, 'knock on the door.' So he came out and he said, 'Oh yes, you've done all right, you've done quite well,' he said. And we had a little chat with him and then we left. And I always remember Mrs Newell, who was a great character actually, we were both on our bicycles and just as we were getting on our bicycles she was saying to us, 'Boys, stick to your books or you'll wind up like me,' waving her paintbrush. She was a woman with a great sense of fun … she had a great sense of humour.

While the exam process itself was obviously stressful for students, exam papers could occasionally throw up interesting examples of creative thinking for lecturers. Like many of his colleagues, having become a lecturer himself, Prof. Seán Tobin found the marking of exam papers a sometimes fascinating experience:

> Some years ago, correcting a Matric paper, now the mathematics was in no way complicated, but one guy on this Matric paper had made an error, and then another error, and then another one. Quite often what can happen is that a student takes his result from here and goes on to the next page, and brings over a sine or something wrong, and then of course he's in trouble again, but this student that I'm talking about … I counted something like twelve or thirteen distinct mistakes, not just transcriptions, I mean logical mistakes, and yet came out with the right answer at the end. Total, absolute, ultimate fluke, and I said to myself, I must make a copy of this, and make several copies, because I intended to give it to my first-year class next year, asking them to find the mistakes, giving them a correct answer, but there were some mistakes along the way. Ah but damn it, I put it somewhere, and lost it, and I always wanted it because it was the most wonderful example.

27 The witty reference is to the original line 'one may smile, and smile, and be a villain' delivered by Hamlet in Shakespeare's *Hamlet*, act 1, scene 5.

Although students may have found that their very visibility, due to the relatively small numbers, tended to somewhat 'cramp their style', there is also a sense that they very much valued the sense of community that the college clearly provided.

EXAM BOARDS

Some professors, as we have seen, were known to students as being inclined to help them if they ran into difficulties at the exam boards. Dr Ben Corballis recalls that Prof. Tommy Dillon was one such man:

> He was such a nice man and all of his students would always say if you're close to passing, and it comes before the board, Tommy Dillon will set you right, he'll get them to give you another couple of points, you know?

Bobby Curran recalls that Prof. Eoghan McKenna was another who showed great compassion towards students in getting them through, particularly in their degree exams:

> That's where McKenna was marvellous. McKenna was professor of maths physics, but he was also *maor na scrúdaithe*, the supervisor of exams, and McKenna used to fight for everyone. We used to do the same now, myself and X would do the same. I make no bones about it, we'd go in and we'd have a lot of the hurlers and the footballers and we knew they were in trouble. Science, engineering, commerce faculty, I was at every faculty, bar medicine, because mathematics was in all of them. I would be tipped off that A, B, C, D, E, F and G were in trouble. So when I'd go in anyway, and I'd look at the sheet that'd be put in front of us, and I'd see L, M, N and O, nothing to do with football or hurling, in trouble also, and I'd pick on one of them and fight his case. And if that one fell, then all the others would fall in tandem.

Exam Board meetings often had their lighter moments also. Prof. Richard Butler remembers one particular incident well:

> These meetings went on all day, and into the nights sometimes, going through all these students. And we came back anyway after lunch, and there was some student up, I forget the actual details, but maybe he had 37 per cent or something ... and after looking at his performance I said, 'Raise him to 40 per cent, and give him a pass.' And [the president] said, 'Oh, chemistry had a good lunch!' And I never forgot it. He got his pass.

LEARNING THE CRAFT: THE JOB OF TEACHING

In the days when staff numbers were still relatively low in relation to the increasing numbers of students coming to the college, teaching schedules for some lecturers were punishing, as experienced secondary-school teacher and lecturer in education Maureen Langan-Egan explains:

> Young teachers, even if they've worked in other jobs, what really amazes them is how tired they are the first year teaching. And mandatory reading for all teachers I think should be Bryan McMahon's book *The master*. He used to talk about taking the nap, and 'the sediment of the day',[28] and he has never got the notice that he should have I think, I don't know why.

Prof. Iognáid Ó Muircheartaigh recalls having had a very heavy schedule when he took up the position of statutory lecturer in statistics in the Mathematics Department in 1970:

> I was teaching an incredible amount by modern standards. In my early years here I remember teaching fourteen lectures a week, fourteen hours of lectures a week, ranging from second-year agricultural science, right up to M.Sc.-level courses. It was extremely wearing, and stressful. When I came here I had really no experience at all, and had to learn on my feet, and just do it. And I think I'm still learning, I'm still teaching.

Prof. Ó Muircheartaigh is one of the many lecturers interviewed who believed that no matter how involved one became in research, administration or college management work, one should still continue to teach, and have contact with students, even, as in his own case, when he was in the final year of his term as college president:

> This year, I've one course going on still, I never gave it up. I really just believe you should do it, it's what we do, and I think it's good for me to see students. I mean I'm in this office working extremely hard, every day, every minute, and never see a student at all, but at least one hour a week, Monday morning at 9 o'clock, I go in there and stand in front of ninety First Med students and talk about statistics, and I like it, it's good.

With over thirty years of teaching experience, Prof. Ó Muircheartaigh makes the point that preparation is still of paramount importance in delivering a good lecture to students:

> You know even though the course I'm teaching at the moment is First Med, and even though I've taught it thirty times, I still have to prepare every

---

28 Bryan McMahon was a teacher, playwright, novelist and short story writer. His autobiography, *The master*, published in 1992, advocated the practice (which he himself followed) of taking a short nap when he returned home from school. McMahon noted that when he got up he would 'find the sediment had settled and the well was clear'. He was able to begin his next activity with a *tabula rasa* (blank slate).

lecture. I've never gone into a lecture without taking time out beforehand and looking at it, no matter how straightforward it is, nothing new in it, and yet I've to sit down and think about it, you know? I do it still. I'm here every Sunday night.

Reflecting on the job of teaching, Prof. Ó Muircheartaigh believes that essentially it is the equivalent of a theatrical performance:

> I enjoyed it. I liked big classes, I'd the O'Flaherty Theatre full, every time, four hundred people, and I mean teaching four hundred people is like a performance. It's a performance, you're on, it's showbiz. You have to keep them under control, keep them alive, and that's what it's about. But I did it, I enjoyed it. But a lecture like that is an hour, it's extremely draining, because you're performing. But I had fourteen hours of that when I was a young lecturer. I wouldn't be able to do it now.

Prof. Etienne Rynne was another lecturer who believes that giving a lecture to a group of students is, in effect, a performance:

> I never sat down at a lecture. I always stand, and I perhaps walk back and forwards a little bit, I move around, because I have to point at the screen. But I didn't use the microphone, I spoke loud, I learned at school, declamation we used to call it, you learned to speak loud. I always spoke to the slides but I didn't read my lectures. It's a performance in a sense, I've always said that, I'm giving a performance. Getting them enthused … that's one of my aims. I didn't have to teach them, when they got enthusiastic they would teach themselves.

Learning the craft of the lecturer was something that many newly appointed lecturers found exhausting. Prof. Rynne recalls his very first lecture after having been appointed to the Archaeology Department:

> My first memory of my first day in college was when I had to lecture on the Hallstatt period, and this was my first lecture in college, ever. Duignan had always lectured on the Hallstatt period on the Continent, which is in the Early Iron Age,[29] it's hardly in Ireland at all. Now I must have done something on that when I was a student I think, but I didn't know much about it anyway. And I went in and lectured to these six students, second and third years together, on the Hallstatt period, my first teaching lecture. And I came out exhausted, because I had been up half the night trying to find something to say.

29 Michael Duignan was professor of archaeology at UCG from 1945 until 1978, when Prof. Rynne succeeded him.

For many young and relatively inexperienced lecturers, seeking refuge in the staff room and recovering their strength for their next lectures was what enabled them to survive the first few months. But when Prof. Rynne decided to take a well-earned rest in the staff room after his first lecture, he discovered that another initiation into the joys of college life awaited him, as he explains:

> The staff room was in the Quadrangle, in the corner. And I walked in and there were two gentlemen there, two elderly gentlemen, sitting down *agus iad ag labhairt na Gaeilge* [and they were speaking Irish]. One was Professor Ó Buachalla, and the other was Professor Ó Brolcháin. And the two of them were *ag labhairt na Ghaeilge* [speaking Irish]. And so I sat down and they started, '*Oh, tá duine nua ann. Cad is ainm duit?*' ['Oh, there is a new person. What is your name?'] And I had to tell them my name, and I remember breaking out in a sweat, my God I've to talk Irish to these two. Which I didn't mind, but just after giving my first lecture. So I spoke Irish to them, and I answered a few questions, and I do remember they asked me my name, naturally, and what was I doing, *seandálaíocht, agus mar sin de* [archaeology, and so on], a lot of the *mar sin de* [and so on]. I remember well telling them that my name was Stiofán Ó Rinne.[30] And they kept calling me Stiofán till later that day I think, and I was walking to my car, and I heard somebody calling 'Stiofán', and I didn't react. Then I turned around and said, 'Oh my God, it must be one of them after me.' Though mind you I would go by that name quite normally, no bother, but when you don't expect it … I think it was Ó Brolcháin was talking to me about something or other. Of course they made me very welcome.

THE ELUSIVE 'PROFESSOR BRADLEY'

Prof. Tom O'Connor recalls an interesting fact regarding Prof. Ó Brolcháin, who was, as we have seen, a keen Irish-language enthusiast. His determination to use only the Irish form of his name was the cause of some confusion to those who were determined to use the English form, as Prof. O'Connor recalls:

> It was one of the amazing things with the department, a tradition, that students would arrive, the very first day in college they'd come looking for Professor Bradley. And, 'There's no Professor Bradley here, there never was a Professor Bradley here.' … [H]e just didn't recognize it. He'd say, 'It's Ó Brolcháin.'

Prof. Ó Brolcháin's love of the Irish language was one of the reasons he was particularly pleased when Éamon de Valera came to UCG in 1959 to preside at the

---

30 Etienne is the French form of the name Stephen, and Stiofán is the Irish form of the same name.

conferrings, in the interregnum between the retirement of the previous president, Monsignor de Brún, and the start of the presidency of Prof. Martin Newell.

Clearly there were some professors in the college for whom Irish was an extremely important part of the college ethos and identity. Occasionally, however, a professor's preoccupation with the subject gave rise to some amusing incidents with students. The following story, recounted by Tony Bromell, relates to Prof. Tomás Ó Máille, who was professor of Irish:

> Bhí scéal ann faoi Ó Máille. Bhí gluaisteán aige, rud nach raibh ag mórán daoine ag an am, agus bhí sé ag teacht isteach an geata agus deirtear gur leag sé duine dos na mic léinn. Agus bhuail sé amach as a ghluaisteán agus ar seisean 'an bhfuil tú gortaithe?' 'Tá mé' arsa mo dhuine. 'Oh ná habair "tá mé" a duirt sé, 'abair TÁIM, TÁIM'.[31]

> There was a story about Ó Máille. He had a car, something which not many people had at the time, and he was coming in the gate and it is said that he knocked down one of the students. And he jumped out of the car and he said, 'Are you injured?' 'I am,' said the guy. 'Oh don't say "I am [*tá mé*],"' he said. 'Say I AM, I AM [*TÁIM, TÁIM*].'

Having accidentally knocked down the young man and enquired as to whether he had been injured, Prof. Ó Máille went on to correct him on the correct form of the phrase 'I am' he should use in the context of the event being described.

An insistence on the maintenance of high standards in the Irish language was extremely important to a great many professors in the college, but, as professors themselves might admit, even Homer nods on occasion. Tony Bromell relates a story about one of the gentlemen encountered by Prof. Rynne in the staff room on his fateful first day, Prof. Liam Ó Buachalla: 'Déarfadh sé "Tá an Ghaeilge ar fheabas ar fad. Níl aon ábhar chomh teibí sin nach féidir é a chur i ngeibh sa Ghaeilge. Tá sé, mar a deirfeá, an-precise." Agus ní fhaca sé an ghreann.' ('He used to say, "Irish is a marvellous language. There is no subject so abstract that it cannot be explained in Irish. It is, as they say, very precise." And he didn't see the humour.')

Most academics would maintain that they developed their own teaching style in part from learning from the examples shown them by lecturers or teachers who had previously taught them. An early piece of advice received in relation to his own work was very much taken to heart by Prof. Seán Tobin, and was reflected both in his own writing and in his feedback to students on their work, as he recalls:

> I fancied myself very good at English, and remember, you know, that 'pride always goeth before a fall'. It always stuck in my memory, the comment

31 '*Táim*' relates to the Foirm Táithe, where there is a synthesis of the verb and personal pronoun in one word. '*Tá mé*' relates to the Foirm Scartha, where the verb and the subject are in two separate words. '*Táim*' was the correct form in this instance.

written below an essay of mine by a teacher in secondary school – it said, 'Words are like leaves, and where they most abound much fruit of sense beneath is rarely found.' [32]

One suspects, therefore, that the advice 'Brevity is the soul of wit' was best heeded in submitting work to this particular mathematics professor.

Some professors took an unusual approach to the teaching of their subject. Joe McGrath recalls the somewhat unorthodox lecturing method of Prof. Mitchell:

> He was the registrar, and he was our professor of geology. He'd come in and for half an hour, he would lecture us, a solid lecture, and for the rest of the time he would dictate that lecture to us and we'd write it all down. I thought it was an extraordinary method. Yes, he'd talk for maybe a bit over half an hour, and then he'd go over that again and he'd dictate it to you, you could take down every word. Although it would have saved him an awful lot of trouble if he could have copied it out.

Bringing a subject like archaeology to life is difficult without field trips, and UCG was fortunate that Prof. Rynne was committed to taking students out of the lecture hall and leading them on visits to archaeological sites and museums. The first step in establishing a field-trips programme was the establishment of an Archaeological Society in the college, as Prof. Rynne explains:

> I asked why they hadn't got an Archaeological Society? So I got [the students] to start up an Archaeology Society and I gave them some general lectures and led them on most Sundays on field trips, starting with one to the Burren. I also used to take them to see museums and monuments abroad. Well, you can't do archaeology without seeing museums. I can show them all the ringforts they want and the megaliths they want, but I can't show them the objects, and I am very keen on artefacts, having worked in the museum myself. You can't date a ringfort unless you know what's been found in it.

PROFESSORS HELPING OUT WITH SOCIETIES

Becoming involved in the activities of the various college societies was something some academics took on by choice – or in some cases they were 'persuaded' by senior academic staff. When Prof. Seán Tobin returned to the college as an assistant lecturer in mathematics in 1956 he was inveigled into becoming an unofficial chauffeur for some of the societies, as he explains:

32 W. Shakespeare, *Hamlet*, act 2, scene 2, 86–92.

There was the various clubs, the football, hurling, soccer and rugby, and various professors had particular interests in those. For instance Eoghan McKenna, the father of Siobhán, was, when I came here, professor of mathematical physics, a very nice man indeed. But he had a great interest in the football club … and did all he could to help it. The professor of English, Professor Murphy, he was interested in the drama, DramSoc, the Drama Society, and the Rowing Club. And indeed when I came back on the staff, Jerry Murphy, he kind of shanghaied me really, he buttonholed me, 'Oh you might help me.' He had me helping him to transport the Drama Society around the country to odd little halls out in the country and also helping to take some of the fellows on the rowing teams around, and so on.

ADVISING STUDENTS

It was part of the duties of academic staff to advise students on their first days in the college as to which subjects they should take. Prof. Seán Tobin recalls being asked to fulfil this role at an early stage in his career:

When I became an assistant, in the early days I remember being asked by Jerry Murphy, who was the dean of the Arts Faculty at the time, to sit in the Aula, with other members of staff, and meet the incoming students, and advise them on what to do. And in those days it was very, very free and easy, and not organized really. You sat there, and students came along – there was no central applications office in those days – and they'd come along and they'd say, 'I'd like to study English,' or, 'I want to study science,' and you might say to them, 'Well, why? What's your particular interest? I can only advise you, what's your particular interest, what do you really like to do?' So I remember this girl came along, from Kerry. I was sitting at one of these rickety desks that fold up, and I remember that girl coming along and she said, 'I think I want to study arts.' And I said, 'Well that's fine, is there something particular that you want to study in the arts?' 'Yes', she said, 'I like English'. 'Oh', I said, 'well that's a very interesting subject, a very broad subject, and of course if you really like it then I'm sure you'd be very happy doing it'. 'Of course I like it', she said, 'sure I *ates* books'. So I said, 'I'm sure you'll be fine so.'

KEEPING AN EYE ON TROUBLED STUDENTS

While it was primarily the role of the lady superintendent and the dean of residence (commonly known as the chaplain) to provide pastoral care to students who might occasionally be troubled or in difficulty, the small, intimate nature of the college meant that in many cases the role of lecturer or professor was often a great deal more pastoral in nature than would have been the case in other universities, and there are many stories of academic staff putting themselves out considerably in looking out for the interests of students. Maureen Langan-Egan recalls how her Irish professor, Tomás Ó Máille, sought her assistance in relation to a fellow student of hers whom he considered needed some help:

> Tomás Ó Máille was a very caring man – well, he could be. I remember a student who almost cracked up, and went missing … the terrible distress, just with overworking and a more competitive environment, and she would also be the type of girl to put herself under pressure. But I remember him asking me at the time to more or less keep an eye on this one and I reported her … she wasn't that long missing at the time, but somebody gone like that you still worried. And I reported her to the guards in Eglinton Street, and they gave her the forty-eight hours. Anyway she came back, and decided she was going to go home … She worked out alright. But he was concerned about her, oh very, very concerned.

The pastoral care of students is something many professors took very seriously, and in one particular case it may indeed have saved the life of a student. One such student was Pat Lindsay, later a Fine Gael senator, senior counsel and master of the high court. But in his student days Pat Lindsay's political beliefs came to the fore at a volatile time in world politics, as Jo Burke recalls:

> There was a great story about Pat. He was with Prof. Fahy. Fahy was a priest now, and the Civil War in Spain [was on], it was,[33] Franco's thing, there were a crowd of Irish fellas going off in a boat to help. But didn't Pat say he'd go too. And down he headed to the docks. Fahy heard and went down, and took him away. 'Pat, why are you going off there for, will you come back and get your degree, and go better yourself?' He was a brilliant fellow you see. So he rescued Pat anyway from going over to Spain. He brought him back again. He came back and finished his degree. He was a brilliant fella Pat.

THE LEARNING PROCESS OFF CAMPUS: TRAINING DOCTORS

Taking responsibility for the training of young doctors was clearly onerous, and all the evidence would suggest that the professors in the Faculty of Medicine worked their students hard to ensure that they got the best possible training in preparation for their future careers. The life of a student doctor had its lighter moments however, often due to interactions with professors. While on hospital rounds during their clinical training student doctors were required to follow their instructors around from patient to patient. The numbers involved meant that getting close to the professor concerned, and the patient under discussion, was sometimes difficult, especially if, like Dr Ben Corballis, you were a tall, 16-stone American.

33 The Spanish Civil War lasted from 17 July 1936 to 1 Apr. 1939.

Michael O'Donnell, he was one of these very soft-spoken fellas. And I remember one day we were standing at the bedside, and he said something, and then asked me a question. I was in the second or third row. So I said, 'I'm sorry sir, I didn't hear the question.' And he said, 'And whose fault is that?'

The pressures on medical students, between their clinical responsibilities and their studies, was immense, and not surprisingly they took the opportunity, whenever possible, to let off some steam and have some fun. The professors charged with their training were generally amenable to this, provided it did not impact negatively on the student's work, but Prof. Eamon O'Dwyer recalls one situation where his desire to facilitate his students brought him into conflict with the most powerful man in the university – the president, Monsignor de Brún:

> The students came one day, you see they lived in residence in the hospital, there were eight of them living in, and they came to me and said, 'We'd like to have a party.' 'You mean a sort of a drinking party?' 'Oh yes, of course.' And I said, 'Well look, as you're all students of the college, and as the president is responsible ultimately for you, I better ask him.' So I went over to see him and I said, 'Monsignor, the students over in maternity would like to have a party, and I told them I'd come and get your permission for it.' 'There's to be no party,' he said. 'Oh', I said, 'no party! You tell me no party, and the parties you give', I said, 'the soirées that you have over beyond, which we all attend'. 'I said no party.' 'Alright,' said I. So I went back to the hospital, and I met the deputation. 'I'm sorry,' I said, 'The president said no. But wait now', I said, 'I am the professor here and head of the Department of Obstetrics and Gynaecology, but I'm also the Department of Health Director General of this unit. Anybody in this unit works under my direction, be they cleaners, nurses, anaesthetists, pathologists, everyone here, they work under me. I'm the director, so putting on my director's hat, you may have your party, as long as you behave yourselves.' So, they had their party.

GOVERNING BODY MEETINGS

All important decisions relating to appointments, examinations, fiscal and structural planning were decided by the Governing Body, and hence the monthly meetings of this august body were much-anticipated events. The meetings were presided over by the college president, who, depending on his personality, either loved or loathed the task. The meetings were often all-day affairs, so it is hardly surprising that on occasion those attending might have wished they were elsewhere, as Bobby Curran recalls:

> [President Martin Newell] had a hearing aid, he was going a little bit deaf that time. I think some of his deafness now was … polite, or political.

Because I know when I was on the Governing Body with him, he was chairman, he used to turn it down when he didn't want to listen to certain guys, you know?

One long-standing member of the Governing Body was Michael Browne, bishop of Galway. He turns up again and again in the reminiscences of those who served on that body. Prof. Eamon O'Dwyer recalls one particular incident that reveals much about the power the bishop chose to wield over the management team and academics of the university:

> The Governing Body was meeting this day and Michael Duignan was registrar. And he had promised the lecturers that he would put through a monies statute, in which they'd get an increase in stipend. Now a monies statute in the college had to be passed by a majority of the governors, not a majority of governors present at the meeting. You needed a full majority of all of them, a full turnout. The bishop was building his cathedral, and always at about twenty to one at Governing Body meetings he'd begin to fold up his papers, and when he had them folded up neatly he'd bow across the table to Archbishop Joe Walsh from Tuam, and then he'd go to the man from Clare, and then Achonry, and then Loughrea. And then he'd stand up and he'd bow to the chair, and they'd all stand up after him, and then give a little bow and then march off, down to look at the cathedral. He'd go up to Mount St Mary's for a slap-up lunch. So the bishop was gathering his papers, and when Michael saw the bishop doing all this he said, 'President, President, please, please, we should do something. Would you take item twenty-five?' It was way down the list. 'Would you take item twenty-five now before their lordships leave us, because as you know there's a statute that it has to be passed by a majority of the governors, and I promised the lecturers I would bring that up today?' Michael Browne ignored him completely. And then they stood up and as they were passing by our table the bishop turned to Michael Duignan, and was … wagging his finger, 'Let me tell you something, some of us have work to do.' So he walked off towards the door with all the others, and when he got to the door going out, just before he got there he turned around and he said, 'We're not all full-time professors, you know.' And poor Michael Duignan, with a sledgehammer you couldn't have hurt him as much. Anyway, I was sitting there saying to myself thank goodness I didn't get the swipe of the crozier.

One of those who attended the Governing Body meetings in the early '70s, and learned a great deal from the experience, was Pat Rabbitte, who was the first student representative ever to be appointed to a governing body in an Irish university in 1971. For Pat it was a formative experience in his political education, and also brought him into the orbit of the formidable Bishop Browne:

I think you see that as a student leader of 19 years of age, or 20 years of age, you're thrust into an environment where you think you know a great deal more than you do, and you're fearless. And you don't really grasp the politics of the situation, that there were so many different interests involved, and they may not be prepared to come up front, you know? For example, some of the academics would have been very happy to see me prosecute some of the issues that I would raise. There were splinter groups and factions you learned, I mean on the Governing Body, there were frustrated academics, who wanted to make progress on things. There were conservative academics who didn't want to change the way things were. There was Michael Browne, exerting entirely disproportionate influence. So that, you know, it really was a ferment at the time by comparison ... So you had these changing alliances, for different purposes and so on, and they began to get accustomed to the idea of student representatives ... Michael Browne never did, and we had a couple of really stand-up rows, where I did not demonstrate due deference, due respect, etc., as he saw it. And one of the things I remember is we used to go to the Ardilaun after the meetings,[34] for lunch, or dinner if it went on all day. And that was quite an event because that was the main meal that I would get in a month! And there was a special red wine reserved for His Lordship. The rest of us would drink whatever.

As a subsequent president of the students union in 1980/1, Brendan 'Speedie' Smith adopted a different approach to Pat Rabbitte and other previous student-union presidents – except on one particular occasion when, as he relates, pragmatism got the better of him:

Afterwards there was a big dinner, and I never went for dinner because I felt after a few glasses of wine, you know yourself, you became part of the old network, the guard is down. The only time I ever went for dinner with them, I was absolutely broke, during College Week, all my money was spent, and I was starving. I had no choice but to wine and dine with Bishop Casey, for that particular one time, and one time only.

As the main decision-making body in the university, the Governing Body was clearly going to be an important vehicle for bringing about changes in respect of both the academic staff and the student community. However, although students had a representative from 1971, when Pat Rabitte was elected, it wasn't until the mid-'70s that academic staff had designated representatives on the Governing Body, as Prof. Iognáid Ó Muircheartaigh explains:

34 This reference is to the Ardilaun Hotel, on Taylor's Hill in Galway.

At that time a number of professors I think were elected to the Governing Body and the rest were bishops, or county councillors, or whatever. And we said there should be staff, there were no staff, as of right. There were a few professors on the Academic Council, but there was no representative of the academic staff. So we argued, very strongly ... that there should be at least one member of the academic staff elected by all the academic staff. And we won it for the first time around 1976, I think, and John Mulhern of maths physics was elected. And next time round I stood for it, in '79, and got elected, and so I was on the Governing Body representing all the academic staff.

Oh it was great fun. And I felt I had great authority then, although I was a lone voice, but I was representing someone, I wasn't just one of the elite professors who were on there, I was elected by all the academic staff, including the professors. I certainly saw myself as a lone warrior there, representing a whole big constituency out there, and I'd say nine times out of ten, I was a lone voice crying in the wilderness. I mean the number of times I was defeated, like by eighteen votes to two on the Governing Body, or to one, you know? It was lonely. And very wearing. I mean I would be absolutely shattered and exhausted after it. The meetings were three hours, and if you're all the time standing up saying, 'I disagree with this,' and they're saying, 'Oh this idiot.' In those days I was worn out by them.

The Governing Body notwithstanding, the autonomy of the college was somewhat restricted by the fact that most major decisions had to be ratified by the university senate, as Dr Séamus Mac Mathúna explains:

Ag an am sin bhíomar, chomh maith le UCD agus UCC, go mór faoi ordóg Ollscoil na hÉireann, a rabhamar mar Chomh-Choláistí di faoi Acht 1908. Bhain sé sin le torthaí scrúdaithe agus ceapacháin shinsearacha agus chuile shórt mar sin. Ní fhéadfadh an Coláiste torthaí scrúdaithe a thabhairt amach fós go cinnte, mar, go foirmiúil, ba mholtaí, nó torthaí sealadacha, ón mBord Scrúdaithe anseo iad go dtí go nglacfadh Seanad na hOllscoile leo go hoifigiúil, tar éis dá gCoiste Seasta iad a bhreathnú. Go minic bheadh moltaí á gcur ar aghaidh ag an mBord Scrúdaithe áirithe anseo, ar nós go n-ardófaí marcanna áirithe le Pas nó Onóracha a thabhairt do dhuine, nó go dtabharfaí cead do mhac léinn eile teacht ar ais le haghaidh scrúduithe an Fhómhair, nó rud éigin eile den saghas sin – aon rud a bhí lasmuigh des na rialacha díreacha a bhí leagtha síos sa cháipéis Marks and Standards le haghaidh na scrúduithe uiliog. Agus is ag Seanad na hOllscoile a bhí an cinneadh ar na moltaí sin freisin. Ar ndóigh, ba ar chúiseanna eisceachtúla, ar nós tinnis nó cásanna truamhéileacha eile, a chuirtí na moltaí sin ar aghaidh, agus de ghnáth ghlactaí leo. Is cuimhin liom a chlos faoi

chruinniú amháin den gCoiste Seasta ina raibh go leor moltaí den chineál
sin uainne faoina mbráid, go ndúirt oifigeach sinsearach ó Choláiste eile, le
teann spraoi, 'The hand of death is obviously hovering over UCG.' Mar an
gcéanna leis na ceapacháin shinsearacha – ba ag an Seanad a bhí an cinneadh faoi Uachtarán nó Ollúna nó Léachtóirí reachtúla sna Comh-Choláistí
a cheapadh. De ghnáth chuireadh an Coiste Rialaithe, tar éis dóibh moltaí
a fháil ón Dámh áirithe agus ón gComhairle Acadúil, trí ainm, a rogha
féin ina measc, chuig an Seanad, ach bhi de cheart ag an Seanad – faoi
réir, inár gcás féin, forálacha Acht 1929 maidir le hinniúlacht sa Ghaeilge
– éinne den triúr a cheapadh, agus tharla sé sin ó am go chéile, gur chea-
padar duine eile díobh seachas an té a bhí molta ag an gCoiste Rialaithe. Ó
na seachtóidí i leith, áfach, cheap an Coláiste Bord Measúnóirí i ngach cás
agus de ghnáth ghlactaí lena moladh siúd.

At the time we, along with UCD and UCC, were very much under the
thumb of the NUI, of which we were constituent colleges under the 1908
act. That related to exam results and senior appointments and lots of things
like that. The college could not yet issue definite exam results, because formally they were recommendations, or provisional results, from the Exam
Board here pending their official adoption by the NUI Senate, following
consideration by its Standing Committee. Often recommendations would be
forwarded by the particular Exam Board here, such as the raising of certain
marks to give a pass or honours to a particular student, or to permit another
student to repeat at the autumn exams, or something like that – anything
outside the direct rules laid down in the marks-and-standards document
which covered all exams. And the decision on those recommendations also
rested with the Senate. Of course those recommendations would be put
forward on the basis of exceptional circumstances, such as illness or other
sad cases, and they were normally accepted. I recall hearing about one meeting of the Standing Committee which had a lot of such recommendations
from this college before it and at which a senior officer from another college
quipped, 'The hand of death is obviously hovering over UCG.' Likewise,
with senior appointments – the decision on appointment of the president or
professors or statutory lecturers in the constituent colleges rested with the
Senate. Normally, the Governing Body, following receipt of recommendations from the relevant faculty and the Academic Council, would forward
three names, including its own preference, to the Senate, but the Senate had
the right – subject, in our case, to the provisions of the 1929 act regarding
competence in Irish – to appoint any one of the three, and that happened
from time to time, that they appointed somebody other than the person
recommended by the Governing Body. From the 1970s onwards, however,
the Governing Body appointed a board of assessors in each case, and its
recommendation was usually accepted.

GONE FISHING

Outside of the sometimes heated academic and political environment of the college, the attractions of the River Corrib were a major advantage to academic life in Galway – and indeed at certain times they dictated the lecture timetable of some academics, as Bobby Curran recalls:

> When the mayfly came up lectures wouldn't be missed but they would be rescheduled. Because if there was a good wind up from the west and the mayfly was up you could be sure that X was gone fishing. And we'd know that as well, and we'd come back to him then the following week and say, 'You know can we arrange that lecture?' and he'd have no problem with that.

Similarly, Dr Sheila Mulloy recalled that during the mayfly season one of her professors would anticipate his absence by affixing a note to his door which read, 'Béidh mé tinn amárach [I will be ill tomorrow].'

According to Prof. Sean Tobin, students came to expect the temporary absence of lecturers when the call of the river beckoned, and he describes fondly the approach taken by Prof. Martin Newell of the Mathematics Department:

> His students were not suspicious when each year, in early May, he would tell them gravely that he was about to give them a couple of weeks to reflect on their year's work, and that after that he would be back to deal with any difficulties they were unable to resolve. It was only in later years that they realized that the extension of this facility to them coincided with the news that 'the mayfly was up' on Lough Corrib. Professor Power too would vanish and thus did an annual metamorphosis of insect life determine the intellectual biorhythm of the UCG Mathematics Department in those golden days.[35]

According to Seán Mac Iomhair, the mathematicians were not the only keen fishermen: 'Silím go raibh an iascaireacht tabhachtach i gconaí i nGaillimh, agus go h-áiraithe i measc na dochtuiri mar shampla, leis an mayfly. Bhíodh sé an-deacair theacht ar dhochtúir Mí na Bealtaine nuair a bhí an mayfly suas.' ('I think fishing was always important in Galway, and particularly among the doctors, for example, with the mayfly. It was very difficult to come across a doctor in May when the mayfly was up.')

The attraction of Lough Corrib and the River Corrib was not just a boon to academics working at UCG, but, as Prof. Eamon O'Dwyer describes, it greatly added to the attraction of the college to extern examiners:

> I had an extern examiner here from London one year, and after one of the orals in the Aula I said, 'John, will you come out fishing with me?' 'Oh no',

---

35 S. Tobin, 'Mathematics' in Foley (ed.), *From Queen's College to National University*, p. 173.

he said, 'I think I'll put my feet up, and relax Eamon. Aren't we meeting this evening?' 'Oh yes.' 'You go catch your fish.' So I rushed home, put on my [fishing] trousers, went out on the Clare River, near Tuam, literally within twenty minutes I had my fish, about 7 lbs. So I brought him home and put him in the scullery and when John came for the meal he said, 'Well Eamon, I suppose you caught your fish?' 'I did actually.' 'You didn't!' 'I did!' 'Joy, he told me he caught a fish!'[36] 'Oh he did, come out and I'll show it to you.' So I showed him the fish. 'Well, well, well, I never', says he, 'I never'. I was in London examining for the Membership of the College of Obstetricians a month later and a fella came up to me and he said, 'You're from Galway.' 'I am.' 'You're the professor who went out fishing after the oral examination one evening, and caught a fish.' 'Yes, I am.' The stuff of legend! 'Could I come and examine next year?' And I said, 'I'm sorry, there's a waiting list.'

STAFF PARTIES

Although an extremely popular and apparently gregarious man, Monsignor Hynes' presidency was not distinguished by any large degree of entertaining in the president's residence. This may in part be due to the fact that much of his presidency, from 1934–45, took place during the war years when rationing and other restrictions were in place. In 1945, with the war by then over, and a new incumbent in the role of president, things changed quite considerably. During the presidency of Monsignor Pádraig de Brún, parties in the president's residence were commonly held, and everyone was expected to attend and perform their party piece.

The new president was extremely fond of entertaining, with functions organized in particular to celebrate the visits of the variety of academics and artists whom the president invited to the college to give guest lectures from time to time. But the president's penchant for surrounding himself with people may have been due to something other than a love of entertaining. Many of those interviewed expressed the view that as an accomplished, witty and erudite man, the president may often have felt lonely and isolated – an inevitable drawback of his chosen vocation.

For whatever reason, parties were a regular feature of the de Brún presidency, and by all accounts were very much enjoyed by those who attended them. Staff Christmas parties in particular were an opportunity for all of the academic staff to mix socially, and Prof. Pádraig Ó Céidigh recalled his first Christmas party at UCG with great affection:

> Presiding over it was Pádraig de Brún, a great man, he was a hero of mine, and of course he gave his usual rendering, which was 'Lepanto'. He'd stand up, and the leonine head of him, and he'd start 'White founts falling in the courts of the sun, And the Soldan of Byzantium is smiling as they run.'[37]

36 Prof. O'Dwyer's late wife.   37 The opening lines of 'Lepanto' by G.K. Chesterton.

The tradition of staff Christmas parties continued into the presidency of Prof. Martin Newell, and Christmas parties of the '60s and '70s, presided over by President Newell, were, by all accounts marathon affairs, greatly enjoyed by everyone concerned. Seán Mac Iomhair provides a vivid account of the proceedings as he remembers them:

> An sean dinnéar Nollag, thosaigh sé ag a 9 a chlog le seiris san Aula. Ansin bhíodh dinnéar cúig phláta ann, agus tuairim is meanoíche thosaíodh daoine ag damhsa. Thosaigh sé leis na mbean chéile a bhí ag na doctúirí móra, agus dhéineidis siúd damhsa sibhíalta tar éis Mean oíiche. Céad rud ina dhiaidh sin ná disco. Agus ina dhiaidh sin arís dreas céilí, agus bhí tú ag teacht go dtí a ceathar a chlog ar maidin faoin am. Agus ansin a thosaíos an seanchas, agus na party pieces. Agus an uair sin ní raibh cistin ceart sa choláiste agus Ma Creaven dheanadh sí na turcaithe a fháil déanta in áit éicint, agus leagfaí san Aula iad, agus nuair a bhí an béile mór thart, d'fhagfaí na taisi ansin dúinne, chomh maith le mias mór soup. Agus do na daoine nach raibh fonn orthu deireadh a cur leis an oíche, bhí Aifreann ann ag a seacht a chlog ar maidin.

> The old Christmas dinner, started at 9 o'clock with sherry in the Aula. And then there would be a five-course meal, and around midnight people would start dancing. It started with the doctors' wives, and they would dance in civilized manner around midnight. The next thing was the disco. And after that then there would be a few céilí dances, and that took you up to 4 o'clock in the morning. Then the storytelling would start, and the party pieces. And in those days there wasn't a proper kitchen in the college, and Ma Creaven would arrange for the turkeys to be cooked somewhere and brought to the Aula, and when the big meal would be over the leftovers were left for people, and a big colander of soup. And for those who didn't feel inclined to bring the evening to an end, there was Mass at 7 o'clock in the morning.

POOR SALARIES

While teaching jobs in the university were much valued, for a good many years the salaries paid to junior lecturers and assistants were poor. After Jo Burke graduated in 1936 with an honours degree in physics and mathematics, she was offered a position, supervising practicals in the Physics Department, but on a salary that made it very difficult for her to survive, as she explains:

> When I got into the department, I had the princely sum of £90, and £50 for mathematics, £140 a year. And then we stayed in Ward's Hotel for £2 a week, there wasn't a lot left to live on. But Pa Hynes came to me this day and said, 'There's something badly needed in this university, and I wonder

would you do it?' I said, 'What is it?' He said, 'There's students coming in here, and they have no physics at all from secondary school, and they need someone to give them a helping hand in their first year. I'll give you any room you want in college, and take a class at night'. There were so many students passing all the other subjects and failing physics, because very few schools were teaching physics. A lot of schools were doing chemistry, not physics. So he said would you start a new class, and so I started that, and that is really how I managed to survive on my meagre salary in the university. I started grinds then, I used to have huge classes. I had to confine them to forty, any more than that wasn't a help to them, it was more like a lecture. I was giving them the practicals in university, so it dovetailed nicely with what I was doing.

Given the level of highly qualified people being produced by today's universities it is difficult to contemplate a time when qualified graduates willing to take up teaching positions were difficult to come by. But such indeed was the case, and was the reason why Prof. Tom O'Connor, a graduate of UCD, came to Galway in 1956. But as we shall see, the issue of the poor salaries paid to assistant lecturers came once again to the fore, just as it had twenty years previously in the case of Jo Burke, as he explains:

I heard word they were looking for two people in Galway as assistants in physics, because the two honours graduates of that year had failed their exams, so that was the crisis at the end of the first term. So the president, Monsignor de Brún, had known about me in the School of Cosmic Physics, so he offered a place to me, and to Fr Gerard McGreevy, who was a graduate of Maynooth, and who was just doing a master's as well. So the two of us came down here in January 1956 and we were appointed to the position of assistants in physics. And we insisted on having a salary of £450 a year, because that's what you could get from the Post Office or engineering, or some of these other sort of civil-service jobs at the time. And it was much more than any of the other assistants were getting in the university. So we were appointed but the Governing Body, which didn't always agree with the president, and various bishops they had on the Governing Body at the time felt that he had overstepped the mark acting in this way, in appointing us. So he said, 'Look, there's nobody else, this is what we had to do.' So as a result of that we weren't reappointed in June. We had to re-apply for the job, because that time an assistant was employed for ten months of the year, you got paid in ten monthly instalments, you didn't get anything in July and August. Well it didn't make much difference really. You were getting £450 a year, it's about £9 a week or whatever it was. So you paid £3 a week for full board in digs down here as well, so that's what you had to live on. So we came down and started to teach here. And the Physics Department consisted of Prof. Cilian Ó Brolcháin, who'd been a professor since '34, and Declan Larkin who was the lecturer in physics since '47, and then we took over various jobs when we were working there. We had to reapply for our jobs at the end of the summer, and we applied, and we were the only applicants. So that sort of proved that these were the only people that were available.

THE GROWTH OF SCIENCE

Not long into his teaching career at UCG the numbers taking science increased considerably, as Prof. Tom O'Connor explains: 'In 1958 we had a big increase in numbers, because Sputnik went up in 1957, and there was a whole new interest in science.'

UCG has always been good at playing to its strengths, and nowhere is this more apparent than in the development of areas of study related to Galway's maritime environment. Prof. Tom O'Connor explains how this came about in the Physics Department:

We couldn't compete with the MITs[38] of this world but we said we'd get a project which would have the advantage of Galway's maritime situation. So we thought that this was as good a reason as any to look at the maritime air, and that was in '57. And we started looking around for a place where we might do that. Now also, it just turned out that the US Army had been encouraging research in Europe, post-war research in Europe, and they had a research office, and we were the first in fact in physics to get a contract from them, for a year, for the study of ionization equilibrium. We'd put this in, and they had bought it, and they were giving us somewhere around £1,000 for the year, which was very useful.

The funding was just the incentive the Physics Department needed to start the ball rolling on a whole new phase of research, which was to prove critical to the development of meteorological studies. But first there was the challenge of finding the right location to take measurements and conduct experiments – and Prof. O'Connor took a very proactive role in doing just that:

What we wanted was a site where the air was coming in from the ocean, which hadn't passed over any human activity in recent times, so there was no complications from pollution, or roads running around the shoreline, between you and the shore, so that you had pollution from the cars and that sort of thing. But this was difficult to find, everything was on the shoreline. I mean even when you think of Blackhead, the road goes around

38 Massachusetts Institute of Technology (MIT).

between you and the shore. So this was the problem. So I went out in '57 on a bicycle, cycling around. And Paddy Keady was starting in Kilkieran at the time,[39] his research was on Kilkieran Bay. So we spent a while there, and I used to cycle round and go down the various highways and byways. So we came down the Ard Peninisula and out to Mace Head. And Mace Head turned out to be very suitable because it was sticking out into the bay, with just MacDara's Island opposite us, and Croch na Cille, so there was empty space, an uninhabited area, and it was from anywhere from the due south round to north-west, so that's where most of the wind would be coming from anyway, so it was very good from that point of view. And it was on top of the hill, this little head. There was a coastal watch station that had been erected during the Second World War, and it was just abandoned there, some windows were still in it and some of the doors were falling off it, but anyway it was there. And there was a house beside it within about one ESB pole of it, so we were able to get the ESB to put a connection in.

Having found what he considered to be the ideal location for his research station, Prof. O'Connor now needed to gain the approval of his head of department for the expenditure that would be involved in bringing the new facility up to standard. Knowing how the professor of physics operated was a distinct advantage to Prof. O'Connor in this regard:

> Prof. Ó Brolcháin was a very accommodating person in a sense ... so the main thing that you had to do was you had to make the decision and tell him what we were going to do, and he would always agree with it and support it. And so he was very supportive of that ... and we'd got this cash then which gave us a certain independence.

But before he was prepared to sign-off on the expenditure Prof. Ó Brolcháin, not unreasonably, wanted to see the site in question, and the account of that reconnaissance trip makes for an entertaining tale:

> [A]t that time he had – this was '57 – he still had a pre-war car, which was on its last legs, and he was waiting for January to change it. So he wanted to go out to see this, and I'd say it was just after Christmas '57, beginning of '58, and Paddy Sharkey was the graduate student I had, and myself, went out with him, he drove out. But the car had a hole in the bottom of the floor, which the breeze came in through. Which wasn't very good on a very cold winter's day. But anyway, we went out and had a look at the place, he liked it, he said, 'Okay, fine,' and we went back. But I remember coming back one

---

39 Prof. Pádraig Ó Céidigh of the Zoology Department established the Marine Research Lab in Carna, Co. Galway.

of the problems we had was it started to snow. And you know the snow had fallen, and you couldn't see the edge of the road, and the wipers weren't working, so the windscreen was blanked across.

But the snow used to keep slipping down, and he was a rather small man but he used to try and sort of climb over us, standing holding onto the steering wheel and looking out through the gap at the top. And we made our way back across, and we were coming across by Inverin, but we had to stop to look at the Sputnik. Because he used to be always very keen to watch Sputnik passing by so it was due at about half past five, and I remember stopping there in the middle of this vast plain in darkness to watch this little light going across the bottom of the sky. Very faint, but this was out in Connemara, perfect viewing. Anyway, it turned up on time as well, so that was one of his things, he was always very interested in looking at stars and things. We came back, and we got the approval and we gradually got it put together. We got windows put in, and we got a door put onto it, so the thing became habitable, and we started. And our first measurements I noticed in the report were taken on the, I think, 28 June 1958.

The Atmospheric Research Centre at Mace went on to great success, but it is interesting to note that while this was a centre for scientific research, having a good relationship with the local community, and appreciating the rich culture of the area, was also very much in the minds of those operating the station, as Prof. O'Connor explains:

> We had a guy called Máirtín Folan who was living in a house beside us at the time, but one of the nice things I remember, we were out at Mace Head, looking out at MacDara's Island and he said, '*An té atá ar a' taobh MacDara, ní baoill dó* [The one who is beside MacDara need never fear],' I think that's fishermen's lore. So we always sort of felt safe at Mace Head.

TEACHING COURSES THROUGH IRISH

While it might be argued, with some degree of validity, that the Irish language had in many ways been the saviour of the university in the 1940s and 1950s, by the early '70s demand for some courses through Irish had waned considerably, as Prof. Richard Butler recalls:

> There was a first-year course, it was through Irish, and the second-year course in chemistry was through Irish, and Frank Coll and Sean Ó Cinnéide were teaching that. I wasn't asked to teach anything through Irish at that time, but I remember, I think in 1976, when I met Frank Coll coming out of a lecture and he told me that was the end of the second-year class through Irish, there was only one student in there.

TEACHING MIXED ABILITY

Because subjects like chemistry are necessary components of a number of different courses, a difficulty arises when, as is often the case, students come to study a subject but have never studied chemistry before, or have studied it at a very basic level. Prof. Richard Butler developed a pragmatic strategy for dealing with this problem, which by his estimation has always worked very effectively, as he explains:

> There'd be 350 or whatever it was in the Kirwan Theatre, and you got people with As in the Leaving Cert, people with normal Leaving Cert, people with chemistry/physics combined, and then about 50 per cent, 55 per cent, with no chemistry at all, and you're trying to teach all these together. It's very difficult, very difficult. What I used to say to them, with no apologies, is I'm teaching the weakest students in the class, so ... I'd just tell them, look, if you're going to be bored, be bored in silence. That's what I used to tell them. And that we'll start, if you take any topic, if you did chemistry in the Leaving Cert, and you got an A, if you take any topic, probably say atomic structure, I'll give you ten lectures, the first two you'll have from Leaving Cert, but the remaining eight you won't and the remaining 8 is what matters when it comes to the exam here ... So they believed me then.

TEACHING MATURE STUDENTS

The introduction of night courses, and other part-time courses, saw an influx of mature students, some studying at third level for the first time, and others returning to college to add to their qualifications after a long interval. Maureen Langan-Egan returned to college to complete a master's in education, and was delighted to find that she and her fellow students were heartily welcomed by one of the professors:

> We were singularly privileged in our master's years in that there was a specialism in history. And I can remember Gearóid Mac Niocaill coming in to us the evening he started and looking at us and he said, 'Thanks be to God that I've a group here that I don't have to explain what Ireland was like before rural electrification.'

Maureen credits one of her other history professors, T.P. O'Neill, with encouraging her to focus her research on a particular aspect of history where there was much work to be done:

> T.P. pointed out, he said, 'Look, there's a whole lot of work that has never been done on women's history.' T.P. you see, having worked in the National

Library for years, was aware of resources, hugely aware of what was available or not available. Oh we were singularly privileged.[40]

For Prof. Richard Butler the dynamism that accompanied the arrival of a lot of new people in the 1970s was infectious and exhilarating, accompanied, as it was, by a great deal of infrastructural changes:

> The expansion in the place was incredible ... this was all related to the new buildings, the whole policy, the whole atmosphere in the country was education, and especially science, and it was a great time to be involved in it. There was that kind of exciting atmosphere around the place, and a lot of Young Turks all over the place. I mean the faculty meetings and the Academic Council meetings were amazing.

NEW ADVANCES IN TEACHING

While the traditional 'talk and chalk' method of teaching had been the mainstay of teaching since the inception of the college, gradually new innovations in teaching methods and teaching aids began to come on stream, and both academics and students learned quickly to adapt to these changes.

One extraordinary example of an innovative use of new technology came about as a result of the enforced absence, on sick leave, of a lecturer, and given that these events occurred in 1972 must surely constitute one of the first occasions of multimedia learning ever instituted in an Irish university.[41] Prof. Turlough Fitzgerald was appointed professor of anatomy in 1968, and he had big plans to develop the Anatomy Department following his return from the United States:

> In 1972 I got very ill. That was in June, and by September I was shuffling about in my dressing gown and the big thing on my mind was that the neuroanatomy course would start in October, and there was no one to teach it. So, my wife Maeve had been appointed lecturer in histology (microscopic anatomy), and she got the notion why don't I do it on video? So, once a week a particular room was vacated and the audiovisual people came over with their camera and TV cards, which in those days were eighteen inches by a foot, yellow card, and I would spend thirty hours the previous week, preparing felt-tip diagrams of things. And then I would memorize the first three or four minutes of what my next presentation was going to be, and then simply put one TV card after another, and then I'd memorize the final three or four minutes, and go back direct on camera. And Maeve arranged Perspex panels all around the walls of the reading room in the department,

40 Maureen Langan-Egan has since researched and published widely in the area of women's history. 41 The Open University only began broadcasting in the UK in January 1971.

and put them up, and that went right through to the December. I was out
for the rest of the year, but I did some research, writing up things at home,
and then when I came back Maeve got the secretary, Mary O'Donnell, to
type out all I'd said in the hospital and organized what she called TAT, Text-
Atlas-Tape for each topic, with text on the left pages and picture on the
right and a tape I dictated. So the [group of students] were able to look at
the pictures while listening to the tape, then go on to the next and the next,
and they could then review the topic by going back and reading the text.
And this approach developed quite dramatically, to the point that overall we
produced one hundred TATs, between gross anatomy, histology, embryol-
ogy and neuroscience. And the students loved the idea, especially because
they could study it in their own time.

DEVELOPMENT OF MARINE SCIENCE

The development of marine science is one of the college's real success stories. The
process was spearheaded by Prof. Pádraig Ó Céidigh. To those who knew Prof. Ó
Céidigh, the fact that his choice of career had its origins in his childhood would
come as no surprise:

> I was born in Sandymount but I was kind of reared at Seapoint, near Dún
> Laoghaire, and I used to spend all my time out collecting … fishing and col-
> lecting marine animals, shrimps and crabs and things, my youth was spent
> like that. My mother had some idea that I should become a priest or some-
> thing, and that was out altogether, 'cause I liked women very much. So then
> she had an idea that I should become a doctor, but I didn't want that at all
> either, or a solicitor, and I said none of those you see. So she says, 'Well
> nobody's going to pay you for collecting shrimps and crabs.'

But his mother was wrong, and it was his fascination with all things marine that led
to him coming to UCG for the first time in 1954.

While studying natural science at UCD, Prof. Ó Céidigh was given a project
to research over the summer, and he chose seaweeds as his topic. In the summer
of 1953 he came to Cill Chiaráin in the Gaeltacht of Co. Galway to study algae, a
task made all the more pleasant by the fact that, as he puts it, 'I was doing a bit of
courtin' with the lady I'm married to now,' and she was from Cill Chiaráin, and
returned there every summer from her teaching job in Dublin. It was a very productive summer for Pádraig, and so began his long career in the study of algae, and
his long association with UCG, as he explains:

> I was totally captivated by the beauty of the red algae in particular, the red
> fillimentus algae. So I stayed on there for the rest of the summer of '53,
> and had a great collection of algae going back, and I had managed to learn

how to identify them properly and so on. So, when they saw that, when I went back to the Botany Department, they said they'd have to show these to Máirín Dev, and Máirín Dev came up to Dublin some days after that, and I showed them to her, and, says she, 'Oh you'll have to come down and collect with me.' So that's how I came down in the Easter of '54. So anyway I came down and Máirín Dev put me up in her own house in Maunsells Road, and we went out on the beach together.

Prof. de Valera kept a close eye on the progress of her protégé, and when a vacancy arose for an assistant in the Department of Natural History, the professor of that department, Prof. Dinan, approached the recently graduated Ó Céidigh, who was at that stage employed by the Salmon Trust in Newport, Co. Mayo. It was an offer he could not refuse: 'Dinan wanted me to go down and apply for that job and of course it was a godsend to me because I'd get back to the sea ...' Having accepted the position, and deciding that if fresh starts were being made, they should be made across the board, he and Máirín Ní Chonaire got married on 2 October 1956. It was to be a brave and optimistic start to his career at UCG, as he explains:

> I handed in my notice, to take effect at the end of September '56 and we arranged to get married then. So after getting my last month's salary, it was £41, I came down here, we got married in Salthill Church, and we'd the reception here in the Great Southern. And after that I'd hired a car and we took off for the honeymoon. We spent the first night in the Gresham in Dublin. And then we went to Cork, to the Grand Hotel ... and then to west Cork, the Parknasilla, and so on. So after five days I'd spent the £41. So I went back to my home in Dublin and collected the dog, and from Máirín's digs her bicycle, so I arrived down with my dog, and a new wife and a bicycle, on the train from Dublin. And I'd no idea where we were going.

Prof. Ó Céidigh's formal career in the college began soon after, and it began in a typically distinctive style:

> My first class would have been about the 14 October '56, and I went down on a bicycle with my dog running along beside the bicycle, my black Alsatian, so I came up and the class were already ensconced inside in the lab, and there was a young student there and she had a little dog, you know, and I said, 'You can't bring a dog in here, and I'll tell you why: I've an Alsatian here and he'll ate it!' So that got me over my first introduction to them. So they were a nice class I must say, I enjoyed teaching them, and the whole thing was the practical, looking first of all at the whole animal, and then dissecting the insides of it, and dissecting it logically so as to leave things like

blood vessels and all intact. I always used to love looking at the insides of a
frog, it was very colourful.

With the budget for the Zoology Department very small at the time – the total
grant, according to Prof. Ó Céidigh, was £120 a year, with an additional £10 10s.
for books – finding money to do the research he wanted to do was always going to
be a problem. But, as many of his colleagues had already found, where there was a
will there was a way, as he explains:

> I started to continue with the plankton because the young stage of nearly
> every marine animal, or at least an awful lot of them, is spent in the plankton.
> Plankton was the drifting life of the sea, carried along by the movements of
> the sea, the currents and so on. So how you collect that is a silk net, a coni-
> cal net, you tow it through the water and it filters off the small fish and the
> young crabs, and lobsters and things like that you know, little jellyfish. So, I'd
> no boat, that was one of the first problems. So I thought maybe what I could
> do was if I invented a machine that would sample the plankton at speed,
> normally you'd have to tow that conical net at one knot anyway, or about half
> a knot. But there was the boat going in regularly to the Aran Islands, the *Dún
> Aengus*, and I thought if I could put a machine in from that … so I made a
> sort of machine that had a narrow opening and then expanded out so that if
> there was anything rushing in it would reduce the velocity, and then a bit of
> a small net inside. That worked alright. I used to throw it out from the stern
> of the *Dún Aengus*. The captain, Captain Sanderson, he was very helpful, and
> so were the crew, and he even offered to slow down the *Dún Aengus* for me,
> it was great. And then when they'd be drifting off the islands, you see there
> was no quays in the islands in those days, and the *Dún Aengus* used to drift
> and the currachs used to come out to her, so when she'd be drifting she'd be
> drifting at very slow speeds so I used to be using a big conical net there. The
> plankton here was much richer than up in Dublin.

Prof. Dinan's support for Ó Céidigh's research went beyond the verbal, when he
put his hand in his own pocket to support it:

> He said, 'Keep an eye out for a boat, but there isn't very much money.' It
> used all go on buying frogs and rabbits and dogfish for the labs. So any-
> way he bought the boat out of his own pocket, he did, it was a little motor
> launch, that belonged to Lord Killanin.

In addition to his own research, Prof. Ó Céidigh's friendship and collaboration
with his colleague Prof. Máirín de Valera continued throughout the remainder of
her life, and their joint interest in collecting in Connemara was often looked on
with bemusement by some of the locals, as he explains:

We used to go out collecting together on the beach and Máirín, she'd meet the oul' Connemara fellas you see out the bay, collecting their own weeds, and one of them would come up, '*An tusa iníon Rí na hEireann* [Are you the daughter of the king of Ireland]?' '*Is mé* [I am].' 'Well, you'd imagine that your father would have gotten something better for you to do than collecting seaweed.'

Prof. Ó Céidigh recalls another incident, also involving Prof. de Valera, which on this occasion made the local newspapers:

We were on our way out to Inishbofin I remember one year, and there was a big storm, there was no way we'd get into Inishbofin. And a reporter arrived and asked us what we were doing you see. We said it was of no interest at all, we were just collecting things, and so on. What had he on the *Connacht Tribune* afterwards? 'Two UCG biologists seek new life on the ocean bed.'

SETTING UP MARINE SCIENCE IN CARNA

Much as Prof. Tom O'Connor had found just the right location for his meteorological work at Mace Head, Prof. Pádraig Ó Céidigh found Carna ideal as a research site for marine science, as he explains:

In '58 Professor Dinan bought me an old shed, a congested districts board shed on the quay at Carna, for £120. Everything was £120 in those days. And I set that up as my lab out there. I got the lab benches out of the Grammar School . That was the beginnings of it. I found at Mynish such a variety of natural habitats, marine habitats there, you had a total variety. There was the wild, rocky shore of Mynish, there was the sheltered rocky shore with big growths of algae on it, and muddy sand sediment, and then there was the big sandy shore off Mynish, off the north shore of Mynish, which had forests of eelgrass and a fantastic fauna of pipefish and sea anemones and different kinds of worms and things there, and the stony coral out on Crag Rocks.

With an incredibly rich research site now identified, the work of teaching students could begin in earnest, but as Padraig Ó Céidigh explains, there was not exactly a rush of students to the new course he was developing:

In 1957 I got my first class taking the degree, and in that year one fella turned up to do the degree. And he was a Christian Brother, Brother Chisholm. But in the meantime in the second year we were joined by two other students, an ex-nun and an ex-army officer, they were all older than me. So the main thing that we did those years was start the marine course.

THE 'YOUNG TURKS' OF THE 1970S

The influx of new, young, and energetic staff in the early 1970s was the shot in the arm the college needed. Motivated by a keen desire to improve the university, for both students and staff, and to move the college into the modern world, these young men and women proceeded to make waves and try to make things happen. Prof. Iognáid Ó Muircheartaigh was one of those whose arrival in November 1970 signalled a real sea change in how the college would operate for the next thirty years. For him, arriving to find that there was no office available for him was the spur he needed to start agitating for change, as he explains:

> Well it taught me a lot, because I started agitating immediately almost ... I mean how can you do a job with no office? So I became a rebel then, and I'd say I was a rebel then until I became president really. Maybe I'm a rebel still, but I was certainly a rebel for most of my career here, just kind of anti-system, trying to change things. And I remember standing up at faculty and complaining about not having an office, the usual stuff, how can you do your job, how can you prepare, how can you meet students and so on. And one distinguished older professor berated me with the words: 'Oh well, I was here for fifteen years and I didn't have an office,' and whatever, when he came first. But I remember saying, it was really cheeky you know, saying, 'You know, professor, with all due respect, you should realize that the fact that our ancestors lived in caves, is no reason why we should do so.' In retrospect it was so cheeky. I mean, 27 years of age, talking to a professor. So that was the kind of attitude at the time ... I suppose we came from the '60s, and they were years of protest, and stand up for yourself and fight your corner. I mean we had confidence, a bit more confidence. And also we wanted to do something, and also we were looking at an institution that hadn't changed for a hundred years.

The 1970s were a radical time in Irish society, and inevitably some of this spilled over into the universities, especially UCG, as Prof. Jim Flavin explains:

> Níl aon amhras orm go raibh an ollscoil seo níos radiciúl ná a macasamhail i gCorcaigh. Fiú amháin i UCD tá tú ag caint faoin 'gentle revolution', an bhfuil fhios agat? Deirfinn go raibh spiorad níos radacúla anseo ná in áit ar bith eile. Bíodh sé ina shamhlíocht ná a mhalairt go raibh fuinneamh neamhghnátheach anseo an t-am sin.

> I have no doubt but that this university was more radical than its counterpart in Cork. Even in UCD you are talking about a 'gentle revolution', you know? I would say there was a more radical spirit here than in any other place. Whether I imagined it or not, there was an unusual energy here at that time.

The need for a trade union for academic staff was identified early in the 1970s. Prof. Iognáid Ó Muircheartaigh recalls how this came about:

> We formed a trade union … it started as the Workers' Union of Ireland I believe. So the founding members would have been Donal Hurley, who is in maths now in UCC, Tony Christofides, a wonderful guy, Michael D. Higgins, myself, and a number of others, Michael Hynes maybe, Des Johnson certainly. And so we formed the WUI. A very exciting time. And we were looking for … we were looking for trouble really, you know, any excuse.

THE ACADEMIC STRIKE

Although the union did try to initiate change, this was slow in coming, which understandably frustrated the young academics. The result was a strike, the first strike of academic staff in Irish history, as Prof. Ó Muircheartaigh recalls:

> It didn't have any real effect, but it was a great, great experience. I remember it very clearly, the issue was communication – the college refused to communicate with us, no communication from on top, because they were a small group of management and they just did what they wanted to. They didn't interact, they didn't reply to letters, they didn't do anything. I know that when the strike was imminent, about to happen, we were told something like, 'We've always seen ourselves as a family here,' you know? And I remember responding, you know, this is the problem, we are not a family, we're a big organization now, and we're trying to make things happen. So we had the strike. And first of all those of us who were committed to it did it, some people supported us, a huge number went to Dublin for the day on the train, it was only a one-day strike, so there was never as busy a train from Galway to Dublin as that date. Because they didn't want to be going against us, but they didn't want to be seen to be subversive, or difficult, either. So the easy way out was to go off and do research or whatever, not be there. But then the other thing was that when it was over Derry Corvin, who was a very nice guy, but a very tough secretary bursar, wrote out a letter to me, saying please could I supply him with a list of the names of those who were on strike so they could be docked their pay. So we considered that at length and we decided that we wouldn't provide that list, on the grounds that we felt that those that were seen to be members of the union could be intimidated in the future, and we weren't comfortable enough with the relationship with the college. So I wrote back saying we were not in a position to comply with the request. I thought that was the right line. So anyway, nothing came of it in the end, I mean no one knew, there was no pay deducted, and nothing really happened. But there was a photograph in the *Irish Times*.

A NEW RELATIONSHIP: THE COLLEGE AND INDUSTRY

Having been a very active presence on campus during his student days, Brendan 'Speedie' Smith found on graduation in 1981 with a BA and a H.Dip. that, like many of his contemporaries, he could not find a permanent teaching job, and worked as a substitute teacher here and there – until the college came calling with a job offer he could not refuse:

> I was offered a job by the college, by Professor Eddie O'Kelly and Dr James Browne, now the president, to manage an incubator factory in the area of computer-aided manufacturing. They were very good at that. That was in late 1981. And it was interesting, because at that time college was very much an ivory tower. It didn't take outside funding, that was an American concept where you took outside funding from the corporate sector, and it was felt in Europe that that was going to mean the prostitution of research and academia, and the freedom, and you were selling your soul to the devil, you know? But for research to take place, particularly in industry and science, it helped to have money coming from the corporate sector, it was making an impact. So at that time there wasn't money around, so while the money was coming together from the Thermo Kings and Digitals, computer-aided manufacturing, I set up a computer shop, down in Newcastle, at Cooke's Corner, and out of the selling of computers it helped finance third-level postgraduate research in college. Isn't that funny? Selling computers in the corner shop, you know? But out of that we developed a postgraduate research connectivity with the Nortels and the Thermo Kings and the Digitals and so on.

DEVELOPMENT OF INDUSTRIAL ENGINEERING

In the climate of industrial expansion that existed in the 1970s UCG found itself ideally placed to take advantage of the demand for engineers qualified specifically in industrial engineering. The first designated course in industrial engineering began in 1972, with the first graduates emerging in 1974, including, as we have seen, a past president of NUI Galway, Dr James Browne. Having worked in industry for two and half years after graduation, it was the industrial-engineering course that eventually brought him back into academic life in 1977, as he explains:

> The industrial-engineering course was turning out small numbers, industry was impatient to convert people, so there were a lot of people who were civil engineers or mechanical engineers, electrical engineers, who needed industrial-engineering training. So the department created a master's in industrial-engineering programme, a part-time, postgraduate, really a conversion programme. That programme started, I believe, in '76, perhaps '77,

and that programme essentially ran parallel with the MBA, and students who were working in industry came in on Friday evenings, and Saturday mornings. So that created extra resources, and that created a part-time position for me. And I took that position because I could do a master's degree at the same time. So I took a two-year post here to do a master's by research, so I got paid to do the teaching, and that covered my master's.

Asked to teach production engineering, Dr Browne found his experience working in industry, including in Canada, stood him in good stead, and although he acknowledges that there were excellent textbooks on the subject, it was the practical experience of production systems that he believes greatly enhanced his own ability to teach it, as he explains:

> In a sense you were only a couple of steps ahead of the students. Because at the time there was nobody available in Ireland, nobody. If you advertised a post in industrial or production engineering, who was qualified to do it? We hadn't been producing graduates, ever, so there was no great body of expertise available.

The growth of the engineering faculty was inevitable given the rate of expansion in the 1970s and 1980s, but there were still restrictions with regard to the possibilities of postgraduate study in the field of engineering, which Dr Browne found frustrating, as he explains:

> When I did the undergraduate degree, there was no postgraduate possibility, the department was too young. And also I'd say, frankly, that engineering here, even up to about maybe the early '80s, the idea was that BE was a very good degree. It was a professional qualification, if you had a BE degree you then were professionally recognized to be a Chartered Engineer. So in a sense doing a master's or a PhD was very, very rare, and only done in the sense of renewing the academic gene pool, producing the odd lecturer from it, but never considered to be a qualification that was useful outside of that. And that was still the case up to the mid-'80s I would say, that anything else, unless you wanted to be a lecturer, was really a waste of time. And even worse than that, it was kind of devaluing the BE. There was a sense that if you went on and did a master's, then the BE would become less, you know, would lose some of its status. That was there, very strongly. It's also the case that most staff didn't have PhDs at that time. The majority of staff would have been people who would have come into lecturing perhaps from an experiential background, who would have been very good … I think perhaps Prof. O'Keefe was the first member of staff in the core Engineering Department in the university who had a PhD, I think that's correct.

It was with the links fostered with the outside world that the Engineering Faculty really began to move forward and supply the needs of a rapidly changing world, as Dr Browne explains:

> Dr John Roche did a tremendous job, he took a kind of Billy Graham approach to it, he went out and he 'hot-gospelled' it. He was a great enthusiast for industrial engineering. He himself had come in from Irish Ropes … I think he did a master's degree here in statistics, and then went out, got involved in the quality-control business, at the time a lot of quality control was based on sampling, on statistics, and then he came back into the university. And he had great enthusiasm for those type of things, and he was very pro-industry. I think we might have been the first university to have industrial projects in engineering, you know, we had final-year projects with industry. And we had access to factories, and were brought on tours of factories. These were all new plants, just beginning, so it was very good.

THE BUSINESS OF COMMERCE

The opening up of new opportunities in the Irish industrial and commercial world obviously played an integral part in the development of new courses and syllabi in the UCG of the 1970s. It also brought a crop of new lecturers to the college, who were to assume an extremely important role in the way in which the college was to develop over the coming decades. Keith Warnock, for example, was one of those who came to Galway in 1976. Academic staff, as we have seen, came to Galway for a variety of reasons, but Keith's decision came about in a particularly unusual way, as he recalls:

> It began in the summer of 1976. I'd done my undergraduate degree in Trinity, and at that stage I'd been out of Ireland for eight or nine years I think. I was on a holiday in Donegal with my wife and two children and we were living in Manchester at the time where I was completing a postgraduate degree. And we decided that we wanted to come back to Ireland, and didn't want to go to Dublin particularly and so basically we put a map of Ireland on the floor of the holiday house in Donegal, and looked at it and decided Galway would be a nice place to work. So we actually decided to get into the car and drive down and look at the university. I'd visited it once when I was at Trinity, I was running on the cross country team, and I'd come for a competition. I had, I suppose, a very brief look at the campus, I'm not sure if we even had time to stop and go in, we had small children with us, but just drove past the university.

Clearly impressed with what he had seen, Keith then decided to make overtures to the college in respect of possible teaching positions. His timing was fortuitous:

I wrote to Labhrás Ó Nualláin,[42] and the letter ended up with Jim Ward, who was the new dean, and who became dean at a very young age, saying I was interested in exploring whether there was any possibility of a job in my area of accounting coming up in UCG, and he wrote back and said by coincidence there is a job coming up. And I said could I just sort of come and talk about the faculty generally? And so in the Christmas of 1976 I drove across and visited Jim. Beautiful day, a December day, I remember we sort of looked at maps and formed unrealistic ideas of houses we might be able to live in, and I remember driving up on the roads behind Barna, and saying what a beautiful place. So I met Jim, and I also met Leo Hawkins, who was the only accounting lecturer at that time. And what was actually being contemplated was the advertising of a second job, which was the one which I eventually took – which was doubling that particular department. But the Commerce Faculty itself would only have had about ten full-time academics at that stage, so it was very, very small.

So anyway, I was told about this job, and applied for it when it came up. I was, as I suppose a lot of people were over the years, somewhat, shall we say, taken aback by the Irish element of it,[43] but at least knew what it actually meant. In those days, and up until the recent amendment of the 1929 act, most people thought that you had to speak Irish to get a job, and as my undergraduate degree was in law, so I like to think I can read a document carefully enough to interpret it, I realized that that wasn't absolutely the case. And I would have checked with the people I'd been in contact within the faculty. So I came back then, in I think it would have been June of 1977, to interview for the job, full of confidence because I'd just been offered a job in UCC in fact so I knew I had that choice. It's a very nice position to be in, particularly when you find that several members of the assessment board are the same people who were interviewing down in Cork.

Keith was fortunate in that he arrived at UCG at a time when there were a large number of new, young staff, similar to himself, who had recently been appointed:

One of the things that I found immediately, and that I remember still, was going out to dinner with my wife, with a whole lot of colleagues, and their

42 Labhrás Ó Nualláin was professor of economics at UCG.   43 The University College Galway Act, 1929 was designed to establish by law the special status of the Irish language within the college. Of particular significance was Section 3, which stipulated that it was the duty of the senate of the NUI, the governing body of the college, or the president of the college 'when making an appointment to any office or situation in the College, to appoint to such office or situation a person who is competent to discharge the duties thereof through the medium of the Irish language: provided a person so competent and also suitable in all other respects is to be found amongst the persons who are candidates or otherwise available for such appointment'. As a result, candidates for appointments to all posts within the university were required to pass an Irish language test before being formally appointed. The University College Galway (Amendment) Act 2006 removed this stipulation.

wives, I think it was in Kilcolgan, that would have been probably within a month of our arrival. And there weren't all commerce people, there were people there from other faculties. And interestingly, just thinking about it, there might have been ten young academics there, and sort of an interesting fact, but about four of them have ended up on the university management team at one time.

But the influx of new people didn't just add to the camaraderie of the college academics – it also fuelled the formation of the first master plan for the college, which provided for the college's expansion in response to the increasing numbers of students coming to study there, as Keith recalls:

> Interestingly, 1977 was also the year in which the university published its first formal master plan for the campus. But the idea of a master plan would really have been driven by the very significant expansion in student numbers that started … you had what was then regarded as an absolute explosion in student numbers and the growth to the previously unimaginable level of 3,500 students. And one of the fascinating things in the master plan was, and it's a quote that I use continually, they said something like, 'It is unrealistic to expect the university' – or 'the college' as it might have referred to itself then – 'would expand beyond 6,000 students'. And here we are coping with 15,000 at this stage.[44]

Coming to teach at UCG after having already acquired a professional qualification in accountancy provided Keith with a distinct advantage in introducing the subjects to his students, as he explains:

> I like to think that having a professional qualification is not in any way a negative. Basically what I'm saying is that I think if you are lecturing to students who, in a lot of cases, have a distinct ambition to become accountants, the fact that you have been an accountant, and can tell even the most trivial stories, even, you know, in my case, in my later years as a lecturer that might be twenty-five, thirty years out of date, they're still real stories about what happens when you are actually working. I think students can relate to that.

While there was a new, young group of academics joining the university staff in the 1970s, there was also an established group of senior academics already in place, who appeared somewhat daunting to their more junior counterparts, as Keith Warnock recalls:

44 The interview was conducted in October 2007. The student population in 2019 stood at over 18,000.

In many ways they would have lived in what I would have seen as almost as a parallel universe. I remember one of the things that struck me going over to the staff room, there was a group of people who would sit in the middle of the staff room in a circle, which seemed to the innocent outsider like myself as virtually impermeable.

Another of the challenges that faced Keith was mastering Irish for the all-important Irish interview that would be required to confirm his appointment:

> I didn't start actually learning Irish until I was 14. I got my Leaving Certificate. Then when I was in Manchester preparing for the interview I remember driving around the hills around Manchester with the Gael Linn tapes trying to master it. In fact my written Irish was fine because I was able to get a copy of the Companies Act, I studied law in Trinity, so I had the Companies Act 1963, which is one of the pieces of legislation which has the Irish on one side and the English on the other, so there was about 800, 900 pages of it. But I was able to concoct an essay about accounting in Irish.

THE MALE/FEMALE DIVIDE IN SUBJECT CHOICE

With more and more career opportunities opening up for women in the late '70s and early '80s, changes in the subject choices – and subsequently career choices – made by women began to become apparent. Keith Warnock was among the first to notice this change in his own field:

> I remember doing some early statistics on the jobs that commerce graduates took up at that stage. At that stage something like 80 per cent of the males were going into accounting, and 80 per cent of the females were going into teaching. You're talking about let's say 150 students, and they would have been split – because Galway was always, I think, out of line with the other colleges there – would have been split 50/50 male and female, at times it's been up to 60 per cent female, but that would be, for instance totally out of line with UCD. So it might have been close to 60 going into accounting, 60 going into teaching. But it was very much segregated on gender lines. [But] the climate was changing very rapidly then, things like the civil service marriage bar being removed, and I can still remember when suddenly the girls in the class started aspiring to accounting. And what's more I remember one year when I think one of the accounting firms awarded three prizes [...] and first, second and third were all female. And I can still remember some mildly unpleasant remarks made by the male group, who obviously suddenly realized there was a challenge there.

Students' perceptions of the subject were another issue Keith found himself addressing when he began to teach accountancy at UCG:

> A lot of accounting is about communication. When you're training as an auditor, which is the way a lot of accountants train, you have to go into companies, who don't really want to speak to you, and force them to talk to you about their systems and explain it, so a lot of what I'm doing is actually saying to people communication is an essential part of this job. Occasionally somebody will ask a question in a tutorial that is incredibly perceptive, something that you haven't thought of yourself, and you'd say why didn't I think of that? Or something that anticipates the way professional standards are developed years ahead and you think gosh, this guy's so smart. And you're making projections about the future, all of which are inevitably highly subjective. You're trying to work on measurement systems which are all contingent on human behaviour. And I remember discussing a problem in a tutorial and saying well, you could do this, or you could do that, and somebody said to me, with barely bated breadth, 'Tell us what the right answer is.' And I said, 'There *is* no right answer.'

Doubtless there are many experienced academics out there who might add 'and Amen to that'.

6

The well-oiled machine: non-academic staff and the operational life of the college

While academics ensured that the learning process occurred in the classrooms and labs, there was a small army of other staff who ensured that the operational life of the college provided an efficient accompaniment to the core learning environment. The non-academic staff, incorporating administrative, library and catering staff, technicians, groundsmen, cleaners, plumbers, painters, carpenters, porters and security, had the job of keeping the wheels of the college running, and providing whatever support was needed to the college management team, the academic staff and the student body. Being answerable to so many people, in a variety of different ways, was no easy task, but it would appear that the system worked, and worked remarkably efficiently, over the five decades examined in this study. There are a variety of reasons for this, but ultimately it came down to one factor: people simply liked working at UCG, and once employed by the college, they never wanted to leave.

Regardless of their status, everyone in the college, from academics to students, was ultimately answerable to the most important figure on campus, the college president, and non-academic staff were no exception. Keeping on the right side of the president – the 'boss', effectively – was clearly a good idea for all employees. But one story, recounted by Prof. Dan O'Donovan, indicates that in the case of Monsignor de Brún, an ardent Irish-language enthusiast, speaking Irish to the great man almost let one away with murder:

> This guy, we'll call him 'Johnny', he was working in the grounds, and he never did a stroke of work and the staff were really annoyed over this. The Governing Body would say to the president, 'We need to reprimand this man, he's not doing any work.' But every time it came up the president would say, 'Oh, but he has lovely Irish.' And the technique he used was that when the president would have his coffee in the afternoon, you know, he would take a walk around the grounds, and 'Johnny' then would bring up his wheelbarrow and he'd say, *'Dia dhuit a Uachtaráin,' plámásing* him in Irish. And of course when it came up then at the Governing Body, the president would always defend him for fostering the Irish so much. But anyhow, one day the Governing Body said you know, we just can't have this. So the president agreed that 'Johnny' would have to start work every day at 8 o'clock. So, some time after that Professor Mitchell was coming in the gate

one morning at 9 o'clock, and 'Johnny' was coming in as well. 'Good morning, Professor Mitchell.' 'Good morning Johnny.' And Professor Mitchell said, 'Johnny, I understood that you were to start at 8 o'clock, and now it's 9 o'clock, how come?' 'Ah you see Professor Mitchell', he said, 'I do the first Friday's'.[1] And Professor Mitchell said, 'Well, Johnny that's a very honourable thing to do, but this happens to be the third Friday of the month.' 'Ah but Professor Mitchell,' he said, 'I do the first Fridays every Friday.'

For many of those non-academics who worked at UCG, their experience of the college was longstanding, as most were native Galwegians. George Deacy's experience was typical of many:

> A lot of people I suppose at the time were in awe of the college. You know, the college was there ... they might know a lecturer and they might know somebody else, but they were looked on with a lot of awe I suppose, they were maybe a different breed or something like that. The wall and the gate were there at that time, so you wouldn't be somebody travelling in or out around there unless you had a need to go in there.

But George did find the need to go into the college when the chance of a job came up – and it was to be the beginning of an association that would last fifty years.

> I was in the Technical School, and a job came up then in the college. And they sent word home, 'Tell George there's a job up in the college, go up for an interview.' So I went up, I think there were three other people for interview there at the time.

George did the interview with Pádraic Ó Lochlainn of the Department of Engineering, and was successful. The chance of a job in the college was greatly valued, as George explains:

> When we were growing up at the time our main objective was to get out of school, and get a job, and it didn't matter what kind of a job it was, it was to get a job and get some money for the house, to support whatever, that was the thing, that was your main goal. Everyone else was in a job. You know if you were hanging round the streets and you didn't get a job you were a bit different. But I got into the college then. Of course the mother was, 'Oh, a job for life!' Oh you had a job for life once you were in the college and that was it. 'Twas like being in the civil service or CIÉ.

1 The term 'first Fridays' refers to a set of Catholic devotions dedicated to the Sacred Heart, which are performed on the first Fridays of nine consecutive months. On these days, a person undertakes to attend Mass and receive Communion.

But there was still one major obstacle to be overcome: the small matter of the Irish language interview, which was a mandatory requirement for all employees. George Deacy was extremely fortunate in being taken under the wing of his future boss, who went out of his way to ensure his young protégé would make the grade:

> I had to do an interview, in Irish, with Monsignor de Brún. So Pádraic Ó Lochlainn tutored me. There was a nice walkway, it's still there, by the college pitch, behind the tennis courts ... So Pádraic used to walk me up and down and talk to me in Irish. Before that I had just national school Irish, that's about it, so I didn't know much more, I just barely got by, I mean I wouldn't get by now! I barely got by with that. But Mr Ó Lochlainn, he'd walk me up and down regularly, up and down, you know he was going to make sure that I wasn't going to miss that interview. And he was just talking about what we did on the job and what we didn't do, and looking forward to doing, and that was it. I was certainly there a month, if not longer, before I got the interview, and I wouldn't get paid until I actually got that, I wouldn't have been sanctioned as a full-time employee until I got the interview with Monsignor de Brún. And he was lovely. So I got the interview then. I was 15.

INDUCTION

Newly appointed staff had to find their feet very quickly. Induction courses were non-existent, and the advice that was given to them was primitive at best. Dr Séamus Mac Mathúna recalls his introduction to his new job in the Exams Office in 1972:

> An cineál ionduchtaithe a bhí ann ná gur tháinig tú isteach agus tugadh Féilire an Choláiste duit – lámhleabhar an Choláiste, is dóigh, ina raibh struchtúr agus rialacha na gcúrsaí agus eolas ginearálta eile leagtha amach – agus dúradh leat, 'Bí á léamh agus faigh amach céard atá ar siúl.' B'in an méid.

> The kind of induction you got was that you came in and were given the college calendar – the college handbook, I suppose, in which the structure and rules of the courses, as well as other general information, were set out – and told, 'Read that, and find out what is going on.' That was all.

However, in most cases new employees were mentored by more experienced colleagues. George Deacy maintains that he was very lucky in this regard:

> Mel Melvin was the senior technician there, so Mel did structures work, and concrete and stuff like that, and soil mechanics, also he'd show the

films, 60-metre film for the societies. And if there was lights and electrical equipment to be fixed or anything around the campus, he'd fix them as well, so he was doing all that kind of work. So he used to bring me along with him then and that's really where I kind of learned a bit of this, that and the other. A mix all the time, it was good. Then if there was stuff broken in our own place, a bit of carpentry or a bit of steelwork or stuff like that, you know we would do welding or soldering or cutting and that, so you got all that kind of stuff as well because we had a workshop there at the time, and Mel was fairly knowledgeable you know, he was fairly handy with his hands. He could nearly make a fix on anything.

While George's training was going well, he also had to get used to the fact that being the newest – and youngest – member of the college's extended family, he was going to be in for some serious ribbing from his workmates, and indeed some of the students, as he explains:

> I suppose what I mostly remember at that time was, being a young kid, when you went into the Archway for the post, Pat Higgins (the porter) used to be there, and he'd be sitting outside the door, or he'd be sitting in front of the Archway, a fine day now he'd be sitting in the Archway, and he'd look at you coming in. And he'd see a young fella coming in, 'Oh look at him now!' And then outside the Archway as well you see there'd be ten, fifteen ... and I can even see the faces now, I don't know who they were, but you know there'd be ten, fifteen, twenty of the students, and they'd all congregate there, under the Arch and Pat used say then, 'Oh look at him now, he's got new shoes and he wants everyone to know about them! Listen to them squeakin!' Then of course they'd start then, the other fifteen then would start, whistles and shouts, so this was it.

Shy and all as he was, George learned to take the ribbing in good spirit, and, as he says, it was never more than just good-natured fun:

> You know if you got a new hairdo or there was something at the time, whoever it would be, Tommy Steele, or somebody at the time, and you'd have the hair like him, 16 years old you know, and they'd be, 'Oh, will ya look at him, he got his hair cut!' And then the other crowd then, the crowd of students, would be whistling and shouting. And they got to know me then as well, you see. If they saw me in town they'd say hello, they knew me like, but they'd get the jibe in there if they saw me ... whistling and shouting. I dreaded it in the beginning but then, well it became part of it.

George Deacy makes the point that building good relationships with people was the key to the way in which the college operated so successfully, particularly at times when the college was expanding rapidly and changes were happening on an almost daily basis. The friendly banter with people like Alfie Sherlock, one of the groundsmen who lived for a time in the Gate Lodge, was a case in point, being rooted, as it was, in a solid working relationship that ensured the work got done – albeit with a bit of humour thrown in for good measure.

> Alfie was always in good humour, I never remember him in bad humour, he was always a real gent. Or you'd always get a laugh out of him. He'd be slagging us, but always in good humour, always in good humour. And the beauty of that was another thing I was lucky in, I never had to ask twice for something to be done. You know, if I asked Alfie would he shift such a thing, or we needed to do that, he'd be there within an hour. Paddy Lally was the same way, he'd be there in five minutes. And then the electricians were great, and the plumbers. And all the people that I dealt with down through the years, they were great, and that was the support I needed. And now I couldn't manage some place, because you know if we were renovating this today, you know before you'd get someone in and they'd be saying yeah, I'll get it done tomorrow, but the boys were there in five minutes, and you had the carpenters there in ten minutes.

George's relationship with the Ó Fátharta family, who lived in the Archway, was similarly pleasant, and added greatly to the friendly, family atmosphere of the college, remarked on by so many others:

> I knew them before they actually moved into the college, they lived under the Spanish Arch, they had a small cottage under the Spanish Arch. But they were lovely, lovely people. Because at that time you see you had to go into the Archway to collect the post, and 'twas a gift coming in to meet Mrs Ó Fátharta and to meet Pádraig and their kids. Peadar and them were only kids at the time, but they were a pleasure to deal with. They'd never be off form or anything, they were just great.

The staff were always kept busy, and how much change has occurred is evidenced in the following observation from Prof. Seán Tobin regarding the heating system that existed in the college for many years: 'The college boilers were run on turf. I remember turf lorries trundling in through the Archway, and over to one side there were big gratings through which they dumped the stuff down into the cellars below.' For many years fires were also lit in individual offices and lecture rooms, and the labour involved in setting and maintaining these, and cleaning out ashes, was immense.

The hard work of the non-academic staff did not go unnoticed by the students. Peadar O'Dowd recalls one man who worked extremely hard keeping tabs not only on the college boats but on the various activities of the Men's Club:

I think the most interesting man that I knew was Peter Curran. Peter Curran now, he was the man that ran the Men's Club. And he was a very quiet man in his own way, and could be very strict as well, but very nice. And I think in fact most people now that I knew from my era, we had a great *grá* for Peter, you know, he was a gas character. And he had a whole pile of boats, he had to look after all these boats, he had to run the club itself, look after the billiard tables, snooker tables, and so on, and clean up afterwards upstairs, where all the cards were played.

GROWING WITH THE COLLEGE

The physical expansion of the college, particularly in the 1970s, presented many challenges to both students and staff, as new buildings were springing up on an almost continual basis, and older buildings were being remodelled and refurbished. At least for a time, the college must have appeared to have been one large building site. Dan O'Donovan recalls the refurbishment of the Physiology Department in the Quad:

> It was decided that we could put toilets into the basement, and they dug up the Archway. And they found rock that they didn't expect, and it took a long time. And in that process, we decided that our labs downstairs, since they were being uprooted and the floor was being torn up, that we would just use that as the lecture hall, and would move research and everything upstairs, and the telephone was still left there while the men were working on it. And one day coming back from lunch, out of curiosity I put my head in, to see how they were getting on. And the next thing is this man has a wheelbarrow with rocks, and he was passing by the pillar, and the phone was on the pillar and the phone rang, and he picked it up, and he said, 'This place is being demolished,' and then put down the telephone. You can imagine the somebody from the university of somewhere saying, 'I rang University College Galway, and it's being demolished, it's not there anymore.' But he never said hello or anything he just said, 'This place is being demolished.'

THE LAB ASSISTANTS

Professors who conducted labs were dependent on the lab technicians who assisted them in preparing for experiments and maintaining equipment. Most of these lab assistants came to the job with virtually no formal training, but most became extremely proficient in their disciplines, and were very skilled and respected members of the college workforce. Many were also great characters in their own right, like Jimmy Cranny, who became something of a legend in the college. Jimmy worked in the anatomy lab for many years, but he was also famous throughout

Galway for his interest in swimming, and the fact that, as Dr John O'Donnell put it, 'He taught probably half of Galway to swim.' The Cranny Pool at Leisureland in Salthill is named after him.

But before Leisureland existed, in the 1950s Dr Ben Corballis, the young American medical student, who was a former college swimmer, having first encountered Jimmy Cranny in the course of his anatomy labs, was asked by the lab assistant to come and demonstrate his swimming techniques:

> Well nothing would do but that I had to come down to St Jarleth's in Tuam, where he taught swimming, and I went down and they had the water warmed up to the point where the ice cubes melted! I went in for ten seconds and was back out. And I told him, 'I can't live with that.' 'Well, come back.' I came back again, they had it up to 85 degrees, it was like swimming in soup. And so I said, 'Well, could we have a medium temperature, you know, some sort of medium?' But Jimmy and I were good friends.

Dr John O'Donnell, in addition to having been taught to swim by Jimmy Cranny, then discovered the important role he played in the Anatomy Department:

> There was Jimmy running the anatomy room. And taking the roll call and making friends with everyone, getting to know all the medical students and giving out to them if they misbehaved themselves, oh he did, if they were getting rowdy he'd have to.

Jimmy Cranny was so widely known in Galway that nothing got past him – he knew everything and everyone. Dr Dympna Horgan and Dr John O'Donnell recall an encounter they had with him, appropriately enough on Salthill Prom:

> We had been away … Dympna and I when we got married, we lived in Belfast, and later in Canada, and we came back on a holiday. But we were walking out the Prom anyway and we met Jimmy, and he said, 'Ah hello, I heard ye were back.' You know, we hadn't seen him for about eleven years at this stage. It could have been last week.

Jimmy Cranny was held in such high regard that his 80th birthday party was something of a major event, as Dr John O'Donnell recalls:

> He was 80 and he said, 'Are you coming to my party?' The Swimming Club, for Jimmy's birthday, held a party in Seapoint, and it was packed. And we were going out to dinner with people that night, but we went to Jimmy's party first. He'd know if you weren't there. There were up to 2,000 people there, you know? And anyway we wouldn't miss it for anything.

Another lab assistant familiar to many students over the years was Tom Hynes, who, like Jimmy Cranny, was a Galwayman, and was the assistant to Prof. Joseph ('Mossy') Donegan in physiology. Dr Ben Corballis recalls a story about Tom Hynes that reveals something of the difficulties students sometimes had in understanding the strong Galway accent of some of the college employees:

> The story I loved about Tom is this lady had been given some of her exam, she had been given some little thing, and Tom walked by and said, 'Bile.' And so she took the urine and she boiled the urine, and he came back, 'Bile,' and she boiled it again, and he was telling her there was bile in the urine, who would tell her to *boil* the damn stuff. And somebody finally told her. He was a lovely man, Tom was. Ah, he was a gent.

THE PORTERS

For those coming into the college, be they students, academics or visitors, the first point of contact was most likely to be the porters in the Archway. They were, to a large degree, the 'front of house' men of the university, and it was from them that people often got their first impressions of the college. Prof. Tom O'Connor recalls his own first experience of encountering the, at times formidable, college porters:

> When I came first there were two people in the Archway, two old men, long-serving servants of the college. One was 'Tulip' Carroll, he was at the front gate. He was called Tulip because he used to look after the tulips, or whatever it was there. But Pat Higgins was the man that lived in the Archway. He lived where the Information Office is now, in rooms there, but he had a great dislike of people leaving their bicycles in the Archway. And he had this great skill of taking a bicycle and just flinging it out the Archway, and you would be coming in and you would suddenly see this riderless bicycle come out of the Archway and across and down the steps.

The Ó Fátharta family, who lived in the Archway from 1958 until 1969, were a much-loved feature of the college for generations of students. Maureen Langan-Egan's memories, dating from the early 1960s, are typical of many:

> Oh they were lovely. He had superb command of the Irish language, and a huge interest in the place. I remember Peadar as a small child, and Mrs Ó Fátharta was a real lady from Aran, and she had the hairstyle and the most beautiful face, a very gentle person. I have lovely, happy memories of them.

Another student who remembered the Ó Fátharta family well was Pat Rabbitte, who had special cause to be grateful to them:

I have fond memories of them. Because I was president of the Union of Students, I of course had a special relationship with them, and they used to take great care of me. Pádraig Ó Fátharta was the one attired in porter's uniform, and a great big retired Garda, Canny, was his aide-de-camp. And everything, all the buzz, was in the Archway, that was the hub of all activity, exchange of information, posting of notices, and all the rest, it all happened there. And at that stage the chief porter would literally know everybody in college. But a very, very demanding job. He was very good at it, he had a great sense of discretion. And you know, it was a time of considerable student agitation, and a youth culture for the first time in this country was beginning to be recognized, and something like, for example, the birth of the Maoists, would have posed quite a challenge to the chief porter of the time, because the Maoists would invariably have a meeting outside the Archway, and that was always an exciting event.

Prof. Jim Flavin recalls being told a story by the late Christy Townley, for many years the college librarian, relating to Pádraig Ó Fátharta, and the then president of the college, Monsignor Pádraig de Brún.

B'as Inis Méain é Pádraig Ó Fátharta, a bhí san Archway. Bhí Pádraig de Brún istigh ann uair amháin, in Inis Méain, agus bhí de Brún ana-mhór leis an ailtire Michael Scott, agus bhíodar istigh i bpub éigean agus mar a tharlaíonn i gconaí bíonn na locals ag cur is ag cuartú cerbh é an duine sin, an sagart, de Brún. 'Bhuel', arsa duine amháin, 'níl fhios agam cé hé, ach is dóigh liom go bhfuil sé ag obair le Pádraig s'againne,' 'sé sin le Pádraig Ó Fátharta.

Pádraig Ó Fátharta, who used to be in the Archway, was from Inis Méain. One time Pádraig de Brún was there, on Inis Méain, and de Brún was very friendly with the architect, Michael Scott, and they were in some pub on the island and as always happens the locals were wondering who was this person, this priest, de Brún. 'Well', says one of them, 'I don't know who he is, but I think he works with our Pádraig', that is with Pádraig Ó Fátharta.

THE LADY SUPERINTENDENT

Miss Rosalie Kirwan was appointed as lady superintendent in 1914 and retired in 1944. She was succeeded by Ms Sarah Keane, who was appointed in 1944 and who died in 1948. On Ms Keane's death, Mrs Mary O'Driscoll was appointed to the position, serving from 1948 to 1981. Although Mrs O'Driscoll was replaced in the role by Mrs Margaret Fletcher-Egan in 1981, times by then had changed considerably, and Mrs Fletcher-Egan's role was to act as counsellor to the female students rather than as their moral guardian. So the role of lady superintendent effectively ended with the retirement of Mrs Mary O'Driscoll, who is fondly remembered by many of those students who attended the college during her tenure. Pat Rabbitte is one of those who remembers Mary O'Driscoll, or Ma O'Driscoll, as she was more commonly known by students, with great fondness and respect:

> Mrs O'Driscoll, a lovely lady. I ended up on a lot of committees with her because of the Governing Body, and being president of the students union. Her aide-de-camp was the Catholic chaplain, Fr Tom Kyne, a lovely man, did his best too. They were very sensible in terms of how they both conducted themselves. And it still was a pre-contraception era and so on, and inevitably you'd have had some unexpected pregnancies, and so on and so forth, and they both seemed to be able to handle the situation with a great deal of discretion, they were greatly liked.

For Brendan Smith, who was deeply involved in students union politics during his time at UCG, a good relationship with the college staff was essential. Brendan recalls why this was the case:

> The security lads were so good. There's Tim, still there today, from my time. You'd be working late into the night preparing a magazine or political paper or whatever, and they'd come down and have the chat with you at three, four, five in the morning, and the cup of tea in the Students' Office, you know? And there was a friendliness about it, it was great. And there was flexibility, you know college would close at certain times, there was a certain flexibility there you know? So the Security Office was right beside the porter's desk and the two worked hand-in-hand together. And we'd be up all night with our Tippex and our old fashioned typewriters, the real old-style cutting and pasting. And so we always had a good working, friendly relationship with people from the porter's desk and the security desk, and the cleaning staff and all the rest of it. There was no class barrier.

GREENING THE COLLEGE

Brian Finan's long career at UCG (he retired in 2008) began with an interview for the position of head gardner in the college, which was somewhat unconventional. Having studied horticulture for two years at the National Botanic Gardens in Dublin, Brian applied for the job, with no real interest in getting it, as he explains:

> I said I'll try it anyway, and I got a phone call from a person in college to go down for an interview. So I arrived down, I think it was on the 12 October 1965, and I didn't know Galway, and I just drifted along towards Johnny Ward's shop, and I asked where was the university. And at the time the university was an enclosed campus, so the old gateway was still at the

gate lodge, so I remember leaping over the wall to see what it looked like. I saw the old Quad building so I went in, and I met my interviewer, and he promised that he'd have me back on the train by 6 o'clock to go back to Dublin. There was no such thing as a Personnel Officer, Human Resources at that time, you were just taken on the advice of somebody. The person in charge at the time was over exams, and he was a very busy person, so he just threw me a sheet of paper and asked me would I write down a few details, words in Irish. Being only about 20, I was a little bit frightened, but at the same time I didn't care whether I came to Galway or not at the time. So I had the interview and then he said, 'You must meet some other people.' So we went out and we met the professor of botany,[2] on the lawn outside. And then the registrar at the time,[3] I'd to meet him, and he looked at me, 'Show me his hands,' he said, had I good strong hands? So that was the content of the interview.

However unconventional the interview procedure may have been, the college authorities were clearly sufficiently impressed with Brian's qualifications – and his hands! – to offer him the position, and he made arrangements to travel to Galway and take up his new appointment:

I was appointed then to report on the 1 November. At that time it was difficult to get transport from Roscommon into Galway for a Monday morning start, so I had to take the bus in on Saturday night and be ready for my Monday start. I arrived into college on Monday morning, and there was nobody in sight, nobody around. It was a church holiday you see at that time, and the college didn't open on church holidays. So I just met somebody at the Archway and they told me to come back tomorrow, so I came back tomorrow and of course I'm here since.

Brian recalls that the college paid what would have been an attractive salary at the time – £14 a week, with increments of 11 shillings a week for the next three years. Brian found himself working with a very small team of staff, as he recalls:

At the time in 1965 there were two painters, there were two carpenters taken on kind of temporary at the time, they weren't there long, and there were about three grounds people, and myself. I got staff then in 1967.

As an ambitious young 20-year-old, Brian was keen to get on with the task of developing the college's landscaping – but he had a battle on his hands on occasion to source the funding necessary to do his job in the way he wanted to do it:

2 Máirín de Valera was professor of botany from 1961 until she retired in 1977.   3 James Mitchell was professor of geology and minerology from 1921 to 1966, a post he held concurrently from 1934 with that of secretary/registrar of the college.

Money was quite scarce. I remember going in to the person who was in charge at the time and saying 'I want to buy a lawnmower,' and that we'd want to get a reasonable quality one, and it'd cost about £300. So he was a bit shocked at that and he said, 'Well we'd have to think about that.' Is it more important to spend the money in the library now or is it more important to buy a lawnmower? So the question was, do we want the grass cut or do we not?

Brian recalls that in the late 1960s the physical appearance of the college began to change considerably with more expansion of the infrastructure, which somewhat symbolically coincided with a more general 'opening-up' of the college to the wider world and to a broader range of students:

In the late '60s, the corporation, which was under the county council at the time, they started a road-widening programme in the Newcastle area, so they came down Newcastle Road, cut in then University Road, took six meters off the college boundary, so that nice stone wall we see at the front of the college was built in that time. It would have started before I came, they would have finished off around 1966 over near Johnny Ward's shop but there was a lot of controversy at the time between college and the county council. The council wanted to lower the wall so that people could see what was inside. The compromise then seemed to be that they'd lower the portion of the wall along by the gate lodge up as far as midway between the gate lodge and the traffic lights at the hospital there, so that people could look in.

One of the benefits of the handover of college land referred to above was the fact that the college was paid in compensation, and the buildings officer at the time, Gerry Lee, devised an innovative use for the money, which was to pay enormous dividends in the years to come, as Brian explains:

Gerry Lee at the time suggested that we should grow some trees for future development for the college, and he asked me to do it. And that was the biggest challenge I had. We took over an area in Dangan and we developed a nursery then from 1973, up till about 1996 when we finished. The idea was to have a supply of trees to plant on campus – we were planning ahead. And shrubs as well. We raised, and bought, and planted over 25,000 trees on campus in them years, you know, so some of them would be pretty much tree groves here and there and native trees, indigenous types, and others, and most of the campus is the bones of that planting. On the old campus there was something like 200 or roughly 300 trees which sounds small when you're talking about 25,000, but a lot of them were elm trees and they had to succumb to Dutch elm disease, so a lot of them were lost. But you must remember that in those days there were very few nurseries in the country. If you go back to 1965, there was no such thing as a potted plant, they just weren't heard of, plastic pots, so the whole horticulture thing has changed. You can do landscaping all year round now because of containerized stuff, and more machinery and different methods. But as of pre-1980 the nursery would have been in full production, we'd have the four common trees in production, and from then on they were going out on the site. In 1977 we started planting out the perimeter areas, and that's what's in Dangan today.

The enormous changes which began to materialize in the landscaping of the campus as a result of the college's investment, and the work of Brian Finan and his crew, were not only appreciated by those who worked on or visited the campus, but were also recognized by the winning of a prestigious national award, as Brian explains:

> We were gradually developing, so this National Tidy Towns thing came in, and the Galway City Tidy Towns said that we should apply for a section of that competition. So the competition designed for the best condition of a public building, we won the first prize in that in 1974, and we've won prizes off and on since.

One of the big changes Brian experienced during his time at UCG was the fact that interior landscaping began to take on a more important role.

> It has been shown that it's psychologically good for people in offices if there's a bit of real life there, apart from themselves. That it can uplift you. It's like a badly painted room: it can be dull and you can feel down, but if something's bright it picks you up, and the campus is the same. Plenty of people have remarked to me that, 'Oh it's lovely to walk into the place and see the trees,' and so on.

GETTING PAID

Brian Finan vividly recalls the way in which wages were paid to non-academic staff in the days before cheques and automatic bank transfers:

> It was paid by cash. At the time, on the maintenance side, there'd be maybe six or seven people, and they were all paid on Fridays at 11 o'clock. And it was kind of like a religious ritual where people went up, they queued up outside the Accounts Office and somebody handed them out the envelope and they took off their hats, caps, going in, this sort of thing. I could never be part of that. I used to forget about it, and eventually they asked me would it be more convenient if I could be paid monthly, so I opted for that. And

'twas cash payment for quite a good while. Most people at the time would be on weekly wages, they were small wages now, academic staff I think would have been paid monthly. But cash payments continued I'd say until into the '70s. But then there were armed robbers and that sort of thing. Then it wasn't safe handling cash so eventually it was changed over to cheques, standing orders or whatever.

Aside from his gardening duties, Brian Finan occasionally found that the college's quasi-rural location sometimes led to the odd uninvited 'guest' entering the campus:

That was common enough to have 'visitors' like cows and goats, and pigs, because there was a person who had a piggery just at the back of us here, it's on the site of the Arts Millennium here, in that area, and they used to keep pigs, and regularly they'd break in and you could find a sow in campus territory, that was in the late '60s. You see at that time Galway city was quite rural in 1965, so you would have a lot of wandering horses and other animals at the time would break out, it was all farm land around us.

ADMINISTRATIVE STAFF

Catherine Lyons had been working in Dublin in what was then AnCo (later FÁS, now Solas) when she got married in 1972. Her husband then registered as a student at UCG and they moved to Galway. This move actually proved to be fortuitous for her, coinciding, as it did, with the lifting of the 'marriage bar' in 1973,[4] as Catherine explains:

I had to resign on marriage. Tony and I got married and we came down to Galway. He was a student here, he started in 1972. So we got married quite young and came down to Galway. He was a student and I worked. When I first came I got an interview with the university, I was interviewed but I wasn't appointed. And then a year later they contacted me to see would I actually take up a position. The registrar at the time was Professor Michael Duignan, he was professor of archaeology. I had the interview and I was offered a job as private secretary to the registrar of the university. It was temporary, and what saved me was the Anti-Discrimination Act of 1974, they couldn't just offer you a temporary contract. I was made permanent,

---

4 Until 1973, women who worked in the civil service in Ireland had to resign if they got married. This policy was a significant barrier to the advancement of many women in clerical and administrative positions throughout the civil and public service, including in universities. Even after the marriage bar was eventually lifted, in most cases married women were still only offered temporary or part-time contracts, on the basis that their husbands would be the main breadwinners, and therefore they should not be encouraged to take up positions that could be held by single or widowed women.

and all they did was just put me on the next increment, they didn't give me anything extra, I just got permanency.

Catherine's relationship with the slightly hard-of-hearing Prof. Duignan proved to be long-standing, but was not without its challenges, as she explains:

> Professor Duignan, I found him fascinating. He could never remember my name. And he'd come in every morning at about 10 o'clock, he didn't have an office as registrar but he had his office as professor of archaeology, which is where the Buildings Office is now. And he would ring down and he'd say 'Good morning Mrs eh, eh, eh …' and I'd say, 'Lyons,' you know? So every morning we'd have this 'Good morning Mrs eh, eh …' 'Lyons.' So I always supplied the 'Lyons' part. But he was a real gentleman, and I really got on well with him.

Having worked with AnCo, and later for a time with Digital in Galway, there were other adjustments for Catherine Lyons to make, particularly with regard to the equipment she was required to work with in the college, as she recalls:

> Séamus Mac Mathúna and I shared an office, the Registrar's Office, and we were joined by Tom O'Malley, who is now a senior lecturer in law. Now I had come from Digital, which was an American company, so they had those electric typewriters. When I got to college I had this antiquated thing, clackety-clackety, and it used to drive Séamus mad because he couldn't stick this noise. So one day I really got frustrated and I said, 'Jesus, Mary and Joseph, this thing is obsolete!' So there wasn't a word out of the two of them. The next week a brand new IBM electric typewriter, a golf ball, arrived into the office. So Séamus had obviously gotten the message. If he was to have peace and quiet he'd better do something.

Although Catherine Lyons was fortunate in working for only one person, the registrar, Mary Cooke, found herself joining the fledgling administrative team which saw her turn up for work in whatever section required it at a particular time, as she explains:

> I came in '72, I was sent up from Manpower. And I was interviewed by Paddy McDermott, and Miss Joyce. Paddy McDermott was the first administrator of the university really. He actually was instrumental in setting whole new procedures, the new committees, new structures. So I was interviewed by him, and I just happened to be in the right place at the right time. They were setting up the students' services and they needed someone that knew something about accounts, for the clubs and societies. I had worked in America, I had done this, that and the other, and that's how I got

my position. But that man was in charge of personnel, students' services, careers, extramural studies, which he developed with Seamus O'Grady who came in there, he developed extramural studies, supervisor of examinations, what else … he had five or six different things. He was the first administrator, the first, and all of us worked under him.

And it was a time of development, things just started to develop, and he put all the committee stuff, all the committees were put in motion, there was nothing there before then, it was all handled by the academics. Then the office got overcrowded, so they took rooms down in the Crescent. It was the first off-campus office, there were the three of us, and we'd get a phone call saying, 'Come up, we're busy.' A taxi would go down, and you'd roll up in the taxi, and you'd work away and he would say, 'Okay, we're not doing examinations now, we're moving over to careers.' And we'd have him here at the desk, he'd come in, he was very dramatic, a very dramatic character. But he was great, he would bring us everywhere, we were his team.

THE HOUSING COOPERATIVE

The cooperative spirit that undoubtedly existed among the workforce eventually led to an extraordinary initiative between the workforce and the university's management. In an innovative development designed to help college employees get onto the property ladder, the UCG management agreed to support the establishment of a housing cooperative for college employees, and to offer loans to employees who wished to buy new houses. The scheme was a great success, as George Deacy explains:

They were years hoping to get a housing co-op off the ground, and they did. I suppose there was about ten of us, or twelve of us in it, and we looked for sites from the corporation, and the corporation gave ten sites that were up here on Ardilaun Road, behind Ardilaun Road there … Then we asked the likes of Coens then,[5] and people like that in the town, you know would they give us a discount rate on account of we bought the equipment from them. So then they built the houses, I think it was twelve houses. It was just the fellas themselves there, we formed a co-op in the college, in other words that we'd build these houses, and you'd move on and look for more sites you know, and then as staff were being employed by the college then, that they would be able to buy a nice house. So that was it, we just got the leg up. I didn't have one because I had a place myself, I just happened to be on the committee, that was my involvement. They built ten or twelve houses, so there was about ten of them in the one row, all college employees. I think then they were able to get a loan at whatever it was, 9 per cent at the time, I

5 Coens were, and are, a builders' providers company based in Galway.

remember it was cheap at the time, and they were able to get the loan from the college, and that helped them, they were able to pay back the college. Successful as it was it didn't move from that.

TRADE UNIONS

Joining a union was something new employees were very much encouraged to do when they began to work in the college, as George Deacy explains:

> I joined the union when I came. When I was employed first I was told well the best thing to do is to go and join the union. I never got tied up with the political end of it, but saying that it's nice to think that everything ran smoothly, but only for I was in the Union I wouldn't have moved on either, I needed that to progress.

Certainly the trade unions played an important role. According to George Deacy, management recognized that good work needed to be rewarded – but sometimes needed prompting:

> You had to tell them what you were worth actually, do you know what I mean? If you didn't tell them what you actually did they wouldn't have realized it. They weren't reading it. You had to keep telling them and you'd say, 'Ah well you know you're putting me in charge of about £1 million worth of equipment, I'm just not getting the pay for what I'm giving.' There'd be always somebody there that would recognize what you were doing, and you'd get it in the long haul.

After such long service to the university George Deacy was rewarded with an honorary degree in 2005. For George, as he himself put it, 'It was the icing on the cake':

> I can't look back and say I had a bad day in the place. It's lovely to come out with that kind of a feeling. Well at least you'd say they recognized my achievements, and gave me an honorary degree, so it finished up lovely. I was saying if mother was with us she'd say, 'God at least one of them has got a degree anyway.' But I mean after all the hard work and that. I said to myself she'd love that, she'd love that, I'd a right job then.

The recognition of George's long career and the significance of the honorary degree was something which had a resonance even outside his own immediate family and friends, as he recalls:

> I happened to be away with eight or nine lads recently, we were in France, and this fella was there, I hadn't met this fella before, and when I met him he

said, 'God, I was [there] when you got your honorary degree.' He said, 'My daughter was being conferred, and would you believe we spent ten minutes afterwards when we were out in Donnelly's sitting down, talking about you.[6] And it was great to see', he said, 'that you'd come up from the ranks, do you know what I mean, and we were amazed, and we didn't know you, but we were delighted for you.' So it was great, it really was great, I was delighted.

THE STRIKE OF ADMINISTRATIVE STAFF

The strike of administrative staff in 1977 proved a major turning point in the working conditions of academic staff in the university,[7] and particularly the women workers, who made up the bulk of the administrative staff. Pat Rabbitte was involved in the strike and the establishment of the trade union that had preceded it:

> When I was president of the Union of Students I was headhunted by the then ITGWU, now SIPTU, by Michael Mullen, who was the general secretary. And the English unions, the ASTMS in particular, were coming in here, organizing, for the first time, white-collar and professional staffs. And he wanted an Irish rival to that. He wanted to set up an Irish white-collar division of the ITGWU, and I was brought in to do that job. And whether it was through my connections in the college, or whether it was growing dissatisfaction with some of the practices in the college, the administrative staff felt that they were a backwater, that nobody listened to them, that the academic staff had won a voice, and were heard. And they made a connection to me at that time, and I took them on into membership. And the membership grew. And there were some very strong personalities in the leadership of it locally. Ms [Mary] Cooke was not a lady to trifle with. Catherine Lyons, Mary Colleran, Tom O'Malley was a member of the committee, and spokesman, Des McSharry, all of those, Liz Walsh was the other woman who was involved at that time. But we ran a very effective dispute, and it was relatively quick and we did quite well for the people out of it. But it was part of the changing times, you know? In those days people at all levels were very happy to have a job in UCG, and they were prepared to do whatever they were asked to do and it was just part of the changing times that … industrial democracy was in the air at the time, and you had sacred cows being challenged. So all of these things began to be challenged as the years went on and there was a big woman thing in the decision of the administrative staff. They felt that women were being passed over, and they were beginning to assert themselves.

6 Donnelly's Restaurant, in Barna, Co. Galway.   7 The strike, involving 85 administrative staff, lasted from 17 to 20 January 1977.

As we have seen, the administrative staff, or 'team' as Mary Cooke described it, was largely under the direction of Paddy McDermott, and for many years worked extremely well. But the harmony of the team was somewhat undermined when the almost exclusively female administrative staff began to be supplemented with male graduates, who were invariably given more senior positions. With the prospects of advancement for the women – most of whom had their Leaving Certs and secre-tarial college training but no third-level qualifications – effectively stymied by the arrival of the male graduates, there was increasing support from among the female workforce to secure a better deal for themselves. As Catherine Lyons put it, 'It took a while for us to find our voices.' But find their voices they eventually did, albeit tentatively initially, as Catherine explains:

> Eventually, we started putting our little complaints about how we saw the way things were going, just because we weren't graduates that we were being discriminated against. We weren't given the same opportunities, promotion, even training, absolutely nothing.

In time, the decision was made to join a trade union, and it was a former UCG graduate, and president of the UCG students union, now employed as a trade-union representative, who swung the decision for the female administrative workers, as Mary Cooke explains:

> We decided that we would join the Irish Transport and General Workers' Union. Pat Rabbitte was there, Pat Rabbitte was a graduate of UCG, so there was kind of a contact there. And the union was very anxious to set up inside, we'll say, the semi-civil service, because they had no foot in the door.

Catherine Lyons and Mary Cooke recall that another important deciding factor for the women was the fact that they would be allowed to establish a branch on their own, as Mary Cooke recalls: 'The fact of having the autonomy of our own branch, that was the first time that was done.'

Having joined the union, and enlisted most of the female administrative staff as members, the next step was to negotiate with the college authorities: principally for better working conditions, access to promotion, better pay, and access to educa-tion. But first they had to win recognition of the union by the university – which led to the famous strike of administrative staff in 1977.

A negotiating committee was formed, comprising Mick Conlon, the branch secretary, Catherine Lyons and Pat Rabbitte, the representative from the ITGWU. Catherine Lyons recalls vividly the events leading up to the calling of the strike:

> We sounded out the members to see how did they feel about a strike, and they had said there was to be a full-time strike if the union was not recog-nized. The next day we were negotiating with them, and I always remember

Pat, sitting in the waiting room, waiting to come in, reading the *Irish Times*, he always did this, he would read the *Irish Times*. And they filed in, and they nearly had to prise the paper away from him, and he would carefully fold up the *Irish Times*, and put it aside, and say, 'Well?' And then they asked for the keys, and he said, 'Well that's very unfortunate.' It kind of pre-empts any kind of discussion. Our keys would have to be given up, and that meant not just us, that meant everybody in the union who did have keys to an office would have to hand them up. So this was the first thing that he said. But I think Pat Rabbitte said, you know, 'Have you got anything else to say?' And they said no. And he just got up and walked out, and we walked with him. And I always remember the Bursar turning round to the IBEC representative,[8] and saying, 'What do we do now?' And him shaking his head, 'I don't know.'

And to be fair to Pat Rabbitte, and I worked with him for a while, I found him great. He would always hold his nerve and our dignity as well, which I felt was very important. And that he really stood up, and Mick Conlon as well. But then we were on strike.

The result was the first strike of public-sector administrative staff, in January 1977. The women organized themselves for action, and found great support among the women workers and some of the academic staff. There were those, however, who, as Catherine Lyons recalls, 'came over the wall at 8 o'clock in the morning', to the great disappointment of the striking workers. There were other members of staff for whom the mere notion of a strike was abhorrent. Mary Cooke recalls an encounter with one of the college's longest-serving female administrators:

The next day we were on the gates anyhow, and we were on it for a while, and she pulled the window down and she told me I was a roarin' disgrace. Ah but she was a different generation of course, I wouldn't take any offense.

Word of the strike spread quickly once the women had taken up their picketing positions at the various entrance gates into the college. The atmosphere among the workers was upbeat and determined, as Catherine Lyons recalls:

I was on the front gate, and I felt like Maud Gonne. I was on the front gate with my group. And we were marching up and down, you had to keep walking. And next I see Stan Shiels.[9] Now it was cold, it was January, so I saw Stan Shiels arriving up to take a photograph. But of course I, being me, I

8 The Irish Business and Employers Confederation is Ireland's largest business lobby group. It works to promote business interests by lobbying and advising governments, policymakers and key stakeholders, and also supports member companies with advice on industrial relations and management of employees. 9 Stan Shiels is one of Galway's best known press photographers, who worked for many years with the *Connacht Tribune*.

said I wasn't stopping. I said, 'Girls you just have to keep walking up and down. We're not here for the fashion pages.'

The atmosphere altered considerably when the college authorities made an approach to the workers, as Catherine Lyons recalls:

> I said, 'Keep walking, keep walking.' So they advanced, the four of them advanced, and we were just walking up and down. They had to ask us to stop. Because we weren't going to stop for them, they wanted to read something out to us. It was a court injunction. And they read it out saying that Mick Conlon, who was our branch secretary, or his agents, and whatever, that we weren't supposed to be picketing. And of course me in my innocence said, 'Well can I have a copy of that?' And he, in his innocence, says, 'No, you can get it in the courthouse.' And of course the implication of that is that if he had given me a copy of the injunction, I would have to go, because I would be in contempt of court. But he didn't give it to me because he said I could get it in the courthouse. And then, of course, when he realized his mistake about an hour afterwards they were mad trying to give us copies of it. But we got word from Pat Rabbitte that we weren't to accept anything. So this went on for about three days.

The publicity generated by the strike was considerable, and there was a great deal of support for it from within the academic and student community, as Mary Cooke recalls:

> You had people ... coming down to say, 'Anybody that intimidates ye, you're to let us know.' The Academic WUI, so they were very supportive. The academics were very nice to us. The students brought coffee and teas. And they didn't break the strike, they just stood, they didn't cross the picket.

Both Catherine and Mary recall that the women were determined to succeed, no matter how long the strike was to last. Catherine recalls the measures taken to end the strike:

> We were getting very entrenched. It's amazing, the women, the ones that were kind of dubious in the beginning, really got strong, and they weren't going back until they got X, Y and Z. So the longer it went on the more militant the women became. Which was a good support to us, because they were always undermining you about what support have you got, but they could see that actually we had good support, you know? We had support from the transport union, the Galway branches, the students union.

The strike was eventually resolved following a labour court hearing in the Great Southern Hotel. The result was a resounding victory for the striking women, as Mary Cooke recalls:

> We got everything we wanted nearly at that meeting. And then after that we got a thing that was very unique, that they couldn't advertise posts without internal notice, that posts should be advertised internally, and that was a big coup. And we couldn't be transferred either without consultation. And we had a consultative committee.

The fact that the striking women were docked two and a half days' pay after the resolution of the strike did rankle somewhat, but the end result was a victory, something which the women involved in the strike are deservedly proud of.

THE COMPUTER AGE

The late '60s and early '70s witnessed the dawn of a new age: the age of the computer. While the new technology was still something of a mystery to most people, including most of the academic community, the new computer that was installed in the college in 1968 transformed the educational and professional life of the institution forever. It also provided a unique challenge to the college staff who were charged with operating and maintaining it. George Deacy found himself at the cutting edge of this new technology, as he explains:

> Professor O'Keefe came in in '56, '57, about a year after I came, and then John Finnegan came I think in about '66, '67, just before we got the computer.[10] And he was the instigator, Prof. Declan O'Keefe, in getting the computer in there. So then they asked me would I help run that as well as the Soil Mechanics Lab, and then I was helping out in the Structures Lab as well. So I said okay, grand, I would do it. At that stage we ran it as an open shop, that the students would come in, that they could punch their own cards, or there were one or two ladies there that would punch the cards for them, they could actually put them into the computer themselves, threw the switches and stuff like that as well. They'd come in, 'twas like an open shop, and that's the way we ran it, so they were able to come, and they'd be there at 12 or 1 o'clock at nighttime.

The dedication of George Deacy and some of his colleagues in effectively 'minding' this extremely valuable piece of equipment was extraordinary:

> I was still only working there from nine to six or half six, but you'd drop in around 9 o'clock or 10 o'clock to ensure everything was done right. It

10 Mr Finnegan was appointed statutory lecturer in civil engineering in 1965 and lectured in computing. He was responsible for the installation of the computer system and managed the centre under the direction of Prof. O'Keefe.

was a big responsibility. That was a serious piece of equipment, a serious
investment of money, so ... and you know you'd say students going in,
they're going to wreck everything, but we never had any trouble. But it was
a source of awe though for people, I mean this really was the new technology. Because I mean Mr Finnegan and I, we went down to Shannon, down
to de Beers, and this fella says to us, a security fella, and we were looking for
somebody, and he said, 'That's not them, but do you see those fellas over
there?' he said, 'Look at the cut of them. They're the programmers, and you
know them because they have a gimp on them.' And at the time, anyone that
knew about computers, you know they kind of kept it to themselves, they
didn't like to spread it around. Whereas when Finnegan came and he had
the computer he wanted, that's what he wanted, *everyone* to know exactly
what was going on. He taught me everything about computing. He said he
wanted [people] to know, and he wanted it hands-on, it was very hands on.
And so they gave the lectures, Finnegan gave the lectures and they typed
up their programmes, and then they put them in the manuals to ensure that
everything ran alright.

George read all the manuals and became extremely knowledgeable about computers, something which, he acknowledges, was actively facilitated by his superiors, as
he explains:

What you'd pick up was where they were learning how to programme, you
saw the course and you could see what they were doing and what they were
learning, because then it ended up that what you were doing, you were cor-
recting the programmes for them. They came in and you corrected them.
They'd come in and they'd run them through, and they'd have errors, well
you could look through and you could see there's an error there, because
you know it was repetition even though it was better. So when programmes
got more sophisticated then you got more sophisticated as well.

The advent of the computer age provided a wonderful career opportunity for
George Deacy, and the shy 15-year-old who tentatively began his career in 1956
ended it as head of operations at computer services in 2005.

THE STAFF ROOM

Having been emboldened by their success in the strike, the women administrative
staff subsequently set out to establish their rights – and the rights of all non-academic staff – in another area of college life, as Catherine Lyons recalls:

The staff room used to be where the Academic Secretary's Office [is now].
And I remember looking into it once or twice, and it had the armchairs

beside the fire, and there were only two inhabitants, I think, it was Professor Coll on one side of the fire, and on the other was Professor Máirín de Valera, reading the *Irish Press*. Gerry Lee wanted to convert that staff room into an office and have the staff room over where it is now. So before that it was called the academic staff room. He organized that anyway, and the staff room, it was called 'staff room', was being opened on such and such a day. So we all decided that six or eight of us would march in on the first day. Which we did, and they all looked up, and all the older professors were there, and they nearly died, when they saw us marching in. And we marched up and we ordered our tea and coffee and we sat down. And they used to have these kind of seats in the centre, that's where the academics sat, you know, the satellites would be outside. But we sat down in the middle, we were just making a point, and I think Professor Coll … I always remember him shaking his head. Nobody said anything to us. And so we established a right to go there, that's how that right came about. Well it said staff room and we said well we're staff. I was on the first Staff Committee.

A GREAT PLACE TO WORK

Catherine Lyons, having worked at UCG/NUIG for thirty-six years, regards the college as the best possible place to work:

> Oh I love coming in to work. I've never lost that enthusiasm for work. Of course I've been very lucky where I actually work, I work in the Quadrangle. So I started off over in one corner, I'm now over in another corner. So I haven't quite gotten around the four corners. But I really love coming to work every morning. And I love the students, I think they're wonderful. And I always liked the staff. I always felt, no matter what the difficulty anybody had, that I'd like to say that I gave them time, you know, because I'm a firm believer that there's always a solution to every problem. After so many years I like coming in to work. And the kind of job I have, I don't know who's going to come through my door, you know, what kind of problem is going to come in. You just have to deal with it.

The very active social life of the college was also a significant factor in the staff's enjoyment of working here. But Catherine recalls one famous incident when a staff Christmas party held in the recently refurbished Aula Maxima almost, literally, brought the house down:

> We were upstairs in the Aula, the second floor was just put in. And we had our Christmas party, and you know the song, Tony Christie, 'Is this the way

to Amarillo?' Well Colm Ó hEocha was downstairs with Gerry Lee,[11] and they thought we were going to come through the floor, they thought the floor was going to give. And they [wouldn't allow] anything else after that in the Aula. I always remember 'Is this the way to Amarillo?' and we all banging away on the ceiling, and down below they were all looking up at the ceiling wondering was this going to give way.

LIVING IN THE ARCHWAY: THE Ó FÁTHARTA FAMILY

For some members of staff, as we have seen, the college wasn't only where they worked – it was also where they lived. Peadar Ó Fátharta's association with UCG goes back over fifty years, and indeed it could truly be said that he grew up there, he recalls:

My first association with college was in 1958. My dad was appointed as live-in porter in December, and I remember walking in with him, through the main gate, holding his hand, I was 5 years old. I was so excited when I saw this big house, and I said to dad, 'Are we going to live in a castle?' My eyes lit up when I saw a football pitch with goalposts, and this field would play a major part in my football education over the next nine years. And there was a big wall around the college, but the student population in those days was very small, there were less than 2,000 students. There was everything within the walls of the college. We spent from 1958 to about 1969, about eleven years, living in the Archway.

Our accommodation consisted of the Archway as it is now, the entrance door, our kitchen was to the right when you came in the door, and we also had a dining room to the left. There was a small reception desk, there were keys for the different buildings and rooms, and directly behind that there was a telephone kiosk, as Dad and Mam looked after the switchboard as well. Off of that there was a walkway, a little anteroom, and we had a bedroom in there. Our other two bedrooms were on the first floor. And I remember when I went in there first we'd two beds in it. And as you head up into the clock tower, that's where our toilet was. There was a big range in the kitchen, and the kettle was always on the range, and academic staff and students alike were always welcome for a cup of tea. People such as Monsignor de Brún and Máirín de Valera could often be found there.[12]

Dad's job was, as a porter, he was security as well, he looked after the keys, because at that time there was no security. He also looked after all

11 Dr Colm ÓhEocha, a former professor of biochemistry, was president of UCG 1975–96. Under Dr Ó hEocha's presidency, student numbers doubled, and the present modern campus took shape. A year after his retirement, the university changed its name to the National University of Ireland Galway. Gerry Lee was UCG's buildings and development officer for many years.   12 The original kitchen would later become Peadar's office, when he became head porter.

the mail, information, opening of rooms and also setting up some of the theatres because everything was in the Quad. The Quadrangle was the heart of the university at the time. Dad's hours really were from early morning till late at night, there was very, very little relief for him, it was hard going. Mam helped out as well, and we used to help out Mam.

Limited enough as it was, the Porter's accommodation in the Archway often had to stretch to accommodate not just the Ó Fátharta family, but their various relatives who came to visit from time to time, as Peadar explains:

> It was a halfway house. Dad and Mam were from the Aran Islands, Dad was from Inis Méain and Mam was from Inis Oirr, and of course on the Lá Aonach, the Fair Day, we'd have all the *col ceathracha* [cousins] and uncles or aunts coming down, and there was many a time that we wouldn't have a bed to sleep in because they were putting up people.

The Ó Fáthartas soon established themselves as the college's resident family, and the porter's lodge became a refuge not just for visiting relatives from the Aran Islands but also for the college community as a whole, from, as we have seen, the college president himself down to lecturers and, occasionally, troubled students, as Peadar explains:

> Máirín de Valera, Éamon de Valera's daughter, she was professor of botany, and being a botanist Máirín spent many of her summers on Inis Meáin, studying the rare plants that grew there. She had many photographs of the islanders, including the children, and Dad was in some of those photographs. And she used to come in and sit down at the fire in the kitchen, and loved nothing more than to speak, in Irish, about her Aran experiences. On a nice day she would often say to us, '*Ba bhréa liom bheith in Inis Méain inniu* [I would love to be on Inis Méain today].' Even the students used to come in, and my parents were always so welcoming, especially during exam results, which in those days were read out in the Quadrangle. The announcement of exam results was an anxious time for students. Many were consoled by Mam in our kitchen with a *cupán tae* [cup of tea].

In addition to the pastoral care given to students, and the many and varied tasks which Pádraig Ó Fátharta had to perform on a daily basis, the hard-working porter used what little free time he had to create a productive garden to supply his family with vegetables, as Peadar explains:

> We had a garden, which was at the back entrance of Newcastle Road. The garden was like a jungle when we went down there, and it was quite big. And Dad cleared the whole area by hand, with a *speal* [scythe], as they call it.

Over a period of time he transformed an overgrown jungle to a very productive vegetable garden which produced many kinds of vegetables. Being an islander, his gardening skills were second to none. These skills were evident in the garden he produced.

He'd a shed there as well, it was a big long black shed, and Dad fixed it up and transformed it. He reared chickens and ducks there by installing overhead lighting.

For the Ó Fáthartas the family atmosphere in the Quad was greatly enhanced when Monsignor de Brún retired in 1959, to be replaced the following year by Prof. Martin Newell, who subsequently moved into the president's residence in the Quad with his family. For young Peadar it was not so much the president himself who impressed him, but rather his famous footballer son, also named Martin Newell, a member of the three-in-a-row All-Ireland senior football team, as Peadar explains:

> For me it was a great thrill that Martin Newell,[13] of the famous Three-in-a-Row team, lived in the college. Martin was studying in Heidelberg at the time and he was commuting to play matches for Galway, Martin was a left half-back on the team. And he used to come home and his younger brother Johnny and myself were great friends, and we played a lot of football on the front pitch, and Martin would come out for a kick-around. Now it was something like the equivalent today of meeting, say, one of the soccer stars like Beckham, because we were young, he was a hero you know? But there was a funny incident, and Martin still jokes about it, where he arrived for a match, if memory serves me it was a semi-final in '64, and he had forgotten a pair of laces for his boots. And of course he called over to the Archway to me and he borrowed a pair of laces. I gave him the laces, and I never saw them again. And he was always slagging about that day, that he never gave me back the laces. I always used slag him, 'Ah sure, the laces carried you round.' There was always good banter between the Fahertys and Newells.

The two families became great friends, and fortunately for Mrs Newell, Bean Uí Fhatharta was, in common with herself, a great baker, and their skills were often called upon for college social events, as Peadar explains:

> Mrs Newell was a lovely woman, a real lady, and they used to have a coffee morning at end of term, and the Quad would be closed off. Tables would be placed in the Quad, near the grass margins, and were draped in white linen

13 This is a reference to Prof. Martin L. Newell, the son of mathematician and college president Martin J. Newell. He played at left half-back on the winning Galway teams in the All-Ireland Senior Football Championship finals of 1964, 1965 and 1966. Like his father before him, Prof. Newell taught in the mathematics department of UCG/NUIG.

cloths. The tables would be laden with beautiful cakes and bread, produced by Mrs Newell and Mam, who were both great bakers. All the professors and lecturers would be invited. It would be once a year and it was always a lovely occasion.

The Newells and Ó Fáthartas were not the only families living on campus. At that time Alfie Sherlock and his family lived in the Gate Lodge also: 'Another lovely family, and we were all very close friends, there was a big family of them in it. And Alfie Sherlock spent over fifty years here, from a young boy till he retired, he was a college steward.'

For Peadar Ó Fátharta, particularly as a young lad, the college's location right beside the river, and the availability of boats from the college's Boat Club, only added to the magical atmosphere of living in the college, as he explains:

We were very privileged in the university to have the Men's Club, as we call it, the Boat Club which is down at Earl's Island opposite the cathedral. So, on the Sunday the great thrill was to go on the river. And the caretaker was Peter Curran and his wife was May. He looked after and maintained the boats. The boats would be lifted annually, and painted by George Williams and Seosamh Ó Liatháin, who were the college painters at the time. Apart from the boats there was a snooker hall there, and training facilities for the Boxing Club, and other sports. Sunday was just a fantastic day to go down to the club and the thrill for us kids to get a boat. We used to go up to Mionloch, old Menlo Pier. Dad and my cousin would do the rowing. The river was like a flotilla of boats, you could literally walk across the river there were so many boats, with students and college staff. We'd moor the boat in Menlo and we would walk up the village to a little shop owned by the Corcoran family, and we would buy a mineral and biscuits and we would go back down to the pier and relax on the water's edge, where Dad would listen to some GAA matches on his transistor, he was an avid GAA fan.

Another magical time for the Ó Fáthartas, and indeed the other families living on campus, was Christmas. With the students and most of the staff away, the college was a quiet, enclosed enclave for the families who lived there. However, children being children, Peadar remembers one particular Christmas particularly vividly:

When it snowed and the place was completely white, it was like something out of another world. And I remember one Christmas Dad was sick, he had mumps. And Mam was expecting a baby. But Dad was sick that Christmas, and I remember Mam asking me to go over to the shed, in the back of the college, and she killed a turkey. And my biggest worry was, being Christmas, and Christmas Eve and Santa and everything, how ... *ba ceart dom bheith i mo chodladh* [I should be asleep], I should have been asleep at a certain time, for Santa, because Santa won't come. And I remember I was very, very upset, it was around 12 o'clock at night, and she was a woman that worked into the night sometimes, like a lot of them in those days. And we killed the turkey, and plucked the turkey, and we had the dinner for the following day. But of course Santa did arrive, he mightn't be as *flathúil* [generous] as other years, but I remember her saying that Dad was sick and we weren't able to do this, or we weren't able to do that. Innocence was a great thing.

The fact that the Ó Fáthartas were native Irish speakers proved to be extremely important, particularly for those students who came from Gaeltacht areas and were away from home for perhaps the first time. Peadar recalls that his father Pádraig became an important figure to such students:

Dad and Mam were like father figures to a lot of them. Peadar Mac an Iomaire of Roinn na Gaeilge often told me that when he came here Dad was a guy he always looked up to. He was always there for the Gaeilge and the bit of chat, give them a bit of help, a bit of comfort, when they were away from home. It was like a little bit of home, here on campus, especially the Archway.

The hospitality extended by the family living in the Archway did not just extend to students – occasionally academic staff were also in need of some timely reassurance:

There was a nice little story, where Professor Declan O'Keefe, who was professor of civil engineering, Declan O'Keefe told me that he was coming for an interview, about 1960, when he got the job, and he came in to the Archway, and he came in looking for directions to the interview room. And he was met by this man who was cleaning a noticeboard. And Declan said he got delayed because of traffic, but he was late for the interview. So Dad had got word that there was a delay in the interviews, and Dad reassured him, sat him down, gave him a cup of tea, and Declan said that made him feel very, very welcome, and it reassured him.

Having lived almost all of his life in the college, when Peadar had done his Leaving Cert, and a job came up in the college, it was almost inevitable that he would apply for it, as he explains:

I did my Leaving Cert in 1972, and that summer a position as porter, became available. I applied and got the job from Mr Gerry Lee. As I was the first porter taken on for some time, with the Leaving Cert in my back pocket, Mr Lee told me that there was every possibility of promotion down the line. The university under Gerry Lee's stewardship was expanding, and true to his word, five years later, in 1977, I was promoted to head porter. I was now supervising my dad, Pádraig, that was very strange. Now we got on very well, I needn't have worried, everything worked out fine. Our workload consisted of sorting of mail, internal and external, record of keys, telephone queries, general information to students, staff and general public. Porters and security worked side by side, some of our work overlapped.

Even before becoming head porter, as a boy, Peadar had access to practically every part of the college, as his father was the custodian of the keys. One of the places that particularly attracted him was the college library:

> As I got older, I realized that the library was really special. It was an absolutely beautiful place, and we were privileged, because we had the keys. And on Sunday I used to sneak a key off the key board, and a group of us kids, Sherlocks included, we used to go up to the library, put socks on over our shoes, and would slide down the linoleum floor the full length of the library, down to the back door nearly, if you got a good run at it. It used to keep us amused for ages. We felt safe on Sunday because the librarian, Mr Townley wouldn't be there.

Another attraction for the college's youngest occupants was the original college staff room:

> As kids we would visit the staff room, because it had both biscuits and newspapers. When we visited the staff room, one of us would keep nix [lookout], in case one of the staff came. As I was one of the youngest, and unable to read, it was left to one of the Sherlocks to read the cartoons in the *Irish Press*, and the one we loved was 'The Cisco Kid', a serial cartoon, and we used to love following it, week after week. And if we were lucky, and there were some biscuits left over, we would help ourselves. And if someone came, the window would always be left open and we'd just hop out the window.

WORKING IN THE QUAD

For many, the Quad was, and indeed still is, the heart of the university. So, as Peadar Ó Fátharta explains, leaving the Quad to work in another part of the university was something that staff, both academic and non-academic, did with extreme reluctance:

> I remember, when the college expanded in the '70s, the Arts and Science Block, Ma Heavey, a very close friend of our family, said to me one day, '*Meas tú má bhíonn brú curtha orm le athrú, an rachfaidh mé amach as an áit seo?* [Do you think, if pressure is put on me to move, will I leave this place?]' and she said '*Ní dheirfinn é, tá an dúchas sa Quad, tá stair ag baint leis* [I

wouldn't say so, the heritage is in the Quad, there is a history attached to it].' When you walk in to the Quad, as Ma Heavey used to say, there was an atmosphere of learning. There was something magical about the Quad. Even the secretaries, when they come to work in the university, and if you were lucky enough to work in the Quad first, I've noticed this over the years, a lot of secretaries hate leaving the Quad if they're transferred, it takes them a while to adapt to a new place.

The long careers that so many of those interviewed have had at UCG is a testament to how much they enjoyed working there, and enjoyed the interaction with the other staff – academic and non-academic – who worked there also. What is also striking is how important the student community was to those who worked at UCG, regardless of the nature of the contact they had with them. Whether it was Ma Creaven, ensuring that precious study time was not wasted in her coffee shop or the porters, providing a friendly ear and the comforting cup of tea when required – there is no doubt but that the college worked as it did because of the quality and commitment of its non-academic staff. They did their jobs, conscious all the while that they were working in a rather special environment. They, like everyone else who ever worked, taught or studied at the college, adapted to the changes that time brought about – and even, on occasion, introduced significant change themselves. But they ensured that the college worked, so that students could learn, and in having such a well-oiled yet human machine working for them, generations of students were extremely fortunate.

Index

Numbers in bold are plates